Anne Forester
Margaret Reinhard

With a Foreword by Renate N. Caine

The Learners' Way

Brain-Based Learning in Action

PORTAGE & MAIN PRESS
(PEGUIS PUBLISHERS)

Winnipeg • Canada

Portage & Main Press acknowledges the financial support of the Government of Canada through the Book Publishing Industry Development Program (BPIDP) for our publishing activities.

Printed and bound in Canada by Kromar Printing

00   01   02   03   04   5   4   3   2   1

Canadian Cataloguing in Publication Data

Forester, Anne D.

    The learners' way

    Includes bibliographical references.
    ISBN 1-894110-55-2

1. Language arts (Elementary).   2. Learning, Psychology of.   I. Reinhard, Margaret, 1931–   II. Title.

LB1576.F68 2000   372.6   C00-920091-6

Book Design: Suzanne Gallant
Illustrations: Robin Thomson

PORTAGE & MAIN PRESS
(PEGUIS PUBLISHERS)

100-318 McDermot Avenue
Winnipeg, Manitoba, Canada R3A 0A2
Email: books@peguis.com
Tel.: 204-987-3500
Toll free: 800-667-9673
Fax: 204-947-0080

Contents

Foreword

What an intelligent book! One does have to ask, however, why something as sensible as the learner's natural way of learning is often so difficult to implement in schools. It is as if schools were invented to take children out of the native world capable of filling them with a sense of wonder and providing infinite opportunities for learning in order to confine them to what can be formally taught. Why would we ever think that formal instruction "delivered" in limited environments called classrooms could possibly approximate or match the power of the human brain to make sense of information that comes with everyday experience? Children come biologically equipped to add new patterns (from vocabulary to concepts) and learning takes on lightening speed when linked to their need to know.

There are ways to increase the natural intelligence of children, as this book so amply demonstrates. Embed real life in their formal learning. Genuine conversations about things that matter, research projects that make use of children's innate search for meaning, teachers posing challenging questions that are open ended, embedding sophisticated vocabulary and concepts in spontaneous, innovative ways are all things that teachers can do and that ultimately encourage hard work and lead to genuine expertise.

Yet while this entire enterprise of teaching the natural way may sound simple, for most educators it requires profound learning. It often takes effort to drop the artifice and artificial teaching strategies that function independently of the student-centered sense of wonder, excitement, discovery, and hard work generated by intrinsic motivation and joy.

It is one thing to *be* the kind of teacher who does the natural thing. It is another to practice strategies and techniques meant to help children master something they have no interest in learning. It is as if we all entered school believing that the world and our place in it were connected and whole, only to discover that school learning meant that there were subjects separate from other subjects; that learning didn't have to make sense or bring pleasure. Learning was the purpose of taking exams. The real reward comes from people praising you for doing well on exams, not the learning itself.

It is as if fear, anxiety, and pressure to perform came to be the new values that broke the fabric of an interconnected world filled with possibility of our own development. Teachers are all too often people who survived this process and came to believe in it. Sadly, teachers have to first find out how to be learners themselves. They have to learn how to put the fabric back together.

The Learners' Way is a wonderful book, and I plan to recommend it widely. I will recommend that teachers read it with two purposes in mind: first, to look to their profession; second, to remember that they themselves continue to be learners and to aid them to learn again and again what is most natural for all of us and what constitutes our gift for a lifetime.

Renate N. Caine, Ph.D.
Professor Emeritus,
University of California, San Bernardino

Preface to the Second Edition

Whether teacher, parent, or administrator, you have known all along that a happy, active classroom produces meaningful learning that children eagerly apply. In the first edition of *The Learners' Way*, we offered you suggestions for creating the same productive ways of teaching/learning in the classroom that taught children so effectively when they first learned to talk. Now, scientific research expands and validates the principles and practices that constitute "the learners' way" of teaching.

Brain research has become more specific about learning processes. Physiological and neurological evidence confirm that learning functions best when children interact freely with learning materials in a rich and varied environment. The same research documents that memory depends on emotions and sensory input. Mind and body work in harmony and the brain functions as an integrated whole.

Intelligence has many facets, and the theory of multiple intelligences adds weight to the observations of teachers who have always known and built on the special strengths their students brought to learning. Now that knowledge is reinforced by scientific evidence, and teachers can use the successes students achieve in one area as a solid foundation for further and more varied learning, I.Q. is no longer seen as fixed.

And now there is also E.Q. – emotional intelligence – that can be expanded, and that affirms the importance of fostering curiosity,

Now science validates what teachers have known all along

cooperativeness and feelings of belonging. Working with the full range of emotions to enhance or tone them down creates a climate that fosters effective interpersonal and social skills and at the same time produces ease of learning.

Active involvement with the learning materials, in an environment that encourages children to take risks in order to gain understanding, is key in all of the scientifically based learning models. The same factor undergirds the theory of constructivism that holds that true learning and understanding are not simply acquired but constructed by the learner through active exploration and enquiry. The interactive, multifaceted classroom work we describe in *The Learners' Way* fosters that kind of constructivist learning at every turn.

To connect the scientific findings with the down-to-earth classroom practices of *The Learners' Way*, we provide a picture gallery of the basic principles together with vignettes of their classroom meaning. Within the text, icons or brief quotes in the margin will connect the effective ways of teaching/learning with their research bases (see page xxi for a key to the icons and their meanings). If you are ever in doubt whether the practical work you do in class is truly sound and valid, take a look at those icons and know that your work is solidly supported by the most up-to-date research on learning and the brain.

We are indebted to many people who have helped and supported us as we shifted our philosophy and practice of teaching to the learners' way. Dr. Norma Mickelson brought us together when she approved and encouraged our initial research. She has never wavered in her support for our joint work. Ken McCulloch, principal at Fairburn School where we began our work, trusted us to evolve new ways of teaching when no one so much as talked about the learners' way of learning. He took the time to listen, to read our research, and to hear the children read. He believed in the soundness of our research and the effectiveness of Margaret's teaching. Without his support our research would have remained in the realm of theory.

We also owe a great deal to colleagues who shared ideas with us, allowed us to visit their classrooms to observe their interactions with children, and who gave us copies of writing and artwork produced by their students. June Domke, Margaret's team teacher, was first to contribute. Diane Cowden, Shelagh Levey, Ann Domke, and Linda Picciotto have also shared generously and enthusiastically. Anne Reinhard Peterson took our work north and introduced it. During her visits home she has helped with proofreading and editing, as well as contributing information about her students who were different in background and experience from students in Victoria.

Keith Crowley – exchange principal from Australia at Fairburn School – gave us enthusiastic support and warm encouragement to extend our work even further. Trevor Calkins, principal at South Park School, invited Margaret to join his team and has fully acknowledged her contribution to the entire school.

But most of all we are indebted to all the children who have taught us so much over the years. Close observation of these children and their ways set us on our path. They keep us learning and evolving from year to year. To them and especially to Judy Norget, our editor and to all those who encouraged and aided us along the way our most sincere gratitude.

The impetus for this new and revised edition came from the many teachers who, to this day, keep telling us how much teaching the learners' way means to them. They have given us their enthusiastic support and have asked us to continue to write. In responding to that call, we were able to draw together the new material for this edition because of researchers who have presented their findings about the marvelous functioning of the brain in terms that we could relate to. Our special thanks go to Renate and Geoffrey Caine for allowing us to translate the imagery they used in their work into graphic representations. And here our artist, Robin Thomson, added not only his artistic talent but a keen interest and a wonderful willingness to look and look again at learning and learners to create the images we wanted to present to our readers.

For this book, too, we have been blessed with an editor, Annalee Greenberg, who valued our message and contributed much to bringing clarity to it. Peguis Publishers were first to accept our early manuscript and have been our staunch supporters. We are grateful to them and to all the learners who continue to teach us so much.

The Icons and Their Meanings

You will find these icons in the margins next to descriptions of classroom activities. This list is provided as a ready reference to remind you that teaching-learning is solidly based on research and can be explained in these terms to parents, supervisors, or the children themselves.

In the city of the mind, many things function together and serve each other

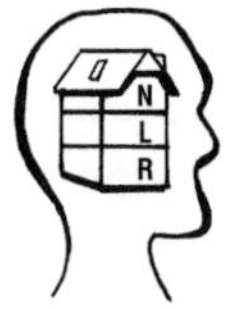

All three brothers cooperate to produce learning

Repto, the basic brain, and its patterns guide behavior – imitation, repetition, flocking, routinization

Limbo is functioning optimally based on safety and positive feelings that enhance learning and memory

The shut-down of Neo's domain in response to the fight-or-flight signal

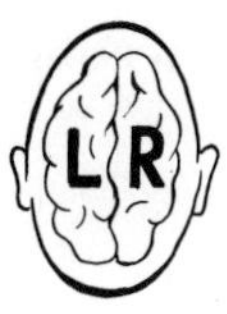

Left and right are integrated

Planting neural trees through active learning and physical involvement

The power and importance of physical movement to enhance learning and grow neural trees

Map learning – the effortless absorption of what the environment offers

Route learning – the careful memorization of information presented by others

Modeling takes many forms

Building on the eight intelligences students bring to learning

Enhancing or reining in the emotions to optimize social and emotional intelligence (E.Q.)

Constructing knowledge, creating inner paradigms

Introduction

In this book we are describing our classroom experience of helping children use their ways to read, write, and spell. Years of in-class observations formed the basis of developing the learners' way of teaching. Now a broad range of research corroborates the effectiveness of fitting our teaching to the children's ways of constructing their own knowledge.

In the chapters that follow we will describe how to help children to learn to read by reading, write by writing, and spell by spelling. As the research confirms, learning flourishes best in a rich context that engages the emotions and makes learning meaningful; therefore, we are devoting an entire chapter to creating a learning climate, and the descriptions of how to fit teaching to the children's ways of learning include all-important social skills and emotional intelligence. In the same spirit, assessing progress is fitted into the overall learning while still fulfilling district requirements. The chapter on multi-age teaching acknowledges the unique pace and development of each learner – something all teachers know and that we confirmed in our in-class research.

O ur work began with in-class observations and videotaping of children at work learning to read and write. At the time, structured lessons in phonics and basal readers with carefully limited vocabulary dominated our reading lessons. Children were learning to read, but careful analysis of the videotaped interactions in class revealed that practice moved the children toward reading

Teaching is aided by observing learners' ways

more surely than our structured lessons. Context, familiar patterns of language, and knowledge of the world around them helped the children more than exercises and worksheets on consonants and vowels. Put in terms of current research, "map learning" – setting learning into a meaningful context – contributed more to effective literacy learning than detail work.

We had begun our observations with the basic assumption that children have an effective language learning system when they come to school and will continue to use their own ways, if you give them the chance to do so. Once that view of their in-class learning was confirmed, we took a closer look at how children learn at home and gradually revised our teaching to fit the learners' ways of constructing knowledge.

What is "the learners' way"?

By the time children come to school they are highly effective learners. They have learned to understand and speak the language that is spoken in their home; they have classified thousands upon thousands of items and events in their efforts to make sense of their surroundings; they have developed interpersonal skills, and, to get what they want, most of them have become very adept at manipulating the people around them.

Since we are concerned with the learners' ways of acquiring knowledge and skills, let's take a closer look at the ways in which infants and young children proceed to learn. We know that they watch, try things out, and gradually become better at understanding and doing things around the home. If we analyze their learning activities and describe them in terms usually reserved for academic enquiry, we find that the young learners are in fact highly effective researchers and explorers.

As you look at the list of what both scientists and children do (Table 1), think of toddlers exploring their home; recall the efforts they made trying to discover how to use everyday implements, how to take things apart and fit them back together. Ask yourself how a baby learns to discriminate between males, females, uncles, aunts, Mommy, Daddy – could you teach him/her such distinctions?

Fortunately, babies draw their own conclusions about what they perceive and then look for confirmation or new evidence. "If Daddy is the only one to respond to dada, maybe the other people who look somewhat like him are not Daddy." If it sounds too far-fetched to talk about drawing inferences and testing hypotheses, keep in mind that when children call all vehicles *cars*, they are not simply guessing but are generalizing and hypothesizing based on previous evidence. Once their hypothesis has proven incorrect, they update their category for vehicles to include trucks and vans. In the best tradition of scientific enquiry they constantly explore the world for new evidence and maintain an open mind that allows them to correct their earlier, less accurate findings. They are insatiably curious because their very survival depends on continually updating their knowledge.

Language learning involves active research

While the junior scientists are eagerly exploring the physical world of their homes, they are also developing their ability to understand and use language. They are asking questions, making demands, cajoling, or voicing loud protests, using readily recognizable patterns of intonation even before their language is fully developed.

In the course of expanding their vocabulary and sentence length, toddlers also generate more sophisticated rules of grammar. At an early stage, baby may come to Mommy with the request, "Pick you up," based on hearing Mommy's "Shall I pick you up?" But before long, s/he will have the correct pronoun references sorted out without specific lessons. Simply based on close observation, experimenting, hypothesis testing, then updating and refining knowledge, the junior scientist accomplishes the learning task effectively and accurately.

Though parents generally don't think of baby as a researcher, they nevertheless know that s/he is an effective learner and trust him/her to learn all s/he needs – including language – without specific lessons. They simply model what they want baby to learn, provide feedback that acknowledges and expands what the child is doing, and let baby practice to his/her heart's content. They focus on meaning and receive even rough tries at talking in a positive manner. Parents make trial-and-error learning safe.

**TABLE 1
METHODS OF RESEARCH AND ENQUIRY USED BY
SCIENTISTS DOING RESEARCH AND CHILDREN EXPLORING
THEIR WORLD**

Both will

Decide what *they* want to investigate, what is important to *them*

Observe, listen, physically examine, test, use all their senses to gain knowledge

Use prior knowledge and previous experience to aid information gathering

Follow the lead of their peers

Draw on the experience of others to aid research, ask questions

Note recurring patterns, similarities, differences, predictable patterns

Develop hypotheses about the materials or activities they are testing

Experiment to test hypotheses

Draw inferences on the basis of experiments and observations

Make retests to confirm or deny findings

Anticipate what will happen next

Generate rules and theories based on observed patterns

Update or correct previous findings on the basis of new evidence

Refine knowledge and test its fit with prior information

Consider the entire situation or context to interpret findings

Work actively to acquire new knowledge

Use imagination and intuition to further their research

Stay with a problem of their choice

Take risks in exploring and putting forth new findings

Are curious and love to explore unknown territory

Work hard to solve problems and overcome obstacles

Under the open teaching-learning interactions in the home, learning moves

- from whole to parts
- from concrete to abstract
- from gross to fine

In other words,

(1) children take in overall patterns before focusing on parts of language,
(2) they examine the concrete world before being concerned with abstract symbols of speech, and
(3) their understanding and talking evolve gradually from rough approximations to ever greater refinement and accuracy.

When we compared these ways of learning and the parents' ways of teaching with the teaching-learning interaction in our own structured classrooms, we came to realize that the two were almost diametrically opposed. Table 2 juxtaposes the ways of the home with the ways of our structured, teacher-directed classroom. It shows clearly that the teaching we were doing at the time of our early research did not build upon the learners' ways of learning.

As we gradually shifted our teaching to fit the learners' ways more closely, we looked for reassurance to writings of researchers like Harste, Goodman, Graves, and Holdaway, who confirmed the correctness and importance of encouraging children to use their own ways of learning. Now the brain research described in chapter 1 validates and expands the principles and practices of teaching the learners' way.

Teaching the learners' way begins with modeling meaningful, enjoyable reading and writing. It gives the children a chance to become familiar with stories and written messages *before* they have to learn the parts of speech. While it may seem impossible to teach children to read by reading when they don't know anything about letters and sounds, it makes perfect sense when you consider that they learned to talk by talking. They can certainly listen to stories, watch how others handle books, and recognize familiar words or messages. In fact, they are building the foundation of literacy – an understanding of the joys of reading and the functions of written language.

How to teach the learners' way

TABLE 2

LEARNING TO SPEAK AT HOME COMPARED WITH LEARNING TO READ IN A STRUCTURED CLASS

Speaking	*Reading*
The child learns to speak without formal speaking lessons.	Structured reading instructions guide the learner.
Learning to speak is an integral part of everyday experience.	Reading is frequently taught as a separate skill.
Whole language and meaningful talk surround the learner.	Parts of written language are introduced one at a time.
A normal flow of language addressed to him/her and to others is available to the beginner as a model of fluent speech.	Little modeling of fluent reading is available to the beginning reader who listens only to his peers.
Familiar actions, concrete objects, and the context or setting give meaning to spoken language.	Context and practical applications are used minimally to help children make sense of initial reading.
The amount of oral language a child has available as models is varied and vast.	The type and amount of written language available to the beginner are often carefully controlled.
The child generates and applies rules of language.	Rules are introduced by adults.
The child decides when s/he is ready to move to a new level.	The teacher sets the sequence and timing for learning.
Gross performance with sounds and syntax is acceptable. (Few parents attempt to have beginning speakers correct their early language.)	Fine discrimination and accuracy are generally asked for. The teacher usually requires the beginning reader to correct imprecise readings of the text.
The child has ample opportunity to practice speaking.	Reading practice is often limited to minutes a day.
Meaning or the truth of a statement – rather than its form – guides the response of adults to the child.	Form – sounds and graphic symbols – are stressed more than meaning or the content of the message.
Parents confirm what the child has said using feedback that expands and elaborates the child's words.	Use of feedback to confirm meaning is minimal in many classrooms.

(Note: the examples of structured, teacher-directed learning are based on our in-class observational study)

Modeling fluent reading teaches beginners more about reading than does introducing particles of speech one at a time. Imagine lecturing aspiring baseball players on how they must move each muscle. Think of the trouble you would have getting children to practice if they never saw or participated in exciting ball games. So to foster both interest and skills in reading and writing, teaching relies heavily on modeling or demonstrating what children need to learn, on having children practice as best they can, and on providing feedback that encourages children while showing them in a positive way how they can move further ahead. Like the parent reading to children at home, the teacher uses predictable and familiar stories that make it easy for children to begin to chime in and get a sense of reading along.

Teaching the learners' way may begin by introducing children to reading stories, but it does not stop there. In fact, because writing is such an integral part of teaching, children have more practice in the use of letters and sounding out than they do in a more structured program. From the first day of school and all through the year, the teacher will write messages based on the children's dictation and will encourage them to write their own. In order to produce these messages, children need to learn about letters and their sounds. Here is where their ability to generate rules comes into full play. As they work at writing, they make sounds, test their previous experience with letters, and discuss how something should be spelled. They are actively involved in figuring out and applying information about letter-sound correspondences. In the process they learn not only about sounds but about spelling patterns as well. While the children write or dictate, the teacher provides on-the-spot individualized lessons in phonologic awareness as the children need them. If context and syntax fail to reveal the meaning of an unfamiliar word in their reading, they apply their knowledge of spelling to sounding out that word.

In spelling, as in reading, meaning guides and motivates the young learners. Just as a baby is eager to practice making the right kinds of sounds to communicate, so young writers try hard to produce the right written symbols to convey the messages they have composed. Thoughtful, sustained, voluntary practice helps children generate rules in the same effective ways that babies generate rules for speaking. These active ways of learning provide a very solid base for sounding out unfamiliar words and internalizing the difficult rules of English spelling.

Since observing how children learn has been the foundation of evolving this kind of teaching, it will come as no surprise that teaching continues to rely heavily on watching how children respond to the activities and materials in class. Capturing teachable moments, noting what moves children ahead and what seems to puzzle them are the crucial teaching tools that will tell you a great deal more about the children and their learning than worksheet exercises. Shifting the focus from looking for "the right answer" to describing how individual children are handling a reading or writing task makes your teaching both interesting and exciting. But it takes practice to move from focusing on the finished product to the children's ways of producing it.

The bonus for you and the children is that assessing progress becomes a highly positive way of helping children move ahead. Acknowledging every small step forward signals to children that they are being successful and they build on those successes. By not asking beginners for precise work with letters, sounds, words, or printing, you make the classroom a safe place for venturing into unfamiliar territory.

Acknowledging the individuality of learning is another key element of teaching. Knowing that each child brings a unique background and level of maturity to learning tasks makes it important to let children set the pace of their learning. They need to feel free to practice reading and writing with materials of their choice and to take their time. The voluntary practice and choice of materials build confidence and also foster independence of learning that frees the teacher to give extra attention to children who need and want individual help.

Teaching the learners' way builds on children's strengths

Teaching the learners' way acknowledges that children bring both five or six years of living experience and a well-functioning learning system as a foundation for their school learning. Therefore, reading and writing are not seen as first steps but as continuations of previous learning. Knowledge, experience, thinking and research skills, methods of learning, special intelligences, and personal qualities all support literacy learning.

Knowledge
- of language, its sounds and uses
- of everyday things and events
- of people and their interactions

Experience
- with abstracting information from overall impressions
- taking things apart
- being independent in learning new information

Thinking skills
- hypothesis testing
- ability to draw inferences
- ability to generate rules
- willingness to self-correct

Methods of learning
- use of models
- observation skills
- trial-and-error learning
- active exploration, use of the senses

Personal qualities
- curiosity
- imagination
- perseverance, willingness to practice
- energy, enthusiasm for learning
- keen interest in the environment or other special intelligences

Building on that foundation calls for a partnership in learning and the same holistic methods of teaching that functioned so effectively at home.

Children thrive when they are encouraged to talk, to draw on what they know about the world, to listen to stories, to look at written messages, to guess or speculate, to look for patterns, and to follow models. They love to explore their classroom physically and become active, careful observers and listeners. When left to choose many of their activities, their attention span is remarkably long and their energy and enthusiasm rarely flag. In school, as at home, they are eager learners.

Instruction that is too teacher-directed can undermine learning

Reviewing the well-organized lessons we used to present revealed that many of our well-intentioned aids to learning actually stripped children of the thinking and learning tools that had served them so well at home.

- Using books with stilted, limited language hindered the children's use of their own language to aid reading.
- Limiting discussion to answers that closely followed the book denied the children's knowledge of equally valid answers.
- Telling children not to guess or anticipate gradually eliminated hypothesis testing and inference-drawing.
- Discouraging the use of pictures blocked the use of general knowledge and context to aid reading.
- Asking children to sit still for long periods of time failed to draw on their natural inclination to explore and use their senses to learn.
- Supplying too many rules eliminated the need for the children to generate or test rules of reading, writing, and spelling.
- Staying with prescribed basal readers failed to generate the excitement and enthusiasm evident in classrooms where children construct their learning.

What has changed?

Comparing our somewhat rigid teaching of the past with the active classrooms of today, shows clearly that the changes we have made involve far more than the addition of story reading and modeling writing. The most fundamental and far-reaching change lies in our attitude toward the learners. Over years of watching for their ways of learning, we have come to acknowledge the effectiveness and reliability of the children's knowledge and methods of learning. We now *know* that their gradual progression from the use of natural language to an appreciation and use of letters and words will bring them to the very same skills that are part of the standard curriculum. We have learned to recognize the global, communication activities of children as the very foundation of true, functional literacy and to feel comfortable with the seemingly slow evolution of accurate decoding skills. Each year we have observed those skills emerge from the children's interactions with written language in all its uses and forms. Stories, name tags, labels, picture captions, news items, written messages will generate phonic skills, printing, spelling, decoding, *and* a love of reading and writing.

Studying the workings of the normally functioning and developing human brain has taught us that physical movement and active sensory exploration are fundamental needs for the full evolution of the network of neurons and attendant cognitive development. Hence, making room for physical movement in class, encouraging sensory exploration of the environment, and fostering independence and choice in learning activities are not indulgences but integral parts of fostering the children's mental and physical growth. Instead of fretting about discipline or the precise adherence to a scope and sequence chart, each year we experience the excitement of noting yet more signs of the children's own meaning-making, pattern-matching, rule-generating, and self-correcting in their reading and writing activities.

Our role of authority figure and dispenser of knowledge or rules has changed to that of co-learner. Our questions have shifted from "is this child doing the *right* thing?" to "what is the child doing, and how is s/he dealing with this learning task?" As a result, we are doing in-class research every day. We are modeling learning behaviors, listening and observing behaviors, and we are participating genuinely in the children's learning. We are as excited about new learning as they are.

Learning by doing and observing what happens are two key components of teaching the learners' way. Apply these two elements in using this book. Read through the book, decide what would feel comfortable to you, and use those ideas in your classroom. Perhaps you will decide that reading to and with the children is a safe first step. Maybe news time with its unison spelling and positive feedback appeals to you. Whatever you decide, give the new activity a good try and keep observing how both you and the children react to the change.

To aid your observations, refer to some of our descriptions of children's behaviors. Better still, discuss your findings with teachers who are launched on ways of teaching that build on the children's ways of learning. Using the methods of assessing progress described in Chapter 8 will reassure you that children are indeed learning.

How to use this book

Keep in mind that learning is a gradual process and that, like the children, you need safety and trust to evolve your own learning. Be kind to yourself and accept that your changes in teaching may at first be rough approximations. Continue to refer back to parts of the book that appeal to you and then gradually expand into areas that seem a bit more scary.

We hope that using the book will add joy and energy to your teaching. Look upon it as an invitation to new learning for you as well as the children.

What Does the Brain Have to Do with Education?

1

Surveying our work table scattered with research notes and illustrations of the brain and its constituent parts, a young visitor asked, "What does the brain have to do with education?"

At times when rigid curriculum requirements and scope-and-sequence charts prescribed what, how, and when children should be taught, the answer might have been, "Not very much."

That type of teaching did not concern itself with the functions of the brain and now seems akin to a doctor informing a patient with heart problems that the functions of the heart don't interest him. Those days are long gone, yet much of the vital information about how the brain takes in, sorts, stores, and at times blocks new information is not readily accessible when it is presented in language that is foreign to us. Rote memorization of the parts of the brain and their functions is as unproductive for many of us as the rote memorization of rules of phonics and multiplication tables is for children. Like the children, we don't apply learning freely when it remains unconnected to our own base of knowledge and ways of learning.

> *My goal is to dispel the notion that the mind can be understood in the absence of biology (Edelman 1992, 211).*

Translating brain functions into meaningful images

As we struggled with a wealth of overly technical information, we discovered images created by researchers that imbued their

findings with meaning we could relate to on a personal level. To make these images yet more concrete, we had an artist convert the verbal images into visual ones to illustrate relevant knowledge about the brain and its processes into learning and classroom practice.

City of the mind

With the advent of electronic scanning devices, the brain has yielded many of its secrets about specialized functioning of its different areas. The findings confirm the right-left split that assigns special functions to the two hemispheres and add details about every part of the brain. Each lobe, each tiny area or part, does its particular job, but the overriding fact is the "brain is a parallel processor," a "city of the mind" in which many parts function together at the same time, supporting each other, or working side by side, much like the many parts of a city function simultaneously and cooperatively (Caine & Caine 1991). Simple activities like talking, reading, or moving about will light up the screen of a brain scan of the city of the mind, showing activities in many neighborhoods simultaneously. Learning activities draw on a whole range of brain functions that are interconnected and mutually supportive. Thoughts, feelings, physical movement, sensory input,

A city with its thousands of inhabitants and different places to live and work functions moment to moment without the need of a central controller to govern the multitude of spontaneous interactions that respond to the needs of the moment.

The brain functions in much the same way. Its many areas and parts communicate and collaborate to meet the demands of the moment. No central controller could match the effectiveness of the free interactions that characterize the workings of the city of the mind.

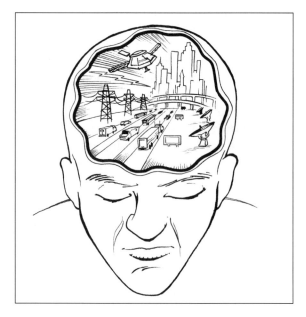

and memory combine to create new learning. The city of the mind thrives on complexity and cooperation. It prospers and grows in a classroom filled with interesting reading materials, real-life math activities, centers that stimulate many intelligences, and art supplies that invite creative work. That kind of environment encourages interaction and mutual support from many areas of the city of the mind as they connect and work together.

The brothers Triune: The brain in three stories

Just as cities have distinct neighborhoods designed to meet different needs, so the brain has special neighborhoods that function as cohesive units. One theme that recurs in the research is the idea that we actually have three brains in one. There is the earliest or oldest layer (the *reptilian* or *r-complex*) that deals with survival – respiration, heartbeat, our vital energy system. The next layer (the *limbic system*) adds feelings and conscious memory, and deals with the reception, analysis, transmission, and storage of incoming sensory information. The latest addition to the growing, evolving brain is the celebrated *neocortex* that does the elegant, creative thinking and planning that make each one of us unique but is not yet fully grown when children first enter school.

The brothers Triune

What makes this "triune brain" so important to us as teachers is that its three layers or modules have open lines of communication between each other, and at any given moment, one or the other is capable of taking charge of our actions, thoughts, and feelings. Learning is not simply a matter of activating the neocortex, but is very much connected to feelings, sensory input, prior knowledge, old habits, and ingrained behaviors. To highlight that interconnectedness, Caine and Caine (1991) created the image of the brothers Triune – three brothers living in the same house and communicating with one another. At times, one or two take control of the whole house.

Repto

Repto is the oldest of the brothers and lives in the basement. His part of the house is connected to the vital supply lines that carry fuel and energy to the whole house. As Repto is concerned with basic survival, he strongly resists change and likes to assert his habits and ways to maintain the comfort and security of the whole family. To that end, he'll go into "fight-or-flight" mode when Limbo sends down a "danger" signal.

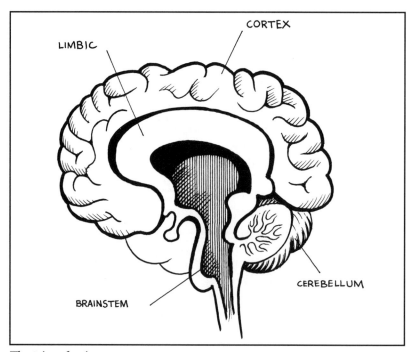

The triune brain

Limbo

Limbo is the middle brother. He occupies the center of the house, the place where sensory information comes in from the outside world. He is deeply involved with emotions, monitoring them, connecting them to memory, and keeping a balance between the oldest and youngest brothers to keep them from dominating the family. To deal with emergencies, his breaker switch can signal Repto, "Danger: activate fight-flight energies," and at the same time blank out the whole upper story to stop Neo's planning and thinking.

Neo

Neo, the youngest brother, is the largest and most versatile of the brothers. Along with engaging in logic and complex analysis, Neo creates and uses language and plans for the future by processing sensory information coming in from Limbo's intake system. He programs physical movement and communicates actively with his two brothers to enhance their ways of being or to suggest a reasonable alternative to fixed behavior patterns. Capable of wonderful growth and development, Neo, too, responds to feelings and incorporates them into his decision-making.

Downshifting means moving into the basement complex

If you have ever wondered about "downshifting" as applied to learners who have shut down their higher order thinking for the moment, the house of the brothers Triune provides a metaphor. When unsure, tired, anxious, or confused, there is great comfort in shifting into the basement complex to be with Repto. Once there, children don't have to think about what to do or how to do it. They fall back on the habits and routines they have grown up with at home or developed at school. They automatically activate strongly entrenched thoughts and behaviors (Caine & Caine 1991, 69). For Pat, it may mean withdrawing, or refusals to answer when spoken to, to pick up a pencil, to move, or to make eye contact. For Noel, uncertainty triggers the "fight" response – acting out, hitting other children, kicking the teacher, and using abusive language. Then there is Robyn, who wants to hide and sticks to the teacher like glue, refusing to eat lunch without her and holding on to her until mommy arrives at the end of the school day.

When stressed out, have you ever looked for the reassurance of being with friends, of familiar work around the home? Have you lashed out verbally or reached for your favorite comfort food (or drink)? Children do just that when they feel unsure.

Safety and familiar routines are the domain of the basement complex of the house of the brothers Triune. When children first enter school, everything around them is unfamiliar. The routines and habits they have learned at home have been displaced. So it becomes vital to establish a classroom climate that radiates safety and joy to reassure children that new habits and routines offer the same comfort and familiarity as their home environment. Once they feel safe, they will readily move out of the basement complex to explore and learn with the other two brothers. When you assure that their basic needs are catered to, they will soon be honing their creativity in Neo's attic. We found that Toby dried his tears during snack time, the more active kindergarten children settled down to paper-and-pencil work when they perceived that moving around, lying on the floor, or sitting under the table was permissible. Marty abandoned lashing out when work in the classroom took on more interest, action, and challenge.

Lashing out or withdrawing – fight-or-flight responses – are by no means the only innate behavior patterns observed by brain researchers and neuropsychologists. A child's brain is not an empty slate onto which the environment draws its scenarios. Patterns of survival, of fitting into the world, are deeply inscribed, and as teachers we have observed most of them in our classrooms. They are not new, but merely confirm that here are behaviors that need to be acknowledged as natural and innate. At the same time, with the collaboration of all three brothers Triune, these behaviors are open to being modified or enhanced in the interest of learning and the full social development of the individual child and the classroom community.

The basic brain

We need to value action as a factor equal to thought, imagination and feeling (De Beauport 1996, 235).

Acknowledging the importance of Repto's domain in the overall functioning of the brain family, De Beauport calls the *brainstem* or *r-complex* the "basic brain" and refers to it as the "brain of action." Connected directly to the spinal cord, the basic brain governs our nervous system and establishes the behavior patterns needed for self-preservation – moving away from threat, seeking out nourishment and warmth, and following instinctive patterns of behavior that become ingrained habits and routines. Several researchers comment on these basic behaviors and their universality and resistance to change. Ignoring for a moment the preening and mating rituals that generally show up as children mature, here are some of the patterns that emerge in the classroom.

Imitation

Learning by imitation – by following a model – is the most fundamental method of learning from earliest childhood. Babies mimic facial expressions and gestures. Toddlers watch their siblings and playmates with the most intense concentration in order to "do what the big guys are doing." Playing house, dressing up, and getting into Daddy's tool kit all attest to the drive to follow the models around home. In this fundamental learning, actions count far more than words. In school, watching the teacher, classmates, and older children at work and play remains the best teaching-learning tool. Modeling social behaviors and lessons produces results where rules and lectures fail.

Repetition

Repeating familiar games and routines provides a sense of competence and safety. Running a noisy toy truck back and forth endlessly may drive Mommy to distraction, but makes a very satisfying sound to baby, who is exercising both muscles and senses. The exercise of filling, emptying, refilling, and emptying a cup or bucket with water or sand is intriguing, builds eye-hand coordination, and can go on for hours. No problem with concentration or time-on-task here.

That kind of intense voluntary practice can extend into the classroom. If movement is encouraged and learning materials captivate the senses, hands-on materials are eagerly sought out and used again and again. When learning to read, children may opt to read and reread the same small book time and time again before feeling ready to move ahead. Reciting nursery rhymes or learning raps add rhythm to repetition and build learning as children opt to recite to themselves or in small groups.

Routinization

Routines arise naturally as repeated patterns of behavior settle into rituals that feel comfortable and right. At home it may be the daily rituals of bedtime stories, of meals served at fixed times. At school, the morning meeting, story time, center time, and the ritual of talking over "what we have learned" at the end of the school day become established routines that make for comfort and an effective flow of learning. An abrupt change in such routines can become a source of stress and can disrupt the harmony of familiar ways of interacting. De Beauport reminds us of the stress we experience when changing our job, home, or spouse and adds, "Routines are to the deepest brain what rationality is to the left hemisphere" (1996, 226). So establishing and maintaining a familiar flow of routine activities can smooth the path of learning. On the negative side, the routinization of the basic brain "explains why antisocial routines, habits, rituals and values become as deeply entrenched as any socially rewarding values" (216).

Flocking

Like adults, children are social beings. They feel comfortable and safe when they have a sense of belonging to a group. Aside from sitting or playing together, children demonstrate their sense of belonging by adopting the mannerisms, dress, or playground activities of the group they feel drawn to. That sense of belonging can be encouraged in many ways and can pay wonderful dividends

in harmonious interactions and productivity. Examples include working on group projects, planning with the class for special events, interacting during the morning meeting, being with classmates and parent helpers during field trips.

Establishing social hierarchies

Dominance patterns emerge early. Children who are self-assured will take the lead in games, projects, or class discussions. They can become models for the less mature or more timid children – an emergent reader we know promptly picked up the British accent of her more proficient reading buddy. The more dominant children are sure to lead while reading big books in unison, doing group spelling, or providing news; so at times, it becomes important to suggest less dominant children participate: "Today we need to hear from Lucy" or "You have been really helpful; now Sergei wants an opportunity to spell without any help." The "leaders" readily heed such suggestions. Because of the spirit of cooperation, helpfulness, and caring in the classroom, they take pride and pleasure in watching the more timid children come forth to speak up or try their hand at an unfamiliar task. Leadership, when affirmed tactfully, can develop positive social patterns and reinforce the power of positive modeling.

Deception

For humans, as for animals, playing dead – becoming invisible – can often become a matter of survival. Hiding is one way of being invisible. Do you remember the time when you avoided your instructor's gaze by studiously concentrating on your notes so you wouldn't be called upon? Children find all kinds of ways to hide when they feel shy or unsure. Once they perceive that they are safe from being put on the spot whenever they are not yet ready, they *will* volunteer to read, spell, or participate in groups. They no longer need to hide when voluntary participation is an integral part of teaching and learning.

Pretending falls under the heading "Deception," and for young children it is a powerful mode of learning and rehearsing. We have all witnessed children trying to do or be what the teacher wants, feigning competence when there is uncertainty. In an exercise designed to convey the mysteries of probability to first-graders, one teacher

Hiding can be part of deception, and early in the year when children still feel insecure, hiding or avoiding the teacher can take a number of forms.

put three red and twenty white balls into a bag, and made it quite clear that to find one of the few red balls was very improbable – "special." Half the class gave a show of hands when she asked, "Who has a *red* ball?" The lesson on probability had gone over their heads, but pleasing the teacher was a well-ingrained habit, so they pretended! Some observers in our classrooms have objected to memory reading, pretend writing, and invented spelling on the grounds that children will never move to genuine skill building. But in class, as at home, the confidence of pretending to know more about the ongoing work is both a confidence builder and a powerful way to rehearse for more polished performance.

The basic brain supports overall functioning

Wakefulness depends on the brainstem more than on the "higher centers" (Restak 1979, 24).

Though the brainstem is relatively small and its functions seem less important to learning, it is the crucial and powerful brain regulator in charge of survival. All of the nerves rising out of the spinal column connect with the brain via the brainstem. In fact, wakefulness and attention depend on the brainstem. If you have ever wondered why a correctly placed karate chop to the base of the skull can knock a person unconscious, the answer lies in the blow being struck to this crucial part of the brain. When it is put out of commission, everything else comes to a stop.

Since the basic brain looks after survival needs, proper nutrition, plenty of water, and fresh air are among the nutrients it needs.

Catering to the brainstem's basic survival functions includes attention to proper nutrition – we can discourage snacks full of sugar or salt, encourage students to drink water to hydrate the brain, allow them to go to the restroom as and when the need arises, and see to it that the air in the classroom is fresh. If these factors seem to fall outside of the realm of education, ask yourself how much health and comfort contribute to your best functioning when working on new learning.

Modeling, meaningful routines, voluntary repetition of material to be learned, and interactions with peers in a safe environment are ways to affirm the natural functioning of the "basic brain." Add to these learning basics the sense of curiosity, feelings of excitement about new discoveries, and the joy of actively exploring new learning, and you have moved up one story into Limbo's domain, the feeling brain.

Memories depend on emotions and sensory input

*Thoughts and emotions are interwoven: every thought,
however bland, almost always carries with it some emotional
undertone, however subtle (Restak 1995, 21).*

Taking a look at Limbo's domain in the house of the brothers Triune confirms once again that learning is by no means the exclusive realm of the neocortex. Sitting on top of the brainstem like a cap (a *limbus* or border), the limbic brain comprises several vital structures that receive and process incoming information that is then transmitted to both the upper and lower story of the house of the brain. At the top of the brainstem, the thalamus is the major relay center for incoming sensory information. That information moves to the neocortex for analysis or to the *amygdala* for emotional screening and storage in memory.

Prior experience, memory, and the feelings connected with those memories determine our reactions and the decision to store or reject incoming information. Sylwester likens the selection and classification done by the amygdala to that of a "librarian who subjectively selects the materials to add to the library" (1995,5). Experiences of interest, pleasure, excitement, curiosity, and hands-on sensory involvement aid selection for storage. Negative emotions – anxiety, fear, pain, frustration, anger – make for

The feeling brain

Long-term memory storage depends on emotions to classify material to be stored or rejected. The amygdala is the arbiter of what to accept and store and when to react strongly to negative input.

rejection. A classroom climate that makes learning safe and meaningful to the children is sure to generate the "store" signal that transmits new learning for long-term storage in the *hippocampus* through its multisensory input systems of touch, sound, vision, and movement.

When school is less inviting, fear of failure, anxiety about "doing things right," or frustration with so much that is unfamiliar can be

"Most incoming sensory information is sent first to the thalamus, and then it's relayed to the sensory frontal lobes for detailed analysis and response. A second, quicker pathway also sends any emotionally laden information from the thalamus to the amygdala. to activate an immediate aggressive or defensive response" (Sylwester 1995, 73).

the negative triggers that cause the "feeling" brain to shut down. If the incoming signal is sufficiently strong, the amygdala can declare an emergency and contact the *hypothalamus* to trigger the fight-or-flight response by shifting to the pituitary for a surge of energy. The neocortex has been hijacked, and lashing out or hiding become automatic responses, giving Neo no opportunity to come in with more reasonable responses.

When endorphins flow

Aside from its physical structures, brain chemicals form part of the feeling brain and affect both our moods and levels of energy.

*The tiny hypothalamic nuclei
– the pleasure and pain centers
– sit right next to each other
and instantly respond strongly
to incoming messages. Love and
hate, euphoria and terror,
sit side by side.*

Depression, sadness, and boredom leave us with little or no energy. Pleasure can quickly turn to anger, as violence and pleasure centers of the brain are in such close proximity. On the positive side, happiness and the drive to explore raise energy levels by degrees. Both within ourselves and in our students, we have all witnessed the instant shift in energy from dullness or apathy to alert interest when something new and interesting arises in a routine class. Creating "a climate of delight" filled with positive social contacts, movement, music, successful experiences, supportive comments from teacher and friends musters the support of *endorphins*, the "internal chemical response that can increase the possibility that students will learn how to solve problems successfully in potentially stressful situations" (Sylwester 1995, 39). The positive learning climate is stimulating both learning and "enhancing serotonin functions (that) reduce aggression and favor social behavior" (Damasio 1994, 76).

Brain chemicals are powerful messengers that affect our entire body as well as our state of mind. "Gut feelings" are just that, "the emotional brain system governs every organ of our body" (by means of the autonomic or involuntary nervous system). "Emotions are the vibrations of the limbic brain, just as thought and imagination are the vibrations of the neocortex" (De Beauport 1996, 88). Limbo exerts a powerful influence on our ways of being and stays in close contact with his creative younger brother.

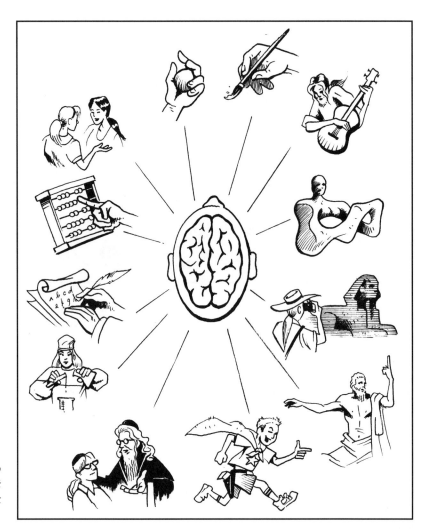

Though dedicated to different functions, the left and right hemispheres work in close harmony.

The brain of creativity, reason, and language

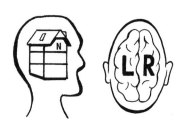

Neo is definitely the best known member of the brain family. His capacity for logic, rational thought, planning for the future and, of course, language contribute much to learning, but that is only half of his unique creativity. Neo's domain has two sides that complement each other, each receiving the same stimulus but extracting different information from it. The two sides – right and left hemispheres – are joined together and collaborate closely to add intuition, imagination, association, and relationship skills to Neo's overall intelligence. Just as the three brothers are in constant close communication, so the many facets of Neo's complex world interact

*Neurons with dendrites that reach out like limbs of a tree are the links that
connect the different parts of the brain. Like trees, the neurons grow and reach out
when they are nourished in a rich environment, in soil that offers many nutrients
and "showers of information, sensations... from the outside world" (Diamond &
Hopson 1998, 25). Established neuron trees grow larger and stronger with
repeated learning; new trees are added as experience and stimulation expand.
New growth and old combine to form a neural forest with thousands upon
thousands of connections to weave a canopy of networks and circuits that keeps
on growing. The forest of neurons changes on the basis of learning.*

and support each other. Complexity and challenge rather than
overly simple tasks fit Neo's ways of learning and growing.

The magic forest of neurons

> *The more researchers have learned about the dendrites in
> our nervous system and brain, the more appropriate seems
> the term "little trees" (Diamond & Hopson 1998, 23).*

Where society once viewed the child's brain as static and
unchangeable, experts today see it as a highly dynamic organ that
feeds on stimulation and responds with the flourishing of branching,
intertwined neural forests (Diamond, 1998, 1).

Physical activity, mental challenge, novelty, social interactions, emotional involvement, and success experiences are the stimulants that make the forest grow, as it is moistened by liberal showers of *serotonin*. The growth of their neuron forests manifests itself in the children's learning, their steps forward, and their growing self-assurance. Success builds on success. Gaining proficiency in the gym was the impetus for a very noticeable spurt in classroom learning for Chris. When Les finally mastered the times tables during Easter weekend, other skills suddenly improved. Finding a new friend in class gave Robyn the confidence to venture into group projects and new areas of learning.

As the neural trees thicken with repeated use, their *dendrites* spread and interconnect to transmit information more readily. Learning deepens and communication expands. These solid, well-established trees become the confidence builders that invite children to climb higher or swing into new areas. We have all witnessed the versatility players can develop in sports and music once they have become proficient and highly practiced in one area. Academic learning works much the same way when it builds on the confidence of ongoing practice and refinement of established skills. Knowing that pattern building is a good foundation for emergent reading, Margaret had encouraged Brett to use pattern blocks at every opportunity. Once he had produced a huge design all by himself, Brett's reading skills took a leap forward and evolved successfully from there. Visitors to the classroom have commented that the children are always eager to respond to suggestions – working in a new genre of writing or tackling an unfamiliar book or activity. Their neural trees have been well nourished over time and are ready to branch out or support climbing to new heights.

Pruning the deadwood

> *Just as muscles are programmed to grow smaller and weaker with disuse, the dendritic trees and spines will shrivel and the cortex grow thinner with lack of mental activity (Diamond & Hopson 1998, 29).*

In the forest of *neurons*, lack of use, stimulation, and proper nutrients can produce deadwood that must be pruned. In *Endangered Minds,* Jane Healy (1990) writes of declining scores on IQ tests and the lowering of children's reading abilities. Like many of the researchers, she emphasizes the role of the learning environment and children's interactions with it to *sculpt* the brain. As teachers we have the awesome responsibility not only for the learning of our students but for the actual physiological development of their brains, which, in turn, will become the basis of lifelong learning. Emotional barriers – fear, anxiety, frustration – can block that growth, as can lack of sensory stimulation and movement. In class, as at home, young children need to explore and manipulate their learning materials and environment to make sensory-motor connections preparatory to building neural networks for more abstract, formal thought patterns. So the classroom climate and resources become crucial factors in keeping neural forests alive. Learning is a physiological process, in which we are quite literally building brains as well as learning.

Plant a new tree

Children's brains are wonderfully malleable. New dendrite trees are planted easily when activities invite participation and offer new ways of learning or interacting. Pruning of deadwood makes room for more advanced skills or activities. At home, crawling gives way to walking as a means of effective locomotion. In school, memory reading is succeeded by accurate decoding and use of context skills; writing evolves from crude beginnings to sophisticated compositions and ever more accurate spelling. Counting on fingers is replaced by paper-and-pencil math. In a classroom built on cooperation, counter-productive aggressive behavior gives way to new, more sociable ways of interacting. The new trees grow and flourish in a climate of sensory stimulation and positive interactions.

*"If a connection, a branch,
or an entire dendritic tree withers
from lack of use, plant another
through stimulation of the
senses and multiple intelligences"*
(Diamond & Hopson 1998, 255).

Movement and sensory stimulation are crucial to learning

If you asked me to think of times when my students are completely still, I couldn't think of a single one (Margaret Reinhard).

When children first enter school, their learning relies heavily on the sensory-motor explorations that have served them so well at home. So as they embark upon learning in class, their eyes and hands are

exploring, their body language responds to stories and activities, and their interactions are lively and full of physical expression. As Margaret points out, they are never completely still, but that does not mean that there is pandemonium in class. Instead, school learning replicates the natural learning children did at home where they had to respect the needs of others but were free to move, to talk, to touch learning materials, to interact freely with the people around them and, as necessary, to be still.

In class, as at home, learning is stimulated and cemented by interaction and sensory-motor input. Learning to read begins with listening to stories and handling books with lots of pictures; writing and spelling are aided by manipulating colorful movable letters, by physical practice at the blackboard, by using large-motor movements on paper or whiteboards, and by active discussions about composition topics. Games of all sorts develop eye-hand coordination, quick reaction, and attention. Effective learning is both multisensory and social. A wealth of research confirms that when all three brain brothers interact freely, learning takes on depth and joy (Caine & Caine 1997).

In Margaret's class, Invention Day stimulated amazing creativity, as children interacted with each other and a large assortment of "junk" materials to design, construct, mold and animate their very own creations – boats, castles, windmills with movable wings, and the like. The classroom hummed with the give-and-take of working together or consulting with each other. Movement included climbing up, over, and under chairs and desks, as cardboard castles and storefronts were erected out of large boxes. Focus was total, energy high, and social harmony absolute. "We are busy doing important work," was the feeling that pervaded. As the children talked about and wrote descriptions and captions for their inventions, language-arts skills were honed. The sense of accomplishment and interest generated by the variety of inventions definitely strengthened existing neural trees and very likely planted a number of new ones.

Manipulatives of various kinds create a feel for number values that move well beyond the reciting of number words or copying of written symbols. Unifix cubes inspired a twin boy and girl to put together 1001 pieces, moving into the hall and all the way to the front door of the school to do the job. Other children joined in and added colored markers to introduce counting by tens – all this in grade one and based on voluntary exploration of materials and

Movement and sensory input shape learning and sculpt the brain

A look at the constituent parts of Neo's domain shows the sensory and motor cortex lying side by side in a broad band stretching right across the top of the neocortex. Then there is the cerebellum *that contains "over half of all the neurons of the brain, and links movement with higher cognitive functions" (Jensen 1998, 83). As physical movement activates these areas, their neuron trees reach out to connect with other parts of the brain to activate thought, feelings, and alertness.*

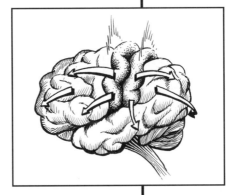

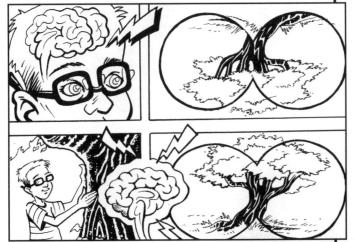

Experiments reveal the effects of action and inaction

Touch educates the brain and turns the world right-side up in an experiment in which students were given glasses that inverted their field of vision. Simply trying to right the world while sitting still did not work. In class as in the experiment, sensory input is highly important to orient learners in space and activate all areas of the brain.

Kittens are born with their eyes closed. Left free to roam and explore their environment, they open their eyes and develop naturally. Kittens strapped into a basket and towed around are deprived of the sensory motor stimulation needed for normal development. As a result, they remain blind. Humans, too, must have sensory motor stimulation to develop normally. Healthy neural development requires *physical movement and sensory input for young learners. The President's Council on Fitness and Sports says that all K–12 students need thirty minutes a day of physical movement to stimulate the brain (Jensen 1998, 87).*

Restraining physical movement has a powerful effect on overall functioning of body and mind. Adults who volunteered to wear neck restraints became disoriented, profoundly upset, and unable to function normally. If you have ever tried to hold an entire class to total inactivity, you know the children's reactions. Now research shows that prolonged inactivity actually impedes the physical development of the immature brain.

Field trips add the magic of discovery to rich multisensory learning. Sights, sounds, smells, and touch combine with balancing on rocks and tree trunks. Learning and growth of neural trees are at a maximum as serotonin flows and the neural fibers of the cerebellum are fully activated.

space. Activity and cooperation were high, and when the twins' mother arrived in time to admire the amazing structure, the glow of success and feelings of accomplishment pervaded the entire class.

Confidence, willingness to venture forth into new fields of learning, persistence with tasks, and remarkable creativity are the hallmarks of children's response to classroom work when their physiological need to move and use their senses is acknowledged and encouraged. Varieties of art materials will evolve motor skills from large to fine. Cooking adds the dimension of taste and smell to the reading, writing, and counting tasks of following recipes. Active games both indoors and out are essential components of building and strengthening the neural connections that pervade the entire brain. Jensen (1998) offers a wealth of biological and classroom research that documents the crucial part active physical movement plays in learning and developing the brain's neural networks and how dance and music can effectively stimulate or calm down an entire class.

The power of music to energize or relax

*Music has an uncanny manner of activating neurons for purposes
of relaxing muscle tension, changing pulse and producing
long-range memories which are directly related to the number
of neurons activated in the experience (Campbell 1988, 17).*

Do you remember the instant energy boost you felt when hearing a lively, familiar tune at a time when you had felt tired or lethargic? Creating a musical break for your students can have the same effect on them, and if you add some movement, body, mind, and spirit will respond. Even a very short break can work wonders to boost energy and stimulate alertness. As Don Campbell (1997) puts it, "The best audiences, I've found, are those that have the opportunity to move in some way before they sit down to listen. Dancing or moving for five to seven minutes … energizes the ear and brain – and so the rest of the body listens better" (57).

Patterns of music, like patterns of language, activate the brain and stimulate complex interconnections that enhance both learning and memory – the more complex the patterns, the more complex will be the memory trace. Planting neural trees of musicality confers wonderful benefits to other areas – language, reasoning, mathematics, pattern recognition, physical coordination, and well-

Dr. Alfred Tomatis speaks of "charging sounds" that bring energy to the cortex and spread to the entire body. Citing the work of Tomatis, Jensen (1996) writes "Cells in the cortex of the brain act like little batteries. ...Amazingly enough, the brain's own batteries were not charged by metabolism, they were charged externally, through sound. ...high frequency tones sped up the brain's recharging process....low frequency tones discharge mental and physical energy."

being. The successes Dr. Tomatis has achieved in alleviating both learning and physical disabilities bear witness to the power of sound therapy and music.

Because of its profound effect on the overall metabolism and nervous system, music can orchestrate the rhythms of your day in class. By playing slow sixty-cycle Baroque music (Pachelbel's Canon in D) at the beginning of the day as children came in and settled down to personal reading, one teacher got a grade-four class off to a mellow start as the entire class responded to the slow rhythms. Playing more lively music or asking the children to sing along as you play familiar songs perks up energy; it also stimulates reading when you provide written charts of the words. If you are playing an instrument or like to sing, you know the benefits and joys of weaving music into your day. But a collection of tapes or CDs can serve you equally well, particularly if you include your own as well as the children's favorites in both slow and lively selections. Jensen (1996) suggests adding popular show-business themes, which have particular local appeal. Don Campbell's *The Mozart Effect* offers a list of music selections that work well in learning situations.

Rhythms of learning

The brain along with all living things must accommodate itself to an environment punctuated by powerful rhythms: day and night, summer and winter, high and low tides. In recent years scientists have discovered that one way the brain may do so is by fashioning powerful rhythms of its own (Restak 1984, 101).

When children are absorbed in their work, they have remarkable attention spans. Creating a special piece of writing, listening to their favorite story, or working on an interesting project can hold their attention for a good part of the morning or afternoon. But like adults, children need breaks and time to reflect in order to think and function effectively. Watching children during writing workshop, Margaret observed that Caitlin did her best work after she had gazed out of the window for some time; Robert needed to doodle before beginning his writing; and Noel took breaks while creating a

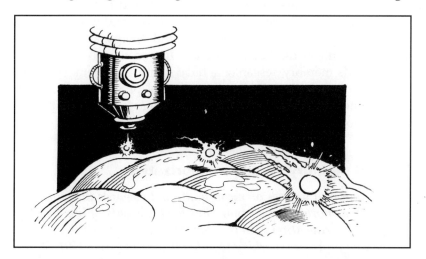

"Our ability to maintain attention is affected by normal cyclical fluctuations in the efficacy of the neurotransmitter molecules that chemically regulate attention. These fluctuations occur in 90-minute cycles across the 24 hours" (Sylwester 1995, 81).

lengthy story. Pauses punctuated productive work. To build habits of independent thought, "it is essential not to force a continuous stream of information into the developing brain but to allow for periods of consolidation and assimilation in between" (Diamond 1988, 161).

In the ebb and flow of work in the classroom, activity alternates with more quiet times. Interpersonal exchanges give way to quiet intrapersonal reflection that consolidates learning; movement can lead to being still. If you think back to your own student days, you know that these fluctuations aided your learning, and that if you attempted nonstop study in order to cram for an exam, there came a time when the brain balked and information overload demanded a break. "Aha" insights rarely appear while you are going full tilt. Instead, relaxation, physical movement, or even daydreaming give the brain the opportunity to let the branches of the neural forest make a new pattern or strengthen existing ones. "Our brain … sometimes is most efficient when it is idling. Think of how many creative ideas have occurred while a person is relaxing or daydreaming" (Restak 1984, 360).

Getting to know your students will help you to orchestrate their rhythms of learning and honor individual patterns and personal rhythms. Providing breaks or time for intrapersonal processing will move the whole class toward a natural ebb and flow of learning. Gauging the overall energy level of the class – and yourself – will help you capitalize on a surge of natural energy after recess or adjust to a lull in the late afternoon. "In addition to noting how rhythm aids memory, researchers have found that memory has its own circadian rhythm. Short-term memory processes are at their peak in the morning, while long-term storage is best attempted in the afternoon" (Campbell 1997, 177).

Memory | Natural memory versus memorization

Education that focuses on memorization disregards the immense "natural memory" that everyone has for the events of life. The key to enhancing education is to find out how, most effectively, to have the two processes working together (Caine & Caine 1991, 38).

Before coming to school, children use "natural memory" to learn the intricacies of their mother tongue and the myriad skills and facts that are part of the events of their lives. They do so by being immersed in their learning environment and exploring it with all of their senses and feelings. No one devises structured lessons or tests for getting along, for classifying thousands upon thousands of objects, or for learning and then refining motor skills. Children actively explore the world around them "to make sense of things and above all make sense of what people do.... They reason deductively and carry on inference at age four or so, much more skillfully than had been previously supposed. It also seems that a child first makes sense of a situation and of human intentions and *then* of what is said" (Donaldson, in Edelman 1992, 244).

The combination of "making sense" of the world and being immersed in a context that imbues learning with meaning recurs in discussions of learning and memory. It seems that the human brain is ideally suited for functioning in the rich complexity of the everyday world. On the other hand, "the brain is poorly designed for formal instruction. It is not at all designed for efficiency or order" (Jensen 1996, 5). It seems that our best intention to simplify learning by stripping it down to the bare essentials may actually be counterproductive in many cases.

Routes versus maps

To create a unifying image for both natural memory and the memorization of details within the curriculum, Caine and Caine (1991) offer the metaphor of map memory – creating a rich inner map that is constantly updated by experience, guided by curiosity and interest, rich in detail, and set against a familiar background. They juxtapose it with route memory – following a preset route and having to work at memorizing that route through repeated rehearsals.

Route memory

Route memory refers to a path that must be followed exactly and does not allow for detours lest one get lost. The route is laid out by someone else and offers only bare details without the enrichment of context. "The curriculum," when interpreted too literally, can become the route or path, something that is followed to the letter in order to reach a specific goal: passing a test, fitting school-district requirements, "covering" the material. In that case, route memory, though very useful for acquiring specific facts, can work to the

Letters and numbers have little meaning when they are divorced from a larger context. Placing them into route memory takes hard work, and negative feelings connected with the work may actually impede learning.

detriment of real learning if students simply memorize what is taught without the desire or ability to apply what they learned.

Route memory generally relies on extrinsic motivation – external rewards and punishment. But once established, it is resistant to change, although not easily transferred or applied in new situations. Items placed into route memory are often unconnected to the learner's personal experience and initially may have little or no meaning. Memorizing rules for math or spelling are examples that come to mind as the work lacks personal meaning and is difficult to apply in new situations (Caine & Caine 1991, 39–41).

The structured phonics lessons Margaret dutifully offered (in the past) according to the then prevailing "requirements" produced mechanical responses on the part of students. They simply followed the route provided by the teacher in a classroom, which at that time provided very sparse context for written language and its many different uses, or for the intriguing values numbers can represent. Letters, words, and numbers remained abstract symbols to be memorized and rehearsed. Unfortunately, those abstract symbols did not fit into the inner map of communication children had built prior to coming to school. Blending the route learning with the rich contexts of reading and math work added the personal meaning the children needed.

Map memory

Map memory connects us to our place in the external world. In order to move around, we must constantly be aware of our spatial surroundings, hence map memory forms constantly and spontaneously as we interact with the world around us. Because map memory is part of our survival system, it relies on the hippocampus within the limbic system. The capacity of the map memory is virtually unlimited, and initial maps for new situations form very quickly. As we interact, we update our inner maps constantly and continuously, as their content is open-ended and flexible. Curiosity, novelty, and interest stimulate the formation of maps, and sensory input enhances their richness and acuity. Learning is highly personal and seemingly effortless. Unlike route memory, map memory readily becomes permanent and is easily applied in new contexts.

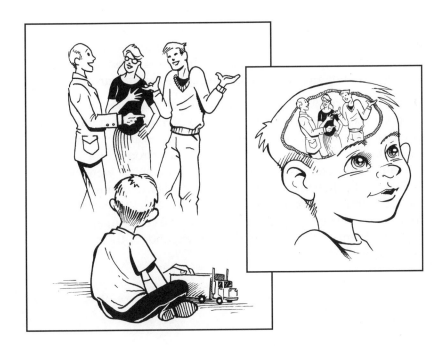

Activities surrounding the learner and taken into map memory without conscious effort are nevertheless easily recalled, integrated with other maps, and updated regularly.

Large thematic maps, such as the inner map for communication, form over time and become enriched by new experience – spoken and written language become integrated and attention to the underlying sense of what is shown by body language adds further depth (Caine & Caine 1991, 41–42).

Creating contexts for memory

Looking back at her early teaching when she was meticulously following the route laid out by curricula and teachers' guides, Margaret remembers how constrained and unhappy she felt. Much of the learning was abstract and inaccessible to the children's ways of natural learning, as she and the children were kept on a narrow path with little room for interesting side trips. Once our in-class research demonstrated to her that her carefully structured teaching route did not fit the children's ways of learning, she gradually shifted to providing the rich context children needed to expand the inner maps they had built at home. To imbue the abstract world of written symbols with the kind of meaning that would create instant inner maps of literacy learning, Margaret shifted her teaching to include the delights of story time, the joy of reading books, and the interest of gathering information from print. For inner maps of written work, she created meaningful contexts for writing and spelling through the daily sharing of news, writing workshop, and writing centers. She gave meaning to math with manipulatives and real-life math work that included handling money, following recipes, dividing up treats, or sharing cherished resources in class.

Dreaded lessons, for Margaret and children alike, about "long and short vowels" gave way to the shared excitement about literacy and numeracy learning that stimulated imagination and creativity. Both students and teacher found learning as productive as home learning had been. The curriculum requirements were not only fulfilled but actually exceeded because the learning now fitted into the children's inner maps. Their experiences gave them the confidence, flexibility, and incentive to take those interesting side trips that enriched, deepened, and expanded their newfound learning and skills.

Blending routes into maps creates added meaning

To teach someone any subject adequately, **the subject must be
embedded in all the elements that give it meaning.** *People
must have a way to relate to the subject in terms of what is
personally important (Caine & Caine 1991, 58).*

A visiting British school inspector once commented to Margaret that
among the very best teachers are those who started their teaching
using a structured approach but then shifted to the open approach
that sets learning into a larger context. While the visitor was
affirming the power of map learning – using a rich context to imbue
learning with meaning the children can readily relate to – he was
also saying that routes are integral to good maps and that the
experienced teacher knows what route the children need to traverse
to reach their important learning goals. In this instance, the route is
not so much a prescribed sequence of teaching, or the presentation
of detailed skills stripped of their context, but the knowledge and
experience of the natural evolution that, say, spelling and reading
will take as children gradually refine their learning. Because of her
knowledge of the route, its landmarks, and its turning points, the
teacher recognizes and acts upon signals that extra help is needed,
acknowledges steps forward, and honors pauses that are needed for

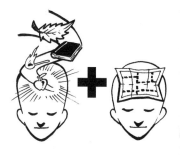

*Morning meeting connects
students' personal experiences
to the details of the written
messages. While demonstrating
how to convert spoken messages
to print, the teacher uses every
opportunity to fit in details about
oral spelling and to conduct
on-the-spot lessons in special
patterns of spelling. Route and
map memories are blended to
enhance each other.*

incubating the next breakthrough. In short, setting a context to create natural learning and to enrich students' inner maps does not mean simply providing materials and standing back "to let things happen." Instead it offers the teacher endless opportunities to observe students at work, to add further details, or to enrich the concrete experiences as and when needed.

Morning meeting, with its sharing of news, is a fine time to linger over interesting spelling words, create a sense of style and composition, or provide extra reading practice for those who need it. After visiting an old-age home and meeting a man 102 years old, children revealed that his venerable age was beyond their understanding. Once back in class, the children put together 102 Unifix cubes, practiced counting by tens, and then created individual number lines for their own ages of six and seven to compare to the long line of over a hundred. By adding their own ages to that of the teacher, they practiced counting, adding, visualizing numbers, and gaining insight into the old age that had been represented by a mere number. It was now visible and comparable to something that fit into their inner maps for number values and differing ages.

Providing guidelines for field trips or projects can become a way of melding route and map learning without the former becoming overly rigid. Describing ways of structuring trips to the beach, Margaret writes:

Since Victoria is situated on the Pacific Ocean, field trips were part of our seashore unit. The children already had some knowledge (a partial map) of the beach and its animals. They were now ready to examine some specifics. We looked up the lowest tides in the tide table and booked a trip at the lowest tide possible to ensure there would be a lot of specimens available (details for route learning). The children knew what they might find, and they had also learned all the safety rules they would have to follow. Once at the seashore, the children, who were full of excitement and curiosity (the stuff that creates instant inner maps) poured onto the beach. They had their nets and other equipment and knew the rules to follow. Each trip was different as to content. Sometimes they had to look for certain animals – crabs, starfish, clams; sometimes they had an activity sheet to fill in; sometimes they had to draw certain animals; and always, all animals were released before we left the beach.

Details gathered on the field trip are learned and rehearsed within the context of the existing inner maps of the seashore that give meaning and permanence to the learning. Feelings of curiosity, interest, and excitement ensure that the new information is filed in long-term memory. The flow of serotonin stimulated by the feelings of personal accomplishment, the freedom to explore and use all the senses, makes for interpersonal harmony free of strife or aggression. In short, the multisensory nature of this integrated map and route learning is sure to strengthen the jungle of dendrites in the magic forest of neural trees.

If we are to encompass adequately the realm of human cognition, it is necessary to include a far wider and more universal set of competences than has ordinarily been considered (Gardner 1985, x).

Multiple Intelligences

Some eighty years after the first intelligence tests were developed, Howard Gardner "seriously questioned the validity of determining an individual's intelligence by taking a person out of his natural environment and asking him to do isolated tasks he'd never done before – and probably would never choose to do again" (Armstrong 1994, 1). That questioning arose when Gardner compared the results of intelligence tests and the successes people achieved in the world outside of education. In his research, Gardner noted that being able to solve problems in everyday life, having outstanding physical or musical skills, and knowing how to produce or create something useful were among the special attributes of people who did not necessarily achieve high IQ scores. Much of what he observed did not lend itself to being measured by the usual tests, yet the achievements were real and at times outstanding. And so Gardner's research focused strongly on what people actually *did* to define the initial seven distinct intelligences; he later added an eighth one.

Teachers recognize and build on students' intelligences

As teachers, we too look at what learners *do,* and in the past we often wished that we had a better way of affirming that Rita or Brendan worked exceedingly well even though standardized tests did not truly reflect their capabilities and potential. Now, having the special strengths of students defined as "intelligences" that have biological and neurological bases, we can assert with good authority that these students are intelligent. Teachers have always been sensitive to their students' strengths; now they can use the knowledge of multiple intelligences to infuse the confidence students need to build on their special strengths and branch out from there into others.

To honor and enhance all of the intelligences, whole classrooms and even entire schools have organized teaching around the eight

Bodily-kinesthetic: *Expertise in using hands and body to express ideas and feelings, to produce and shape things, and to perform well physically.*

Logical: *mathematical: Working with numbers effectively, calculating, recognizing logical patterns, classifying, testing hypotheses.*

Spatial: *The ability to perceive and/or represent the visual-spatial world accurately, being sensitive to shape, color, space and their relations.*

Linguistic: *Using language in all its facets – to communicate, solve problems, produce written works, be creative with language.*

Musical: *The ability to
perform, create, and respond to
music, be sensitive to rhythm,
harmony, and tone.*

Interpersonal: *The ability
to discern and respond to
interpersonal cues effectively,
be aware of moods, feelings, and
intentions of others.*

Environmental: *A sensitivity
to and feeling for the forces at
work in nature, the ability to
observe and interpret natural
phenomena with precision.*

Intrapersonal: *Having self-
knowledge and the ability to
act on that knowledge, a
capacity for self-reflection and
introspection.*

intelligences, creating centers in classrooms, building students' awareness of their special strengths, and encouraging forays into those intelligences that need extra fostering in order to balance students' learning. Though in *The Learners' Way* we are not specifically referring to multiple intelligences, the philosophy of building on the students' own way of learning quite naturally includes them in teaching and learning interactions and the overall classroom organization.

Learning centers encourage the hands-on work that Gardner sees as central to the expression of different intelligences. Writing, art, math, seasonal centers, and the provision of manipulatives of all sorts invite learners to choose their preferred modes of learning, giving the teacher ample opportunity to observe who gravitates where. The freedom to move within the classroom, to change seats and work in different groupings, fosters interpersonal skills and caters to those high in bodily-kinesthetic intelligence, who need to be active.

Modeling, as the principal way of teaching, allows students to shine in their special intelligences. As they select from the teacher's modeling those areas that match their own special intelligences, they build both their skills and their confidence. The proficient ways of functioning in their own intelligence provide models for other children to follow. Group projects draw together teams of students who complement each other's intelligences: To complete a report or diorama, there is the resident artist, the math whiz, the official reporter/writer, the spatial expert who does layout and design. In drama created and produced by the children, the bodily kinesthetic and musical intelligences of players may add that special touch. The open sharing during news time, which is both voluntary and interactive, calls for linguistic and interpersonal skills and provides ample room for student modeling of special intelligences. Children thrive on applying their special intelligences, and their classmates absorb and expand skills they come to value as they watch the down-to-earth applications.

Looking back to her classroom, Margaret remembers drawing out the strong environmental intelligence of Jason, who was both knowledgeable and highly sensitive within that realm but entered school shy and inarticulate. Encouraging him to share his depth of knowledge and understanding built his verbal and interpersonal skills, and Jason blossomed into an enthusiastic presenter of environmental lore. His excitement and dedication captivated his fellow students, who joined him in learning about the delicate West Coast ecosystem. Though his reading and math skills were painfully slow to develop, Jason confidently assumed a leadership role in his own intelligence.

Robyn could work out any math problem using manipulatives and written or verbal calculations. But in spite of her strong sense of math patterns, spelling was difficult until Margaret was able to make Robyn aware of the patterns in spelling. A high degree of spatial intelligence made Noel's artwork a prized addition to books and projects written by students with high linguistic intelligence. Instead of feeling inadequate or left out, students like Noel are drawn into the writing projects and begin to plant new neural trees in the fertile ground of their own intelligence.

Affirming the importance of special intelligences and acknowledging their importance can make all the difference. Margaret's youngest and most needy student showed himself to have wonderful interpersonal intelligence. Margaret encouraged him by making him her official greeter for visitors to the classroom. When it became clear that he was not ready to move to the next class level, Margaret talked to him about his wonderful gift. Over a period of weeks, she convinced him that she definitely could not get along without him as her greeter. She was genuine in her appreciation, and the emphasis on that very strong intelligence made staying behind for another year quite natural and acceptable to a child who could easily have been crushed had there been a sense of failure.

Channeling both intelligence and extra energy into productive realms is yet another benefit of acknowledging multiple intelligences. A principal whose entire school is organized to teach within the framework of multiple intelligences told of a new student who barrelled into school unable to move down the hall without jostling or elbowing people. Once teachers and fellow students greeted him as a bodily-kinesthetic learner and let him know that his strength was much needed in all kinds of projects, the boy happily settled into schoolwork and became the lead in a school play that called for great physical exertion. Given time and the acknowledgment of his special intelligence helped him channel his energy productively instead of aggressively. Interpersonal intelligence received a wonderful boost as positive emotions flowed along with his physical energy.

Feelings are essential to thought, thought to feeling. But when passions surge the balance tips: it is the emotional mind that captures the upper hand, swamping the rational mind (Goleman 1995, 9).

Emotional intelligence

Emotional intelligence is like a spirited horse eager to carry the tandem of feelings and thought forward with powerful strides but is also ready to be reined in when feelings lash it into bolting. Most of the time heart and mind are exquisitely coordinated but learning and practice are needed to train that spirited thoroughbred to serve its owner well, to work enthusiastically for the sheer joy of it, be interested as much in the flow of the work as in the end result, yet achieve more more often than if it had been trained harshly and held on tight reins. Independence of learning and self-motivation are the hallmarks of smooth surges forward. The right environment fosters those qualities effortlessly.

Emotional intelligence has many facets. Starting with the morning meeting that opens each day, the learners' way of teaching gives the development of emotional intelligence free rein. It enhances social and interpersonal skills while teaching the art of conversation with its give and take, demonstrates the need to listen and wait while others are talking, and fosters decision-making and careful analysis of detail when students cooperate during news time. Story time, which forms part of the morning meeting and may also pervade the day, is the ideal medium to bring beginning reading into a flow of learning – reading for the sheer joy of it. Aside from the sense of ease of learning that stems from the unfolding story, "the spontaneous pleasure, grace, and effectiveness that characterize flow are incompatible with emotional hijackings in which limbic surges capture the rest of the brain" (Goleman 1995, 92). Harmony as well as learning flow.

Enthusiasm, laughter, and harmony characterize learning throughout the day and enhance the ability to "think flexibly … associate more freely… solve problems that demand a creative solution." Working at centers makes for independence and responsibility. Here, too, cooperation and effective interactions with others flourish as cherished resources need to be shared and handled responsibly. The open communication that flows at center time makes for a mutuality of learning in a climate that encourages and stimulates collaboration.

To create a climate of delight that sets the right environment for a flow of learning, the teacher models social and emotional responses that demonstrate effective, positive interactions, build empathy and mutual caring. Knowing that lecturing about such interpersonal skills would fall on deaf ears, she *integrates* such learning with the day-to-day work in class. Map learning takes over and makes learning effortless. Learning flows and the ongoing evaluation of progress that is integrated into the day-to-day work makes for an absence of fear and a focus on successes.

Looking at the urgent need for preparing learners to interact effectively in school as well as out, Goleman comments, "Academic intelligence offers virtually no preparation for the turmoil – or opportunity – life's vicissitudes bring" (1995, 36). Building emotional intelligence within the classroom offers that preparation and gives academic learning a boost at the same time. Learners build a repertoire of inter- and intrapersonal skills.

Constructivism

Drawing together the different strands of research on the brain, intelligence, and learning brings us full circle to our own point of departure and constructivism. *The Language of Learning* defines constructivism as "an approach to teaching based on research about how people learn" (Scherer 1999). Among the

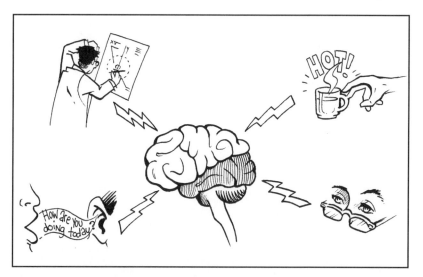

Though the brain has many parts and functional areas, it works as an integrated whole to construct knowledge from the diversity of input.

architects of the theory and philosophy of constructivism are Jean Piaget, Lev Vygotsky, and John Dewey, thinkers whose works formed the basis for our original research into how children learn to read. Today's researchers (Brooks & Brooks 1999; McKeown & Beck 1999; Perkins 1999) are confirming what the children taught us in the classroom. Children structured learning their way – despite our best efforts in our early teaching to structure learning for them. They used context and meaning rather than our adult-designed lessons to make sense of reading. Active involvement and cocreative teaching and learning moved both literacy and numeracy learning to wonderful depths. Students were motivated and energized by their active involvement and by the degree of control and choice they had in structuring their learning. Then, as now, children constructed their own learning. The learners' way of teaching was and is constructivism in action.

Developing a Learning Climate

2

Children who know the joys of bedtime stories approach learning to read with high expectations. They will eagerly search for favorite books and stories and track print with hands or eyes as the stories are read to them. Some of them will come to school already able to read. Feelings of delight, curiosity, and anticipation brought them to reading. No amount of parental coaxing or instruction in phonics could teach these preschoolers the complexities of reading. But their enjoyment of stories and the warm feelings of relaxed sharing – without demands or pressures – produced the learning. Parents and grandparents have enjoyed sharing their favorite stories with children. You have the same opportunity to enchant an entire class, to draw a class full of eager little learners into the exciting world of stories, poems, or songs, and to foster in them that eagerness to share stories again and again. Children have an innate capacity to learn with ease, but you have to provide the external environment and special context that help them unfold their learning.

To create a climate of delight that invites children to enjoy reading and writing, you will want to fill your classroom with books, books, and more books: big books, little books, long books, short books, fat books, thin books, easy books, hard books, picture books, fact-filled books, storybooks, fairy tales, poetry, happy books, sad books, funny books, exciting books, great books, interesting books, mysteries, comic books, riddle books, all the books you can get your

Creating a climate of delight

hands on, not forgetting your own favorites and those of your children. Of course, your treasure trove of books must be readily available to everyone. Invite children to browse, to take books to their seats or even home.

Remember that though they may not be able to read, children are certainly able to listen. As you read stories to children from the first day of school, you will introduce the novices to the joys of story time and reassure those who are more knowledgeable that reading in school is but a continuation of the familiar learning at home.

Be sure to keep the story sessions for enjoyment and sharing. At home parents do not tell their baby how to play. Exploring books and other reading materials playfully can create the same intense involvement that the baby has shown while playing at home. If you stand aside, children will use the learning materials you provide in their own ways. They will invent their own stories or rules for playing games, use books to build houses, pretend to be teacher and read to a real or imaginary audience, invent new endings or reread the same book or story ten, twenty, thirty times. Along with the excitement of discovery, exploration, and invention, there is the warmth and reassurance of the familiar. As at home, more conventional use of the materials will evolve from this free exploration and play.

Variety, surprise, imagination, and challenge are essential components of the climate of delight. Your classroom changes with the seasons; books you borrow from the library or other sources rotate; children's own projects take up part of the classroom for periods of time; and artwork and writing produced by the class are added to the classroom library. Surprise guests, mystery tours, field trips, spontaneous projects (old-fashioned days, pet displays, research initiated by the children) add richness to reading, writing, and discussion. The production of plays and puppet shows is stimulated by the children's reading and is masterminded more and more fully by the children themselves.

Your classroom will rarely be totally silent. Sharing and interaction are the vital components of a climate of delight. Discoveries, new learning, the sheer joy of accomplishment demand expression. Humor and feelings of excitement bubble over not only for the children but for you as well.

Benefits of being allowed to move around the classroom

Having the time to reflect and work independently -

makes for self correction and solid learning.

Teamwork expands the creative impulse.

Liberal access to the blackboard encourages practice and enhances creative work that can be shared or enjoyed individually.

Teachers, too, function best in a climate of delight

Guidebooks, worksheets, and rigid adherence to prepared lesson plans may offer a sense of security, but they can also be quite dull. Shifting to more spontaneity in your planning will add greatly to your enjoyment of teaching. As you read to and with the children, see yourself as a detective who is keenly observing the children's every step forward. You are trying to discover how they learn best, what steps forward they take, and how you can best provide the learning materials that fit the prescribed curriculum. Use your sense of humor and laugh with the children at the amusing viewpoints that emerge. Rekindle your sense of awe as you marvel at the children's astute comments and sensitive artistic expressions. Let yourself enter their world with abandon. Your classroom is one of the few places where your childlike enjoyment of the small pleasures – sunshine, flowers, a hug, an exciting new discovery, a song, a dance – can find uncensored expression. Seeing your excitement and genuine interest, the children put forth more suggestions or cues about steps ahead. The climate of delight is not one-sided but unites teachers and children as co-creators of learning. So do have fun being a co-creative teacher-learner.

Creating a safe learning environment

Learning means taking risks

Learning involves taking risks. If you venture into unfamiliar territory you risk getting lost or hurt. It may take you a long time to reach your destination and those around you may berate you for making detours or taking the wrong turn. If the risks are too high, the road too arduous, or the rewards too small, the safest and easiest course lies in staying where you are. (Remember that the lower brain systems give the shut-down signal if a learner feels under threat.)

But the drive to explore is high in young children. Curiosity, the desire to be surprised, to learn about the world, and to meet new challenges urge them on to new paths. Encouraged by successes and a non-threatening environment, children take in, process, retain, and refine incredible quantities of learning.

The materials we present in school in small easy steps should be absorbed in short order; yet for many children school learning can become a fearful task. For a child, being cast into a totally new setting with a whole group of strangers is difficult enough, but at the same time there are a whole host of new rules of behavior to be learned. To make it worse, the ways of learning that worked so well at home may be unacceptable. Suddenly there are timetables and prescribed ways of doing new jobs. The familiar way of observe-try-and-refine does not work when the teacher tells you what to do, and also tells you not to copy what the child next to you is doing. The choice of what is to be learned now rests in the teacher's hands and much of what s/he demands seems hard, incomprehensible, and unrewarding. Exploring the classroom and moving about to meet other children may be frowned upon. So many pitfalls, so many demands. School can indeed be a frightening place and not conducive to natural learning.

Taking fear out of learning

Over the years of developing the learners' way we have found many ways to make our classroom safe for learning. Trusting the learners and being unworried and relaxed are key factors. Children are extremely sensitive to the moods and attitudes of adults. They have perfected their observation skills during their non-verbal phase of learning and can read adults very well indeed. Thus, cultivating relaxed, positive states of mind has done wonders for us and the children. A sense of humor is definitely an asset, and courtesy and a quiet speaking voice help children abandon their fears.

Courtesy makes for safety and builds emotional intelligence

Have you ever examined your interactions with students in light of rules of courtesy? We discovered some quite appalling behaviors when we examined the tapes of our own teaching during the time of our initial research. We found poor listening, lack of eye contact with children, negative statements about their work, interrupting speakers in mid-sentence, raised voices in inappropriate situations, impatience with a speaker's hesitance, brushing off or ignoring explanations children offered. Can you think of others?

Awareness of our unintended discourtesies helped us to shift to behaviors we wanted children to experience and emulate. We find that being quietly courteous models the behavior we want to foster among children. In the process we also begin to establish guidelines for classroom behavior. After all, a climate of delight and the freedom to learn naturally mean neither a free-for-all nor permissive acceptance of any and all behavior.

At the very beginning of the school year we establish and then insist on the rules of conduct demanded by courtesy and consideration for others. With a quiet, but expressive voice we explain – as the occasion demands it – what behaviors are and are not acceptable and why: "With so many of us together, we need to use low voices so we all get a chance to hear and learn." Or "All these books and games are here for you, but we need to share them. Be sure to take good care of them and put them back where they belong when you are finished."

We keep rules to a minimum but firmly enforce those we do set in a quiet, matter-of-fact voice. Children want and need a framework on which to build and we have found that in no time at all the children themselves become the enforcers of sensible rules about noise, cooperation, and keeping the classroom reasonably neat. If newcomers to the class begin to push, shout, or interfere with their classmates, children who have absorbed our models of courtesy and consideration will inform the disruptive children about the rules of behavior and why they are needed. Visitors to class may be startled to hear a first-grader inform an unruly peer that what s/he is doing is "inappropriate behavior!"

Meaningful work creates a safe climate

Children who are interested in what they do and delighted with their activities soon forget their fears or aggressive impulses. Beginning the year with lots of story reading and lots of talk about the children themselves will ease tensions for those who are fearful. A pat on the head or arm, a bit of assistance with a job, and comments like, "Oh, you are having a bit of difficulty" or "I see you need a bit of help" will dry many tears and demonstrate that the teacher is a helpful person who feels it is all right not to know what to do. In time, these children will learn to ask for help and to turn to the teacher, a peer, or visitors to the classroom with questions.

Keep in mind that you, too, may feel frustrated, upset, or angry when you are asked to do something – in public no less – that is unfamiliar to you or that you know is difficult. Children are no different. To make learning safe, begin the year with familiar topics and tasks. Talk with the children about their homes and their experiences, and as they gradually lose their shyness, you will gain valuable insights into their interests, verbal abilities, and problems. You will find who is quite verbal and who needs a great deal of encouragement. If you keep the focus on topics the children raise, you will elicit more and more participation.

Voluntary participation eases anxieties

Voluntary participation is another factor that makes learning safe. Do you remember that horrible feeling in the pit of your stomach when the teacher called on you to give an answer, read aloud, or recite? Perhaps you knew the material well, but the mere fact that you were suddenly called upon made you go blank and become quite frightened or embarrassed. The children in your class are no different. Even your star students may suddenly feel shy or unprepared if they are called unexpectedly or when a visitor is present. It took us a lot of soul searching to allow children the option not to participate during reading or sharing time. Some took from September until Christmas before they spoke up in a group, but spurred by the model of other children's sharing they finally chimed in. In all our years of observing children we have yet to encounter a child who will not share voluntarily. We make very sure to encourage reticent children but make equally sure that our questions, "Would you like to read this?" or "Would you like to tell us about that?" are truly invitations and not hidden commands. We have learned to accept a child's "no" or head shake.

Observing closely how these children progress will make the classroom safe for you as well as the children. Individual conversations with you or with classmates, the way their eyes or hands track print during unison reading, progress in artwork, all tell you that they are learning, even though they do not speak up in a group. Based on your unobtrusive observations you may want to encourage a child to speak up, but in the safe atmosphere of your classroom there are no command performances and the children know it.

A focus on strengths turns errors into stepping stones

With a focus on strengths and trial-and-error learning, errors cease to be black marks and become stepping stones to further learning.

Once again, recall your own way of learning and what helped you to progress when you learned to play a musical instrument, started to garden, or were developing a hobby. Did your small steps forward and your successes spur you on? Did you puzzle over just how to achieve a particular goal? Did you keep trying different ways to perfect your skills? Did you discover the kinds of questions you needed to ask of those more experienced than you? Could you see or hear more clearly what others were doing to achieve what you were after? In asking ourselves these kinds of questions we have recognized quite clearly that both further learning and our ability to correct errors are largely a matter of attitude. If we had become convinced that making mistakes was an indication of our "inability" to do a job, we simply gave up and often felt angry, belligerent, or frustrated. But if we kept our goal firmly in mind, errors – though frustrating at times – became stepping stones to new growth.

In teaching we make it very clear to the children that errors are part of learning. The feedback we give stresses positive aspects and treats corrections in a matter-of-fact way. Since learning to read and write involves a great deal of hypothesis testing and anticipating, we acknowledge all efforts the children are making. If they suggest *j* as the beginning letter of *giant*, we comment, "*J* sure sounds like it, but in this case we need a *g*." If their reading ability is still limited, we accept meaning and don't demand word-for-word accuracy. If a child reads *house* as *home, mother* as *mom*, or leaves out a word, no comment is needed. Only if meaning is lost do we reread a line or passage and even then we may say, "Good try." Such acknowledgment of approximations, good guesses, and partially right answers is a crucial factor in making learning safe. Children are thereby assured that we listen to them, that right answers are put to good use, and that even mistakes have merit in learning. (Chapter 5 provides more specific examples of giving feedback that acknowledges and expands the children's work.)

Following a model is a safe way to learn

Since learning styles differ, children use different ways of absorbing what is to be learned. Telling them what to do may seem like the logical way to teach because we were generally taught the same way, but many children find it difficult to remember and follow spoken directions. Repeatedly modeling the behaviors and skills to be learned creates a safe atmosphere. Following a model leaves learners free to use the learning style best suited to their ways, and repetitions leave plenty of room to practice and refine new skills. In our own efforts to learn we have become quite aware of the limited value of being told how to do something or how to correct something. Whether learning to folk dance, master French, or use a word processor, feelings of frustration, inadequacy, and anger often blocked our learning when oral directions dominated the lessons. Having models to follow, opportunity to practice without being criticized, and then observing the model again made for far less stress and more productive learning. Children react the same way.

Allowing children to copy each other's work may be hard to accept at first. But the learners' tensions disappear when they can rely on the way in which they learned so effectively at home. Once we acknowledged that copying other learners was simply a first step to greater independence, we relaxed and noted the many ways in which following a model can relieve frustrations or stress. Copying other children offers inexperienced readers a chance to participate, to move away from a place of being stuck, and to be part of the group. At that, giving the same response as another child is not necessarily copying. Do you remember the times when you had an answer ready and the teacher called on someone else who gave your answer? We assume that children want to participate and accept the same response even if given by several children in succession. Once a number of children have had a chance to speak up, we might ask, "Does anyone have any other suggestions?" and move on from there.

Think for a moment about the persistence with which babies explore their environment. That curiosity is their survival mechanism and no outside motivation could be as strong as that inner drive to learn. When children come to school at age 5, they still have tremendous energy for learning and exploring. They can be trusted to learn.

Develop a climate of trust

Parents find it easy to trust their baby to learn to talk. After all, children everywhere pick up their mother tongue. But as teachers we know that learning to read and write can be different. Though some children learn early and without stress, others experience great difficulty, and still others either fail to learn or learn only

minimally. You may find it difficult to abandon your worries and to replace them with the certitude that given time and proper attention all of the children in your class will learn to read and write though some may take longer than others.

Chances are you yourself are a product of many years of education during which tests, exams, teachers' comments, and parents' cajoling kept telling you, "You can't be trusted to learn independently. You need to be made to learn or to abandon your faulty ways." Look back for a moment and try to recall how often your education – particularly tests and evaluation – focused on your errors and weak points. How did it feel to be told, "You did this wrong"? What did such negative comments do for your willingness and desire to learn? How about your self-confidence and your image as a competent learner? Reflect on your experiences for a while and ask yourself how much energy it took to overcome negative assessments. What could you do differently in your own teaching?

Modeling teaches all kinds of skills

After watching the photographer at work during the morning, this kindergarten child decided to pick up a camera to see what he could do in the way of serious work.

Now think of some highly positive learning experiences either in school or out, academic or hobby-oriented. Could you, in fact, be trusted to learn and to enjoy the gradual development of your skills? Were you able to let go of the need to be perfect while still a beginner? Could you enjoy the anticipation of improving a little bit at a time and trust yourself to learn? Compare the effects of the two types of learning and decide which one had more positive and long-lasting effects. If *you* could be trusted to learn, can you move toward that unshakable trust that the children in your care will learn? Knowing that they were smart enough to learn to talk, can you accept that they are smart enough to learn to read and write?

If you have doubts, consider just how clever children are at sensing your every mood and reading your mind (both at home and at school) when it comes to something they want. You may know only too well how positively "Machiavellian" youngsters can be at finding your sore spots and mad buttons and pressing on them with the most irritating persistence. You did not have to provide lessons or guided questions to help them arrive at these subtle but profound learnings. Are the slowest academic learners among those most clever at really getting under your skin? Maddening as it may be, ask yourself what that says about the ability of these children to engage in independent learning. A sense of humor helps at this point as you chuckle to yourself and note clearly that Kevin or Georgina can certainly be trusted to learn *when the learning matters to them!*

Ask yourself further whether you can be trusted to spend a great deal of time and effort on tasks that are both difficult and boring. Do you spend leisure hours musing about such problems or working on building the requisite skills? If you don't, why expect children to? We have learned from this kind of self-exploration that learners of all ages can be trusted to learn. It simply becomes a matter of providing the right environment and learning conditions to allow both teacher and children to use natural learning ways.

How to build trust

Begin your change slowly. Like the children, you need time to try out new learning. See if you can focus more on what the children do *right* than on what they say or do that is *wrong*. Note what changes occur in each child's work over a period of time, what progress is made toward reading and writing. Use the observation instruments and techniques shown in chapter 8 to alert you to new behaviors that emerge from one week to another. Keep anecdotal records of new steps forward. If the children's answers don't match what you had in mind, ask yourself or the children how they arrived at their responses. You may be surprised at some of the sound reasoning behind seemingly strange answers. Note the quantity of work children do as well as its quality and observe subtle changes in their willingness to speak up, volunteer, or try something new.

Refer back to other sections to remind yourself that learning moves from rough approximations and gross performance to greater accuracy, that repetitions and practice are needed, and, above all, that children integrate many skills from the modeling and practice they experience in class. They are learning and making progress even if there are few outside indicators to show just what each child is internalizing.

The children's enthusiasm and self-confidence have become the most important indicators of learning for us. When children see themselves as readers and writers, that positive self-image will surely become reality. Trust becomes a two-way street. As the children sense our trust in their ability to learn they trust themselves; as we observe their self-confidence, we relax and accept that Christine and Billy are doing just fine.

Helping children build self-confidence

If you begin the year with highly familiar reading materials or use poems, nursery rhymes, or stories that have predictable patterns or refrains, the young readers in your class will feel successful from the start. The early memorized readings or rough approximations of text bolster their confidence and help them to move to more exacting tasks. If they see themselves as readers, they will not hesitate to try more difficult tasks. The trust they develop in their own ability is as important as your trust in them.

Trust, patience, and an unhurried calmness are your best allies with children whose learning is slow to unfold. If you keep your attention on each of their positive attributes, you can assure them as well as yourself, parents, or supervisors that the children will read and write. Observing children who progress slowly has given us a chance to see in slow motion what steps they take. Allowing these children to read and reread the same story again and again – if they wanted to do so – helped them establish the brain programs for further reading. In each case, after perhaps ten, twenty, thirty days of always reading the same passage or story, these children would suddenly say, "Today I want to read a new story." From that point onward their independent reading evolved. Trusting them to progress, once they decided they were ready, showed its positive result. Without stress or anxiety for teacher or learner, the children

first day of Kindergarten:
"I'm going to make my chalk
talk for me.

   "Good morning, Kindergarten
      children"

   "Would you like to have me
   put a message on the blackboard
   for you?" someone suggested
   that they say "Good morning Mrs.R."
   + so that was put on the bb. +
   children read it several times.
      During the second day of K. I
   was reading "Brown Bear." + one
   child (boy) was coming up with all ^some
   the words. I kept my eye on him +
   during Big Book reading he was also
   "mouthing" many words. I checked
   with him (later) indiv. + sure enough
   he was ready to read — so with
   that child I will zero in on the
   reading.
      — morning discussion — sharks
   Sept 8. — morning news.
      Some of the children are walking
   to school with their brothers +
   sisters.

*Close observation of children
begins on day one of school.
As Margaret begins with a
simple model of "Good
morning..." on the blackboard,
she picks up on the children's
suggestion to print the same
simple message for them.
Such highly familiar messages
encourage children to
participate, and the teacher
can note who will volunteer,
who is still rehearsing
silently, who pays no
attention, and who is
ready to enter into group
discussions. Noting that one
little boy is already reading
along leads to more careful
checking and a reminder note
to carry forward with further
reading activities for this
young reader.*

moved from the safety of memory reading to greater independence.
Like the baby learning to talk, the young readers can be trusted to
learn. *So hang in there!*

In all our years of teaching the learners' way we have never
encountered a child who did not want to learn, to explore, and to
improve on skills. Before, there were plenty who did not want to do
exercises on consonant blends, answer inane questions about bland

non-stories, or sit still while filling out endless worksheets. But as soon as the focus shifted to activities of interest to them, these reluctant students became lively and willing learners.

A supportive environment makes for whole-brain learning

Creating an environment that fits the learners' ways not only fosters academic learning but has quite pervasive beneficial effects on the overall development of students. The rich, varied environment and active sensory involvement make learning easy and productive, but there is another, highly important side benefit. Brain research tells us that the physical development of the brain – neuron connections and myelin formation growing the magic forest of neuron trees – depends upon the learner's interaction with the environment (Diamond, Hopson 1998). Sensory stimulation and active exploration are the necessary catalysts that actualize the full development of the immature brain of the young learner. Thus, the climate of delight, rich in mental and physical stimulation, not only helps children to learn but actually ensures the full physical development of their brains. By engaging both hemispheres and all three layers of the brain the children are expanding their physical as well as mental capacity to learn.

The elements of safety and trust assure that emotional blocks to learning are minimized and that the lower layers of the brain will not give the shut-down signal but will give full play to curiosity and the impulse to explore. The freedom to move about in class, to talk, and to use all the senses further add to the productive emotional climate. Research has revealed that enforced inactivity not only impedes learning but quite often leads to emotional outbursts and hyperactivity. Another interesting side benefit of sensory involvement and physical movement arises from the fact that the motor cortex of the brain interacts with its higher centers. Physical activity enhances mental activity. Children who are encouraged to be physically active are likely to be mentally active as well. In fact, adults react in much the same way. Pacing up and down does more than simply release emotional tensions created by mental effort. The physical movement activates the neo-cortex and stimulates problem solving.

Similarly, daydreaming, a right-brain activity, has been found to activate the left hemisphere as well. Outstanding scientists like Einstein have attested to the fact that some of their most important breakthroughs have come during moments of inactivity and quietness. As we observe children year after year, we continue to marvel at the evolution of creativity in writing, artwork, and academic work. Making room for imaginative work, for occasional daydreaming or flights of fancy, has opened the door to the development of the full range of research skills we enumerated in the introduction. What may appear to be an overly indulgent aspect of the climate of delight, in fact, becomes the foundation of solid learning and a move toward independent thinking.

Understanding the integrative nature of brain functioning and honoring the way children learn naturally stand at the heart of establishing a learning climate. The longer we observed children's ways of structuring their own learning the more we came to trust their ability to move to ever greater independence in their learning. From the beginning of the year we look for opportunities to let the children do their own work. Letting go of control begins with encouraging children to look after their own belongings and moves from there to keeping the room tidy and following a daily routine without having to wait for the teacher to specify when and how to shift to the next activity. Selecting reading material for sharing, participating in generating the news of the day, and deciding whether or not to share during reading group mark further moves toward greater independence on the part of the learners. Settling their own disputes, forming teams, and generating group projects evolve from there. But composing their own sentences or stories and inventing their own spelling are perhaps the biggest moves toward academic independence. For the teacher they mark a very important "letting go" of the need to "teach specific lessons." Once children accept that they have the inner resources to generate ever more accurate written representations of spoken language, they move ahead confidently and joyfully. Observing that confidence and progress reassures the teacher, even if lingering doubts remain for some time.

A good learning climate produces independence and co-creative learning

Accepting the children's ability to be independent learners has been the most far-reaching as well as the most difficult part of our gradual shift toward teaching the learners' way. But each year, the children demonstrate even more areas that they "can do themselves." As they demonstrate their way of practicing reading, writing, spelling, and problem solving, we learn more about effective ways of acquiring knowledge and skills. We continue to modify our teaching on that basis. Teaching/ learning becomes co-creative. We learn from the children about their ways of acquiring knowledge, they learn from us as we model reading, writing, spelling, and enquiry behaviors.

As we observe closely how children learn, excitement and anticipation mark our teaching days. New discoveries, genuine sharing, and the mutuality of learning make the climate of delight as real for us as it is for the children. If you find it difficult at first to relinquish control over lessons and the children's independent work, hang in there and trust. To help you make the transition, we are providing some specific suggestions that will help you create a climate of delight in your classroom.

Hints and particulars

Fill your classroom with reading material
Books

When teaching the learners' way it helps to be an avid collector of books. No doubt you already have a collection in your classroom, but there is always room for more. So here are some suggestions to help you fill your classroom with books of all kinds.

- Borrow books from the school library, the local library, the school district resource center, your children, your friends, your students, their parents – anyone who has books of interest to your students.
- Ask parents to donate books their children no longer need or want.
- Encourage children to bring books from home.
- Bring in your own children's favorite books.
- If your school district has access to publishers' book clubs, encourage children to order inexpensive books for their own use and get the publisher's bonus books.
- Ask parents to scout book sales for you. If you become known as "the book lady" in the district, people will keep you in mind.
- Consult with your school librarian and suggest what books you would like to see ordered.
- Make books. Have older children or parents make books, put children's own work together into books. Encourage your

young writers to publish. Do group projects – "Our trip to the fire station" or "Our Christmas book."

- Use social studies and science texts as general reading material and keep them available so that children can consult them.
- Get permission to spend money normally designated for worksheets on books instead.
- Buy books rather than expensive kits or skill packs.

Other Reading Materials

- Collect old sets of *National Geographic* and similar magazines.
- Bring in newspaper clippings and Sunday supplements.
- Use children's magazines such as *Cricket, Ranger Rick, Child Life, Humpty Dumpty*, or *National Geographic World*.
- Prepare song sheets, recipe cards, language experience charts.
- Label everything around the classroom.

Cooperation makes for safety

Cooperation and sharing are important parts of a good learning climate. Here are some of the ways to model cooperative behavior:

- Ask for the children's opinions on issues that concern them.
- Cooperate with parents and other teachers on projects or tasks.
- Engage in give-and-take with the children (they soon pick up on this).
- Be quiet and calm in your dealings with children.
- Give children genuine choices.
- Praise/acknowledge cooperative behavior.
- Listen attentively when children talk to you (maintain eye contact).
- Show affection with eye contact and a gentle pat on the head or back.
- Tell children about your family life.
- Tell children when you are upset (be genuine about it).
- Be joyful and enthusiastic in class.
- Listen to the children's problems and hurts.
- Make deals: "I'll do this if you will do that."
- Work alongside children when they are doing projects.
- Take a genuine interest in their concerns, talents, interests.
- Give reasons for classroom rules.

- Keep rules to a minimum but quietly and firmly enforce those you have.
- Model courteous behavior.
- Keep promises you make.
- Have children settle their own disputes.
- Engage in cooperative art projects – you do background, children do rest.

Signs that tell you the climate in your classroom is right

At the beginning of the year Margaret spends the bulk of her time and effort on getting the children settled into the classroom. Here are some of the signs she watches for to tell her that the right climate for joyful learning has evolved.

- Children are getting to work quickly.
- Quiet children are becoming more vocal.
- Noisy children are becoming more quiet.
- Hyperactive children are showing longer attention spans.
- Children are beginning to think of the next step in a task by themselves.
- Children are becoming more independent in choosing activities.
- Children can go to the washroom on their own.
- Children can go to the library, office, gym on their own.
- Children take more responsibility for their belongings; they keep desks tidy.
- Children become good listeners.
- Children trust the teacher; they are not shy or fearful.
- Children are confiding in the teacher.
- Children are sympathetic to others' problems.
- Children rush to someone who has been hurt, asking, "Are you all right?"
- Children greet the teacher warmly.
- Children show their need for a hug.
- Children want to stay in at recess because they like what they are doing.
- Most children are on task.
- Discipline problems have subsided for the most part.

- There is a feeling of calm in the classroom.
- Teacher can leave the room without children noticing or getting out of line.
- Attention spans are lengthening.
- Teacher does not have to remind children of rules as much.
- Parents come in and out of the classroom without their children acting out.
- The atmosphere is one of getting along.
- Other teachers say, "You've got the good, quiet kids."
- There is a feeling of well-being in the classroom.

Space to move fosters independence – become a "space finder"

Children need room to move about and to spread out their projects or writing. Arrange your room to get the most use of space. Push desks together as shown in the sample layout on page 238. Experiment with different floor plans.

Next, become a "space finder" outside of your home room. If feasible, use hallways and spare rooms. Margaret has a carpeted hallway outside her classroom that is just wasted space during most of the day. She puts groups of children out there to work on special projects: making books, rehearsing a play, working on a mural. There is also some space under the stairwell for a kindergarten workbench, and at times, kindergarten children go there to do some hammering. In fine weather the workbench can be moved outdoors for part of the time.

- The library and any special teaching areas are further possible additions to your classroom space. Book them whenever possible and use them for children who need extra room to spread out a project.
- Margaret uses the staff room for cooking with the children, at times to the dismay of teachers who want to come in for a quiet cup of coffee.
- Reading buddies often roam the school to find an empty classroom in which to settle down for reading practice. Classes on field trips, at physical education, in the music room offer possibilities.

The children love to become their own "space finders." Some will settle in the walk-in closet for some quiet work on a book. The corner under the desk, the space behind the pull-down blackboard, and the carpet all invite children to move from their tables and into their favorite spot or physical position. After they have had a stretch, they are quite ready to sit quietly at their tables. Moving about and using space does not lead to chaos or lack of control; instead, moving about and finding personal space keeps children on task and also gives them the physical movement so vital to their overall development.

Focusing on steps forward

Building on strengths and creating a positive atmosphere are key elements in teaching the learners' way. Instead of focusing on error correction, Margaret notes every step forward and comments on it.

She continually comments on the children's positive behaviors: "Good work" or "That's great!" or "You are doing all right." She probably engages in more positive feedback than any other kind of speaking in class. We find that being positive works better than chiding. A usually boisterous child who comes into class without too much noise and disturbance gets, "What a good way you came into the room." In fact, Margaret comments on any improvement, however slight. If a child produces a little more work, speaks up a little more, there is room for a positive comment.

But what constitutes steps forward is relative. A child who has proceeded very slowly would be praised for any slight improvement. Another child who usually does well might not receive specific comments for a very small increase in production. As in all interactions with the children it becomes important to observe carefully and note individual differences. Watch the children and give them feedback according to their best interests. Some children become too boisterous with too much reinforcement while some need much self-confidence boosting. Giving feedback almost becomes intuitive. You come to know just when and where to provide that positive input.

Dealing with "bad" behavior – what to overlook

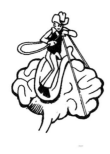

In order not to be a "nag" in her classroom, Margaret overlooks a lot of inappropriate behavior. With Robin, who was particularly slow, she praised even the slightest increase in speed and never commented on his usual dawdling. To have nagged him about catching up, speeding up, and finishing on time would have driven everyone to distraction and done little or nothing to hurry Robin along. Children like Robin sometimes use slowness as a way of getting attention. Since he was getting no attention at his usual pace but did receive it for speeding up, he started to focus on moving along more rapidly.

A bit of talking and boisterous behavior is easily ignored if the overall noise level is still all right. But at times it does become necessary to remind children to use their "indoor voices." Then it is particularly important not to shout, but to model quiet speaking. Instead of shouting directions to a child who is at the opposite side of the room, Margaret moves over to the child, establishes good eye contact and speaks to him/her quietly: "Your loud voice is disturbing those of us who are reading." Such modeling soon establishes the tone, and peer pressure takes over to establish a cohesive, cooperative group spirit.

Here are some behaviors Margaret tends to overlook:

- Talking at quiet time
- Daydreaming, fantasizing
- Forgetting library books
- Slight rough-housing
- Wrong grammar (simply respond with correct grammar)
- Tattling (listen briefly but don't act on what is said)
- Poor printing (just keep modeling good printing)
- Holding the pencil the "wrong" way (model the right way and let it go at that)
- Not getting along (Try to leave them to settle their differences. If Peter complains, "They aren't giving me a turn and that's not fair," suggest, "Why don't you tell them that and ask them to be fair.")

What about troublemakers?

Amanda came into class ready for action. She would wait until the other children had built an elaborate structure with bricks and blocks; then she would stealthily sidle into the group and knock everything over. There would be a loud outcry from the group and Amanda would go off to bedevil someone else.

Amanda's destructive and disruptive behavior continued until considerable discussion among her, the injured parties, and the teacher convinced Amanda that it was much more productive and enjoyable to join the group and build cooperatively than it was to knock things down. Throughout the period of unrest and negotiation, the teacher remained very calm, did not shout or protest loudly, but largely let the discussions, peer teaching, and peer pressure produce the change in Amanda's attitude and actions.

Modeling calm, reasonable ways of discussing feelings and behaviors worked better than punishing or scolding. It seems that Amanda had a little brother who was knocking down her block structures and she was simply taking out her resentments and frustrations on the children in her class. Once she learned how to join them, Amanda no longer felt the need to vent her pent-up resentment on her classmates.

Trusting a child builds independence

On Monday morning, right before story time, Bobby lost a tooth! He proudly showed it off and the big event became the focal point of that day's reading. Instead of the story at hand, the teacher read *The Tooth Fairy*, a hilarious account of the tooth fairy gathering teeth for every imaginable purpose. Bobby enjoyed the limelight, but by the end of the story the tiny tooth had slipped through his fingers and he rushed up crying, "Mrs. Reinhard, I can't find my tooth!"

Since Mommy at home is very much inclined to anticipate Bobby's every need, he fully expected the teacher to drop everything to hunt for his lost tooth. Instead, the teacher merely announced to the class that Bobby had lost his tooth and asked everyone to be on the lookout for it. She also quietly assured Bobby that he would find his tooth if he looked around carefully.

By the end of the day, the tooth was still missing and the teacher once more assured Bobby that if he really looked around he *would* find his tooth. A short while later he *did*. Full of pride and excitement he announced that he had found it, then discussed with his teacher how he could best carry his treasure home without losing it again. With his tooth safely wrapped into a tissue and tucked into his shirt pocket, Bobby went home aglow with his success.

Trusting Bobby to do his own looking and finding without fuss, scolding, or over-indulgence not only became a fine lesson in the joy of self-reliance and independence for Bobby but also for the student teacher visiting the classroom that day. Being kind-hearted and helpful, she had been ready to take over the parents' customary role of doing Bobby's job for him and in the process might have deprived him of an exciting move toward independence.

The spirit of cooperation includes parents

Your job managing a classroom filled with active children will be eased a great deal if you can bring in some help. Look upon every visitor to your classroom as a potential helper and model of skills and invite all comers to interact freely with the children. The cooperative atmosphere you are modeling will be greatly enhanced by the presence of others in the classroom: reading buddies, student teachers, observers, teacher aides, visiting firemen, the custodian, the principal, anyone who enters the class.

But your most important help will come from the children's parents. Invite them to come in any time, ask for and accept help with field trips, jobs around the classroom, snacks, or whatever seems appropriate. Progress may be gradual, *so hang in there*. It may take several years to become known in the district as "parent friendly."

Here are some suggestions that will help you to bring parents into your classroom on a regular basis:

- Have a meeting at the beginning of the year to explain your way of teaching and the philosophy of cooperation that welcomes parent help and involvement.
- Prepare a parent-help schedule a month ahead so parents can plan for their day(s) – or half-day(s) – at school.
- Encourage parents to bring in their younger children.
- Offer tea or coffee at mid-morning to your parent helpers.
- Talk to them about their concerns or problems regarding their children.
- Accept all offers of snacks or help with expressions of pleasure and gratitude. (The occasional sugar-filled treat won't hurt.)
- Encourage fathers to come in – even if briefly – to model reading, writing, or sharing information. Children need both male and female models.

- Reassure non-English-speaking parents that there are plenty of jobs with which they can help – making things, cutting, printing, and the like.
- Give parents jobs that suit them. Some like working with children, some like paper work or artwork, others prefer a combination of activities.
- Acknowledge parents just as you would your students. "You really helped me today." "I wouldn't have accomplished nearly as much if you hadn't come in." Overlook what you would consider negative comments if a parent reads with children, and simply ask for help with something else the next time that parent comes in.
- Have a parent-helper tea at the end of the year and have children cook for, serve, and entertain the parent helpers.

Networking builds confidence, expertise, and enthusiasm

When we started our joint work we very much relied on each other and on our close observations of the children's reactions to our new ways of teaching. Though other researchers were talking about learning to read by reading (Smith 1971), there was as yet little practical advice to be had. There were few opportunities to turn to the literature or to other teachers for reassurance, idea exchanges, or shared excitement. But gradually we built a network of like-minded parents, teachers, and researchers with whom to communicate. Constructivist teaching (Goodman 1986), the young writers' workshop (Graves 1983), shared book experience (Holdaway 1980), and literature-based reading instruction all evolved from observing learners at work. All have a great deal to offer to each other. As researchers and practitioners shared their findings about holistic ways of teaching/learning, we drew ideas and reassurance about our work from them. In turn, we shared our ideas and practical suggestions. Here are some of the ways of networking we have found useful in our work:

- Seek out like-minded teachers in your school, district, area.
- Keep telephone contact with other teachers to compare notes.
- Meet regularly – over coffee, dinner, at breakfast, for potluck – to exchange ideas and raise questions.
- Exchange books, journal articles, teaching materials of mutual interest.
- Invite the principal/supervisor to an idea exchange/ brainstorming session.

- Keep each other posted about speakers, meetings, new books.
- Compare notes on what works for you, how children react.
- Keep parents well informed about your work and their children's steps forward. (Parents will quickly become your strongest supporters.)
- Share the cost of books, journal subscriptions, teaching materials.
- Share special equipment such as a chick incubator, food dehydrator, or video equipment.
- Share the job of organizing workshops and bringing in speakers.
- Offer to give workshops, singly or as a group.
- Develop team teaching with like-minded teachers.
- Coordinate your teaching with teachers in other grades to build on and reinforce the work each of you is doing.

If in doubt – watch the kids, talk to experienced teachers, and hang in there! You can trust children to learn!

When Gale L. returned to teaching after a long absence and a university refresher course, she sought advice and reassurance from Margaret. She began by experimenting in kindergarten and was delighted with the children's positive responses and success. Gale's next teaching assignment took her to a first-grade classroom and she again opted for teaching the learners' way, using a compatible text and supplementing it with story reading, chants, poems, experience charts, and plenty of activity.

The children in her class, who were largely from low socioeconomic backgrounds, stayed happily on task but Gale was worrying about the development of specific skills. Several times a week she called Margaret to seek reassurance. "I'm not sure these kids are learning." "I don't know exactly where these kids are in their reading." Each time Margaret encouraged Gale to simply carry on and trust. One week the call was, "Margaret, I'm worried, other teachers' kids are doing so much better. You can see the results." Again Margaret reassured Gale that measurable results would begin to show.

About January of that school year the phone calls began to change in tone. "Well, I guess they are doing O.K. They are certainly enthusiastic about what they are doing." Finally, in late January, the phone calls became, "I'm so excited. The kids are really doing well. The results are beginning to show. They are reading with great expression and their comprehension is very good." Gale's school had just finished cross-grade testing and Gale's students had done as well as or better than children in other grade-one classes. Her principal began to show her recognition for her work and other teachers began to take an interest in her way of teaching. The children knew all along what worked for them and had fun learning to read and write.

Learning to Read by Reading

3

Once our research had demonstrated that in learning to read children will look for meaning and use patterns of language to aid them, we decided that we wanted to shift our teaching to fit their ways of learning. We wanted to encourage that endless practice that makes for effective learning at home because our observations had shown us that with our structured lessons, individual children were reading no more than a few minutes each day. Our discussions about fitting our teaching to the children's ways of learning led to a number of decisions about how to proceed:

How we made the shift to the learners' way

If children are looking for meaning – let's use material that makes sense to them and builds on their interests.

If children use patterns of language – let's give them lots and lots of interesting language.

If language used at home deals with familiar topics – let's begin reading instruction with highly familiar materials, preferably something the children already know.

If children evolve their own rules of grammar – let's give them plenty of books and stories so that they have lots of material to work with.

If parents model fluent language at home – let's model fluent reading throughout the day.

If parents encourage children to practice – let's fill the classroom with books and writing and encourage children to read and write.

If parents teach talking simply by communicating with their children – let's keep the focus on communicating and making sense.

If parents accept with pleasure and reinforcement the initial crude attempts at talking – let's not worry about exact renditions in reading and writing when the children begin.

As our teaching evolved, our trust in the children's ability to learn by doing was well rewarded. All of the children made good progress and we found that we did not need to worry whether children understood the concept of *word, sentence,* or *letter.* As their ability to understand print increased, those concepts became clear and children used them with greater assurance and accuracy than they had in our days of structured lessons. Introducing fluent reading certainly added enjoyment and excitement to initial reading instruction. But being a conscientious teacher, Margaret did not immediately abandon all of her structured lessons. At first she simply added story time and large charts showing nursery rhymes and similar familiar material. In fact, she introduced them in kindergarten and her students promptly learned to recite and then read the familiar words and lines.

If we had our doubts about the "rightness" and effectiveness of using the holistic ways, the children did not. After Margaret had abandoned her regular phonics drills, a mother told her that her little boy had commented, "I used to hate it when Mrs. Reinhard got out that red book." The red book was the phonics guide. Another teacher tells of the time she let her guilty feelings induce her to put on a structured lesson in phonics. As she worked on the board she noticed that one little girl in particular looked puzzled and not very happy. Finally she spoke up, "Mrs. Cowden, why don't we stop this stuff and get on with the reading?" Her teacher abandoned structured phonics lessons there and then and now the children in her class learn about letters and sounds through their writing and spelling.

Since you, too, may be beset by doubts when shifting to literature-based teaching, we are providing quite detailed descriptions of the different ways in which you can use reading and writing throughout the day. Remembering our own questions about what the children learned and whether or not they were making progress, we are also including comments on some of the things children learn from these activities. It seems to us that for too long we have looked too closely at decoding and word-attack skills and not nearly enough at the very broad range of skills and knowledge that comprise reading and functional literacy. Yet literacy, like the ability to speak, involves far more than knowing words.

Story time

To introduce children to the joys of reading, select lively, enjoyable books and stories and be sure that you take your own preferences into account. Children quickly sense whether you are enthusiastic, bored, or enthralled with a story and they are likely to react in kind. Remember that a parent will talk to baby long before baby is ready to talk, so there is no need for you to pick stories with limited vocabulary or simplified sentence structure. Make enjoyment and fun the key elements in attracting children to reading. In choosing books and stories, consider the illustrations and other physical features – size and style of print, overall layout, or general visual appeal.

When reading aloud, let the children gather around you or in front of you on the carpet and hold the book up so that they can see the pictures as you read. You may want to use an easel or improvised stand to support the book to keep one hand free to turn pages or point to pictures or print as you move along. With very little practice you will learn to read upside down, sideways, and backwards. As you become familiar with the stories you will discover, like one kindergarten child did, that "you can read without looking too!" Though some teachers like to have the children use their imagination to create their own pictures for the stories read to them, we generally find that children stay focused more readily when they can see the pictures and comment on them as the story unfolds. Turning pages quite deliberately also shows that the story progresses from the front of the book to the back and the children like to stay with you as you move through the book.

When reading to the entire class, you may find big books most suitable, but don't limit yourself in any way. Children will eagerly crowd around you to take a closer look at pictures of a story they have enjoyed. You may also want to leaf through the book slowly before or after reading the story to give children more of a chance to look at the pictures.

How to immerse children in reading

Whether you move straight through the story or pause to talk about it will depend on the story, your own preference, and that of the children. Let the moment dictate how to proceed. If the story is exciting or suspenseful, you and the children may be eager to find out what happens next. On the other hand, events in the story may invite comments from you or the children about ways in which the story relates to their own lives. Drawing the children's attention to some of the interesting details of pictures or wondering aloud "what will happen next," models attention to detail for the children. But we make very sure not to turn story time into a comprehension quiz with "What did they do?" "Who was there?" and the like.

Keep story time fairly short at the beginning of the year. Don't make it an endurance test. If the children are unaccustomed to hearing long stories, they may soon begin to fidget, no matter how interesting the story. Keep your eye on their reactions and gradually lengthen stories to help them build their attention span. Once children realize that stories can be talked about, commented upon, and questioned, story time will become a very lively session. As we suggest in chapter 6, story time can be scattered throughout the day. Children enjoy having a fixed time for story reading, but interspersing stories here and there during the day can become a much looked-for treat and often helps to settle children down if they have become a bit too exuberant.

Material to be used for story time is limited only by your imagination and the children's contributions to your stock of reading material. (See suggestions for filling your classroom with books in chapter 2.) Poems, chapters in books, interesting articles in newspapers or magazines, the children's own favorite books, or social science texts all lend themselves to being read aloud to the children.

Leave the stories or books you have read within easy reach and watch the children return to them throughout the day to look at pictures, to read or pretend to read, and to talk about them. If a story is particularly popular, read it onto a tape and leave it and the book in the listening center for a week or so until interest flags.

Skills/knowledge gained from story time

By listening to stories as well as reading books and stories themselves children gain skills in functional literacy and accumulate knowledge that will build the foundation for lifelong reading. *Listed below are some of the skills and knowledge they acquire. No doubt you can think of more.*

Children learn
- to derive meaning from print
- to become good listeners
- to develop long attention spans
- to voice opinions and ask questions
- to become careful observers
- to share what they perceive and discuss it
- to use language patterns to anticipate what comes next
- to recognize phrasing and language rhythms
- to use fluent reading and good intonation
- to build a sight vocabulary for reading
- to distinguish different writing styles
- to glean language patterns for their own writing
- to build their vocabulary and enrich their spoken language
- to use language in imaginative ways
- to look at pictures to help gain meaning
- to distinguish between make-believe and reality
- to build a positive attitude toward reading and the use of written language
- to recognize words, letters, and their sounds on sight

They also learn
- that reading is fun, exciting, and interesting
- what book language is like
- that stories can make you laugh and cry
- how stories unfold with a beginning, a middle, and an end
- that stories reflect personal experiences
- that print, like spoken language, conveys messages
- that stories can be enjoyed again and again
- that story lines and poetry are predictable
- that stories and reading are sources of information

Unison reading in large groups

If, during story time, you hold the book so that children can see the lines of print, you will notice that some of them will begin to read along with you from the beginning of the year. Even in kindergarten, some will actually speak up and talk along here and there, others may simply mouth words, and still others follow the print with their eyes. Hence, story time becomes a good lead-in to more active participation in reading. When the teacher reads their favorite stories, the children love to join in with words or pantomime. Unison reading offers them that opportunity.

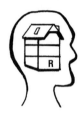

Unison reading (also known as choral reading or echo reading) works very much like a sing-along. The leader intones the words loud, clear, and with gusto, and the participants mumble along as best they can, speaking up more solidly when a refrain or other familiar passage comes along. Unison reading has all the fun and good feelings of a sing-along. Familiar rhythms, sounds, and images invite even the most timid to join the chorus. The safety of participating in relative anonymity engenders feelings of self-confidence and eagerness to learn even more about reading. For the teacher this is a chance to ham it up, to use voice and mimicry to make stories come alive. Children love to hear you ROAR like the lion or speak gruffly like the big bad troll. After you have read a story a few times, you will notice individual children return to the book to imitate your every intonation and gesture as they read or pretend to read.

Big books that all children can readily see, sets of books to give each child a personal copy of what is being read, large charts of songs, nursery rhymes, experience stories, or other familiar material all lend themselves well to unison reading. At the beginning of the year you will find large-scale material particularly useful because it allows you to demonstrate to the entire class how you are tracking print as you read. Whether you use your hand, a pointer or, later on, a bookmark to show that print progresses from left to right and from the top of the page to the bottom, children will watch and then emulate your way.

To keep your hands free for tracking print, suspend charts on the blackboard or wall and place big books on a stand or easel. Run your hand or a pointer along the lines in smooth sweeps instead of pointing to each individual word. The children may want to point to words in their reading, but for your own demonstration the smooth motion of tracking gives less room for the choppy intonation of word-for-word reading that emphasizes all words equally and ignores phrasing. As another step in involving the children, invite two of them to come up to help you hold the book in place and turn the pages. They love to participate in that way and later in the day you will observe groups of them gather around the easel to re-enact that morning's big-book reading.

When first introducing unison reading – whether in kindergarten or grade one – read the whole book to the children first to see how they enjoy it. Then ask, "Would you like to read along with me?" Especially in kindergarten it helps to make such initial readings quite short. Choose books that have just a few words per page or materials – poems or stories – that are either highly familiar to the children or very predictable. If you have a series like Impressions (Holt, Rinehart) or RefleXions (Scholastic) in your classroom, you will have quite a choice of appropriate reading material that is simple yet fun and colorful. Bill Martin's *Brown Bear, Brown Bear,* a story on the rainbow with pictures and just one color per page, "Jelly in the Bowl" (both in *How I Wonder* in the Impression Series), and other familiar poems are sure to be successes with the children.

After inviting the children to read along with you, read the story again a little more slowly, but still with good intonation and a natural flow of words and phrases. If you will leave a pregnant pause just before a guessable word, the children will be sure to chime in. Such invitations to speak up not only hold the children's attention but teach them right from the start to use context and prior knowledge as valuable aids in reading.

Once you get a good chorus of voices during unison reading, begin to ask for volunteers to "read all by themselves" and hand over the pointer to the brave ones. Reassure the children that you will help if they get stuck. Very quickly there will be eager little readers and their successes will encourage others to come forth. Keep any such activities strictly voluntary but make sure that the more hesitant or quiet children get their turns if they show any inclination to come forth when they are given a little reassurance. After individual reading with blackboard work or big books has become established, the children themselves become the helpers. As the volunteer steps forward to do individual reading of a line or page he will announce "I need help," and his peers will read along with him as he does his

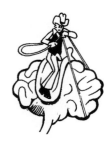

own reading and pointing in front of the group. Yet if the statement is "I can do it myself," the children will not interfere but leave the reader free to read independently.

Once the group becomes restless, end the session and tell those who would like to continue to read that the book will be available to them and that they can read it at the listening station, with a helper, or by themselves later on. Many of the big books come with sets of smaller versions of the same text and children enjoy taking them to their seats to go over the story again. We find that quite often children will select such books for their book time reading.

Unison reading works well in small groups

Unison reading lends itself to small-group reading as well. As you sit down with five or six children, all of you will have a copy of the same book and, again, you will lead the reading using your most expressive intonation. If you hold your book so that the children can see how you are tracking print, they will quickly follow your lead. Small-group reading is a good time to introduce the use of bookmarks to track print. Since fluent readers anticipate what comes next and have eye spans that are ahead of their voice during oral reading, it is important to show the children to keep bookmarks *above* the line they are reading. In other words, they cover up where they have been and leave open the lines of print that come next. That approach gives their eyes a chance to travel ahead and encourages the habit of taking in phrases and chunks of meaning instead of individual words one at a time. One of Margaret's early discoveries after switching to literature-based reading instruction was that children's eye spans increased. She could see that as the children moved their eyes along the lines of print, they were taking in larger chunks than they did before. Of course comprehension is aided greatly by focusing on units of meaning, and using bookmarks in the correct way – moving down from the top without covering up what comes next.

Using the bookmark can also become a convenient way for you to note if the children are following along with you as you are reading together. You will notice how they move from page to page and how some of them glance up now and again to check where your bookmark is, either to reassure themselves or to make an adjustment to their own tracking. If a child is quite off the mark, *gently* reach over and place the bookmark where it should be at the moment. In very short order you will find that most of the children are tracking print accurately even if they are not yet speaking up. Hands, eyes, voice, and thought become coordinated in these sessions, and true reading gradually emerges from the initial mechanical tracking and memory reading. If you keep your eyes peeled for even the smallest steps forward, you will soon see that reading is indeed emerging.

Unison reading also lends itself to individual work with children. It may be more like echo-reading with the child saying the words just a fraction of a second after the person doing the fluent reading. You, a teaching assistant, parent helper, reading buddy, visitor to the class, or a classmate can all become partners in such individualized unison reading sessions. Children enjoy the chance to work individually and to reread stories they have practiced before. Shy or diffident children benefit especially from individual sessions as they tend to speak up more readily in a one-to-one setting. For you, such sessions become opportunities to reinforce skills and to note special needs of individual children. The learning assistance teacher in your school may also find individual unison reading a valuable way of building on your classroom work.

Unison reading builds silent-reading skills and encourages practice

Though unison reading encourages children to read aloud and to practice oral reading, it becomes an introduction to silent reading as well. As the children follow along with their hands and eyes while you and their classmates are reading, they are beginning to track print with their eyes and minds. Particularly when others are leading the unison reading session, you will see the children's eyes move along the lines and pages of print. Since participation is voluntary, the more quiet children still have the opportunity to read along, and unison reading for them becomes their initial practice with silent reading.

If you leave all the reading materials out and children feel free to use them any time, they will lead unison reading sessions in two's, three's, and small groups using big books, charts, or sets of books. They will happily go over the same material time and again as they take turns being the leader. If you want to hear how you sound and see what you do when you read, just watch such peer-led reading sessions. The young teachers will model themselves after your every move and intonation, including the ways you invite children to participate or to volunteer after unison reading.

Skills/knowledge gained from unison reading

When participating in unison reading, children learn all the things they learn from story time.

They also learn that
- print, not the pictures, carries the main message
- written language moves left to right, top to bottom
- language is predictable and can be anticipated
- the same words appear again and again
- personal knowledge or experience aids reading
- the teacher makes no unreasonable demands
- they are free to take their time about speaking up
- they can follow the lead of other children
- they are free to express their views
- it is all right to make mistakes
- it is safe to try even if they are not yet proficient
- it is all right to mumble along before they are sure
- it is all right to do just the parts they can do
- they can remain quiet while figuring things out
- there are more ways than one to look at a story
- it is all right to enjoy a story even if they cannot read along as yet

In addition, they
- expand their repertoire of sight words and phrases
- become more aware of phrasing
- become aware of sounds of letters, particularly initial consonants
- gain confidence in their ability to read
- lose shyness about speaking up
- become aware of punctuation marks and their uses
- learn to take parts or roles in reading
- become more conscious of the reading audience
- expand their imagination
- learn to exchange ideas
- build a memory bank of written language patterns

Writing promotes reading practice

Though writing focuses on producing written messages, it affords endless opportunities to practice reading. Beginning with news time in the morning, the children observe how you convert their spoken messages into letters, words, sentences, and – later on – paragraphs. They will follow along as you say each word, then read the entire phrase or sentence, and then they will join in to read the news of the day with you. Because the messages are so familiar, children readily volunteer to come to the board to read, and if you leave the news on the board, individual children will later in the day come to the board to have some quiet, individual practice. The same process is at work with all the writing practiced in class. Even the picture captions you provide for their own artwork early in kindergarten or first grade will be repeated eagerly by the children. Such familiar and personal written messages often become the foundation of more independent reading. Just as children recognize spoken language that is highly familiar and personal, so they recognize familiar and personal messages in print and internalize them for future use and broader generalizations about writing, print, and reading.

We will discuss the many facets of writing practice more fully in chapter 4 but be aware that every time you and the children put pencil to paper or chalk to blackboard there is reading practice as well as writing practice. With the focus on communication and the production of sensible messages, writing is not simply a drill to produce strings of letters or lists of words. Invitations, notes to parents, descriptions of artwork, letters to pen pals, and stories or projects children produce all offer reading practice that invites voluntary practice and personal involvement.

Writing also creates an awareness of the particles of speech, and enhances phonologic awareness. Though the children don't look at it that way and you may not present it in that light, writing and spelling are the phonics lessons that we have shifted out of reading practice because our central focus rests on meaning and communication. But as we will discuss in chapter 4, the children learn about letters and their sounds very thoroughly and quite readily as they write. Because they work hard to generate their own spelling, their knowledge of letters and their sounds becomes well established and transfers freely to their reading and to sounding out unfamiliar words if the context fails to yield their meaning.

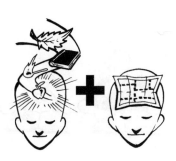

Reading skills gained during writing practice

While focusing on writing, children pick up all of the details of the conventions of print.

They learn that
- sounds can be translated into print
- letters have recognizable sounds
- words can be sounded out
- certain letters have more than one sound
- words are made up of letters
- language can be separated into individual words
- spoken language can be written down, reread, and remembered
- language is segmented into phrases
- there are many different ways to express the same thing
- language can be changed to be more pleasing
- written language is useful in conveying messages

Incidental reading fills the day

The more you focus on conveying messages, the more you will incorporate the use of written language into all activities. As you abandon the concern about keeping language simple, you can expand your reading and writing activities tremendously. In the process you expand the children's vocabulary and stimulate their imagination and curiosity. Just watch the obvious relish with which they try out that delicious big mouthful of a word. Labels around the classroom, written or printed directions and rules for playing games, instructions for making things, descriptions of science projects, directions for getting to the picnic, notes home all become reading material as you weave them into your daily classroom activities. Like the parent who accompanies the daily activities around the baby with a descriptive monologue that comments on what is going on, so you will do a lot of "thinking aloud" as you refer to the many written messages in a matter-of-fact voice. Without belaboring details of words or print, simply talk about needing to read the directions, needing to follow the road map, wanting to make sure you are using the right ingredients in a recipe.

Raccoons.

Procyoninae there are.
Six genera of animals.
that may be classed.

A Raccoon has a mask
of black hair around its
eyes this furry mammal
eats fish and frogs that it
catches in rivers andstreams

The feet of a Raccoons.

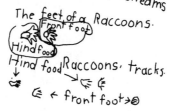

Front foot

Hind food

Hind food Raccoons. tracks.

↓ Ꞙ ← front foot →◉

The Baya's Ragaon'spalyand

The Raoocc̃ns have baow
Fer and blackstrips

***Personal interests spark
child-initiated research
projects***

*Research reports on topics of
interest to the children occupy
much of the reading and
writing time even in grade
one. Copies of passages from
quite sophisticated reference
works serve as the first step in
developing a feel for expository
writing.*

*Here a young researcher is
using her reading skills to find
and then copy some of the
technical information. She
augments her book-based
research with personal
information and her own
illustrations.*

*Composing requires full
attention and spelling goes
by the board for the moment.
The report extends over
several more pages and
concludes with another
passage copied from the
reference book. Reading and
writing are definitely moving
along jointly.*

Children will follow your example and though they will probably make up their own rules for games, they will be aware that the words on the back of the box give the directions you just talked about.

The production of plays – often initiated by the children themselves – requires practice, reading of roles, and sustained rehearsal. Children will research and write their own productions, and work tirelessly on putting on a good show. The same goes for special research projects or the production of stories and books. You will find that you will have to be flexible in your scheduling to accommodate the intense work and extended attention spans of the young scientists and writers.

Center time adds yet more reading practice. Children will move to listening stations, curl up with a favorite book, play word or letter games, and write or read letters. If a cooking center has been set up for the day, recipe cards and charts are scanned as each child takes a turn to prepare some goodies.

Though there may not appear to be a great deal of precision in this kind of reading work, it nevertheless lays the foundation for the functional literacy that we hear about so much. If children are conscious of the many uses of print in their daily lives, they are far more likely to become sensitive to the need to read with accuracy and care than they would be if they were required to be accurate with exercises and worksheets.

Skills/knowledge gained from incidental reading

Since reading pervades the day, children learn a great deal from all the incidental reading they do.

They learn that reading
- helps them find out things they want to know
- can bring messages/greetings
- helps them learn new information
- helps them do things – cook, make things
- gives them directions for playing games, getting to places
- protects them by giving warnings
- is used every day by grown-ups
- is part of many activities

- lets them keep in touch with what's going on in the world
- reminds them of things to do
- is easy when used in daily activities

During book time everybody enjoys books and reading

Once we acknowledged that Uninterrupted Sustained Silent Reading (USSR) was neither silent nor uninterrupted and consisted of little actual reading at the beginning of kindergarten, we simply called it "book time." It is the period of the day when the entire class, including the teacher, sits down with books or other favorite reading material. For the teacher it may be a time to catch up on reading journal articles or new books on reading, or it may be simply a chance to enjoy a novel. After all, enjoyment is the prime object of book time. If you have ever watched children come racing in breathlessly after recess to get settled quickly for book time, you cannot have the least doubt about their eagerness to read.

As at other reading times, the key to success is to have a large stock of books available – both familiar ones and ever-changing additions – to tempt the young readers. You may have to keep a check-out list for some of the favorite books in order to give everyone a chance to read them. Allow children to pick a stack of books to take to their desks so that they will have plenty to look at should their first choice prove disappointing.

In kindergarten book time is most certainly not quiet. Children keep their voices low and there is a steady hum of sharing. If a child wants to read in silence, s/he will find a spot removed from the main group. But most of the children want to share their books with each other. They look at pictures, begin to read or pretend to read, and generally enjoy the interaction with each other and the books. Though you are settling down to read as well, some of the children will interrupt you to ask for help with a word or to ask you to read a passage of interest. Reading buddies may come in at book time and read to and with the kindergarten children. The session expands from just five minutes at the beginning of the year to whatever length of time you decide fits the children's need or attention span.

In grade one, book time quickly expands to more definite reading activities and to longer periods of time. But at the beginning of the year we keep the sessions quite short and allow any interaction with books that the children choose – looking at pictures, going over books read during group time, leafing through quickly, shifting from one book to another. Before long, all of the children settle down to reading and focusing on one book at a time. Margaret finds that children settle down quickly with their favorite book and if she is delayed coming in after recess, she may find the entire class completely engrossed in reading by the time she enters her classroom.

Though book time is much more quiet in grade one than in kindergarten, there still is a lot of quiet sharing. As long as they are not disturbing each other, let the children share in two's or small groups if they wish. Some children like to read to their friends, some like to discuss what they have read or share some fun. As they gain in proficiency, children will also gather together into small groups to read with distributed roles or to share a big book. We allow children to move about quietly to exchange books or interact with each other, but all of them must be considerate of those who do not wish to be disturbed in their individual reading.

At the end of the session most children like to share some of what they have read with the entire group or with a friend. Though by no means everyone volunteers to speak up, it may still be a good idea to cut the session off once it becomes apparent that the children are becoming restless. But you will notice a definite lengthening of attention spans as the year progresses. If you start in September with ten minutes, you may find that by spring book time has extended to half an hour or more.

Grades two and three include an expanded book time and more sophisticated materials for the children to read. Silent reading is coming to the fore and sharing with friends rather than the entire class is the more usual approach. Continue to leave the choice of reading material entirely to the children and provide a special place where children can keep books with their bookmarks for ongoing reading of lengthy books. If your students have been introduced to book time in the preceding grade, they will be ready to settle down for longer sessions right away, and by the end of the year book time may be close to a full hour.

Skills/knowledge gained from book time

Book time teaches the children all of the things they learn during unison reading and story time.

In addition, they learn that
■ there are many kinds of different books
■ some books are hard/easy to read
■ books have different ways of telling/showing things
■ reading the same book many times can be satisfying
■ reading gets easier if you read the same book many times
■ you can pretend to be somebody in the story
■ books can be read in stages, a chapter at a time

They also learn to
■ develop feelings of independence and success with reading
■ pick up imaginative ways of using language, print, artwork
■ become unafraid of new books or tasks
■ become flexible in recognizing different ways of using print
■ generalize information about book language
■ cherish reading as a wonderful leisure activity

Reading groups

Reading groups don't begin until grade one and then not necessarily right at the beginning of the year. We find that it helps to introduce children to reading with story time and whole group unison reading, and to build some knowledge of letters and sounds with news time before gathering for small-group reading. However, if at the beginning of the year you find that there are a few keen readers in your class, you may want to make time to read with them several times a week. For most of the children it is more important to establish the right climate that will serve as a foundation for independent learning. Once children have settled into a daily routine and are beginning to take responsibility for moving from one task to the next without waiting for specific instructions, your time will become ever more free to work with individual children and small groups.

From the introduction of reading groups, we use quite random grouping without worrying about the children's reading levels.

That way there is no chance of labeling children or depriving emergent readers of reading the more exciting stories. If you feel uncomfortable with such random grouping remember that children can listen very well even if they cannot as yet read. As you call five or six children together, keep in mind the benefits young children used to derive from listening to older children in one-room schools.

While early in the year you may want to read a story or passage to the children before asking them to join in, children will soon expect to read along with you during reading groups. After reading a story or section of a book in unison, give the children a choice to reread something silently or to pick a favorite page to read aloud. Keep such reading voluntary and accept without comment or cajoling that a child does not want to read aloud even in such a small group. Just allow the child to return to the center at which s/he was working before group and listen to those who do want to share that day. Eventually all children will volunteer. *So hang in there!*

Skills/knowledge gained from reading groups

Reading groups teach all of the things children learn from story time and unison reading.

Children also learn that
- it is fun to interact with others when reading
- stories give them something to think and talk about
- stories can help them to develop plays
- they can track print with eyes/hands while someone else reads
- they can use context to anticipate what comes next
- stories help them to write
- they can have the teacher's undivided attention
- they have a choice between reading aloud and opting to remain silent
- they can follow the example of other children in reading to the teacher

Individual reading depends on a child's stage of development

The availability of books and other reading materials around the classroom assures that children have ample opportunity for individual reading throughout the day. During center time many children will opt to read, and if you have just put out a new selection of books on the library table or in a new center, you can hardly keep the children away. Such individualized reading affords many opportunities to cater to specific needs that you have noted during reading group or conference time. Children respond well if you furnish reading materials that fit their interests and level of reading development. Adopting Holdaway's (1979) terms, we refer to the different levels as *emergent, developing,* and *independent.* Here are their special needs:

Emergent readers

Emergent readers are just beginning to build their reading skills. In kindergarten and at the beginning of grade one most of the children are likely to be emergent readers. Modeling fluent reading and writing and all of the activities described in this chapter will move them toward reading. But later in the year or in grade two, emergent readers or reluctant readers may need extra attention, encouragement, and inducement to read. From your standpoint, it will be reassuring if you keep in mind that memory reading, pretend reading, and partial sight reading are all part of gradual reading development. If you *know* that these children are evolving toward reading, they will sense your confidence and will develop their skills. Try to find time to sit with them individually several times a week; ask parent helpers or the learning assistance teacher to read to and with these children; have reading buddies for them; and seat them next to independent readers. Allow them to read the same book or story as many times as they want to or listen to it at the listening station as often as they wish, but also read them the same exciting stories all the other children hear.

Be extra sensitive and attentive to the interests or intelligences of emergent readers. A TV program they like, the sport at which they excel, the dog they love, the worries they have, their ability to draw, all can become sparks that finally convince them that reading *is* fun and worth the effort. Again, don't push. Simply continue to suggest, and demonstrate exciting reading material. *Trust* that the children will read. If you do, you will be rewarded not only by the children's successes but also by having a happy classroom that is free of anxiety, stress, frustration, and anger. *So hang in there!*

Developing readers

Developing readers have not yet reached the fluency and ease with which independent readers tackle unfamiliar texts. They are still building their skills and need repetition of familiar materials as well as enticement to move into new territory. If a particular author or topic has captured the children's imagination, bring in further examples and extra copies and encourage the children to find more in the library. The familiar style or topic aids both reading and vocabulary building. Changing the listening center regularly, adding new books to existing centers, and creating new centers or projects will urge your developing readers to pick up books. Encourage those who need or want more personal attention to seek you out, ask parent helpers to read with them, or suggest they partner up with one or more of their classmates to read together, play school, or collaborate on projects. As long as reading material is freely available and you have encouraged the children to take ever more responsibility for their own work, individualized reading will just be a natural part of the children's class time.

Independent readers

Offer your independent readers an ample choice of challenging reading material. Build on their personal interests; send them to the library; bring books from home that you feel they would enjoy; discuss their reading with them; ask for their opinions or for information on what they have read and studied. Encourage these children to talk to parent helpers or to become reading buddies to emergent readers. But be sure not to push or nag. Even if you know well that John or Sarah is able to read far more advanced material, don't insist they do so, as and when you think they ought to. Leave the materials out, suggest, show, or discuss.

They will decide when to move along and may ask for your suggestions or opinions. But there will be many times when they will want to enjoy the easy, funny books that are the oft-repeated favorites in your classroom.

A natural flow of language and concrete experience produce knowledge of parts and rules

At home, children are immersed in spoken language; they observe language in use all day long. Based on that vast input they learn to use language to communicate, and they abstract, then refine rules of grammar. In teaching the learners' way we aim to achieve the same total immersion in written language (See Table 3). The rich variety of materials freely available to the children shows them how to communicate with written language and invites them to explore its parts. Beginning with whole language assures whole-brain involvement from the start. The receptive, holistic right hemisphere first takes in overall units of communication; next the feature-analytic left examines details.

Though we introduce reading and writing as whole communication, there is no dearth of opportunity to work with parts of language and print. Remember that a baby at home spends endless hours of *voluntary* practice playing with sounds, rolling words around to enjoy their sound and feel. Children learning to read will just as happily and voluntarily play alphabet games, shuffle word cards, and spend hours matching and comparing parts of words and sentences. We facilitate that practice by making available all manner of materials and adding verbal input, much like the parent who enters into word games or repeats words again and again at baby's invitation.

The effectiveness of this play with parts of language lies in its voluntary use and the fact that the children are not required to *talk about* these parts *before* being allowed to pursue more meaningful reading and writing activities. By beginning with whole language in both reading and writing, children become very clear about the whole patterns of written language, and they delight in taking it apart, much as they enjoy taking apart toys and puzzles. Like the child taking apart a puzzle, the young readers may not be able to reassemble the parts accurately at first, but the components of print become more and more familiar while the child is playing with them. The parts take on meaning because they fit into a total picture.

Emergent reading evolves from gross to fine

As teachers all of us have studied child development. We all know that fine motor skills develop after the gross ones, that abstract

How reading works when using a flow of language

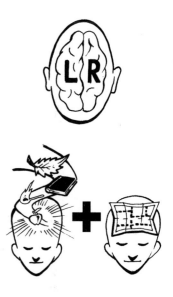

learning is more advanced than concrete work, that children perform many tasks before they are able to talk *about* them. Yet when it comes to teaching reading and writing, we all too often act as if we had never heard of or observed these principles at work. We ask children to learn about the fine details of print and the abstract concepts of words and sounds *before* some of them have a clear understanding of the functions and utility of written language.

Piaget (1955) evolved those abstract principles of development by closely observing children. The progression he observed became quite evident when we observed children's learning in class. Children began their reading with rough approximations of what the teacher presented, no matter how carefully s/he zeroed in on the fine details of print. Holdaway (1979), a devoted child watcher, speaks of emergent reading and gradual approximations as the child moves from reading-like behaviors to greater skill.

"Reading" from memory will often be the beginning stage of reading. During story time and unison reading some of the children will chime in immediately, others may take weeks, even months to speak up. Their eyes may begin to track the print and they may turn pages at the right moment, but that will be all. Mouthing some words without sounds or joining in for a refrain may be the first steps toward oral reading for some children. When retelling stories or engaging in memory reading, these children will be brief, giving the mere gist of the story or just a few words. Even when copying other children, they will produce less and with lower accuracy. Time, practice, and safety to explore will move these readers toward fluency, accurate spelling, and sounding out.

Natural learning is a process of integration

Mastery learning, with its requirement to perform a skill accurately before being allowed to move on, has no place in emergent reading. As in learning to talk, a host of skills evolve jointly. If that seems difficult to accept, think of your own experience, whether learning to dance, skate, write poetry, or speak another language. How was your general performance at the very beginning? Did someone have to make sure you drilled each separate skill before you could – or would – take the first step? Or was it a case of bumbling along as best you could and refining individual skills along the way? Reflect also whether you would have persisted if someone had insisted on separate skill building or mastery learning. Did you perhaps give up on learning another language because you were required to know the grammar accurately and to develop good pronunciation before being encouraged to talk?

The effectiveness of learning at home rests on integrating all of the senses and allowing all of the skills to evolve gradually and jointly. When teaching the learners' way the open organization of the classroom encourages children to integrate all of their sensory experiences. Learning to read is not an abstract task dealing only with sounds and words on a page. Just as babies learn to talk by being involved in their entire environment, so children in school learn to read as they interact with the total learning environment. Reading, writing, spelling, talking, drawing, playing, exploring, making things, observing and discussing science projects, going on field trips, bringing news from home all merge into integrated learning of which written language is an integral part. Specific skills emerge from that overall integrated learning, and children continue to refine and update their knowledge of letters, sounds, and printing in the context of communicating through the written word.

Learning expands in spurts and stops

As children practice their emergent reading skills they decide when they are ready to move ahead, when to move to more difficult reading material, start to use lined paper for writing, or become more accurate in spelling. When they try out new ways, their performance at times seems to worsen instead of improve. As they shift from using primarily memory or sight-word reading to more detailed decoding and accuracy, their intonation and fluency may, for a time, deteriorate. As they try out new rules of spelling, punctuation, or sentence combining, the number of errors they make may increase until the new rules have become fully integrated. (The seeming decline in performance is very much like the slowing down you might experience when first shifting to ten-finger touch typing after being a quite proficient hunt-and-peck performer.) Allowing children time and opportunity to upgrade their performance is a vital part in letting them establish inner rules to guide further learning. Their brain needs time to do the programming based on the massive intake of data, but our experience has confirmed time and again that the inner programming the children do themselves is far more effective than

TABLE 3
TRANSLATING CONDITIONS THAT FOSTER LEARNING AT HOME INTO CLASSROOM PRACTICE

Learning to speak	*Learning to read*
Parents speak to the child from the day s/he is born. They model the use of whole language.	The teacher reads to and with the children from the day they enter school. S/he models fluent reading.
Learning to speak is an integral part of daily life.	Reading is part of all types of classroom activities.
The familiar setting and actions of the home give meaning to the language the child hears.	Familiar stories and nursery rhymes make reading a meaningful activity from the beginning of reading.
The amount of language a child hears is varied and vast. It has many uses and the situation determines what syntax and vocabulary are necessary and appropriate.	A large variety of reading materials is freely available in class. There is no attempt to limit or control the vocabulary. Natural language is used to fit the occasion is used to write the children's own messages.
Parents respond to the meaning of the child's words, to the content, not the form.	The teacher pays more attention to the meaning of the child's reading or writing than to the form.
Parents do not ask their baby to "speak clearly" or "use correct grammar" when s/he first learns to talk. Home is a safe place to learn gradually by trial and error.	The teacher does not demand precise word-for-word renditions or fine discrimination of letters and sounds from beginners. Class is a safe place to try out new skills.
Parents will often repeat back what the child just said. But in giving that feedback they expand the child's ungrammatical phrases into complete sentences.	If meaning was lost, the teacher will reread a short passage or sentence after a child has finished reading. S/he does not ask the child to "think of the rule" or "sound out the word."
Modeling, practice, and feedback help the child to speak.	Modeling, practice, and feedback help the child to deal with written language.
The child is left free to determine when s/he is ready to begin talking and when to move ahead.	The child is given the freedom to decide when to begin to read, when to participate, and when to move ahead to higher skills in reading and writing.
The parents trust the child to talk. No one worries if Bobby or Mary is going to talk. Of course s/he will.	The teacher trusts the children to learn as and when they are ready. All of them learn!

the memorization of rules we used to teach through drills. The children may not be able to talk about their new learning, but their performance will show clearly that they are thinking about what they are doing. No amount of drill-for-skill produces the same profound and productive effect on further learning, on overall cognitive development, and on the physical development of the brain and its forest of neurons.

Stages of reading development

Over years of observing children unfold their reading, we have noted that they will move through a series of stages. They all move along in the same way, but some traverse stages very quickly while others linger quite a while at each point. Differences in development are based on overall maturity, personal background, and experience with reading prior to coming to school.

Whether reading instruction begins in kindergarten, grade one, or later, at the outset, those who are non-readers will accumulate a wealth of foundation knowledge to build their *emergent reading* skills: familiarity with book language, recognition of sight words, familiarity with letters, knowledge of the many uses of print, the importance of using context, recognition of beginning consonants and their sounds. They will engage in memory reading, repetition of refrains, and some pretend reading, and generally assemble the host of skills they will need for more accurate reading.

This information-gathering stage is followed by a period of quiet, when nothing seems to happen and the child appears to drift, perhaps daydream, without taking in any new information. We call this the *pupa stage* because underneath that unmoving exterior an important transformation is taking place. The brain is sorting out all the input and is creating the rules and programs the child needs to move toward true reading in all its complexity. It is adding new trees to the forest of neurons.

For some children the pupa stage lasts less than a week. Others may take two or three weeks before they burst out of their cocoons to announce, "I want to read to you." From that day forward, their reading unfolds! The timing of the pupa stage depends on how the children entered school. If they already knew a lot about reading, it may come early in the year. For children unfamiliar with books and print, it may happen around Christmas or even later. Once again, the advice is, *hang in there!* You will recognize the pupa stage if you look for it and will leave the children room to practice voluntarily whatever they want to use at the time, secure in the knowledge that an important transformation is taking place underneath that passive exterior.

The pupa stage is followed by a new *spurt of growth* during which true reading begins to develop. Decoding, phrasing, using syntax, semantics, and context are some of the skills the young developing readers will apply. Increasingly they will use patterns of language and knowledge of letters and sounds – gleaned from their writing work – when reading unfamiliar texts.

Next there is a *plateau* when once again little or nothing new seems to be absorbed. For many children, this plateau happens around Easter. But each child is unique and both the duration and onset of the plateau vary. Plateaus are not as dramatic or pronounced as the pupa stage, but are quite noticeable. No doubt you are well aware of the slumps in your students' learning. Accept them for what they are – periods of consolidation and solid growth.

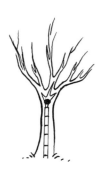

A *second spurt of learning* follows the spring plateau and the period before summer vacation generally evidences yet another *plateau*. It may be that the sunshine outside is beckoning unduly. But this too seems to be a time of consolidation and inner programming. Voluntary practice, shoring up skills that are not yet as solid as they could be, creative work, and lots of reading will serve well in making sure that children benefit from their time in school though they seem to be less active academically.

It may help to compare the children's growth with your own learning. Ask yourself if you move onward continually or need time to stop and digest what you have learned. Remember feeling saturated after summer school or a conference? Children are no different. They too need time to let learning fall into place.

Now reading fills the entire day

Our early observations revealed that the children in Margaret's class were only reading a few minutes each day; however, observers in our language-based classroom often express amazement at the prodigious quantities of reading and writing the children do. Building on the learners' ways has increased both quality and quantity of reading tremendously. In fact, reading and writing fill the entire day and the all-important time-on-task is spent building solid

Michael
We are learning
French.
Mrs Reinhard will be
awak.

March 5
Adam and I played soccer
We will do our work
on a piece of paper
Adam is my best
friend.

Michaell

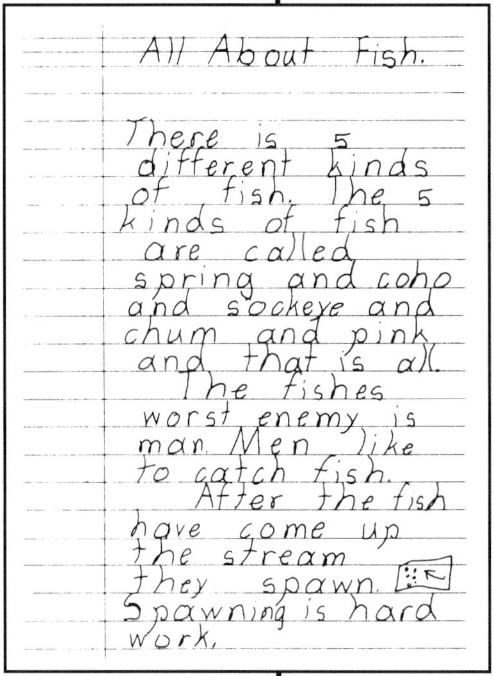

All About Fish.

There is 5 different kinds of fish. The 5 kinds of fish are called spring and coho and sockeye and chum and pink and that is all. The fishes worst enemy is man. Men like to catch fish. After the fish have come up the stream they spawn. Spawning is hard work.

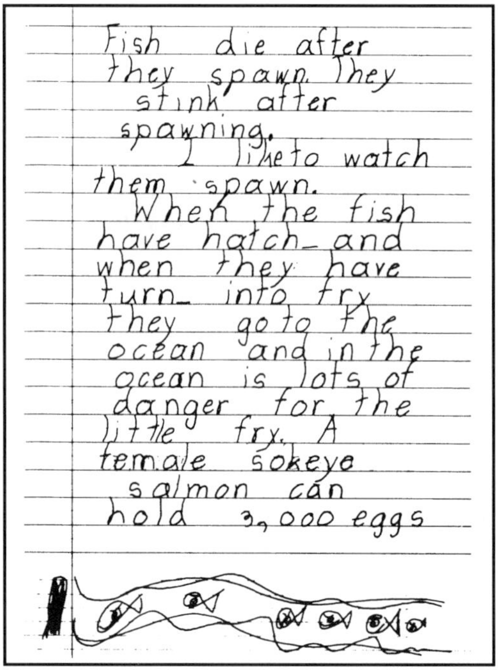

Fish die after they spawn. They stink after spawning. I like to watch them spawn. When the fish have hatch and when they have turn into fry they go to the ocean and in the ocean is lots of danger for the little fry. A female sokeye salmon can hold 3,000 eggs

***Individual progress
comes in surges forward***

*Michael's composition
improved between October and
March, but his printing
continued to be rather messy.
His spurt forward came right at
the beginning of grade two as
evidenced in his research project
on salmon, which extends over
several more pages.*

skills. While teachers who are just turning to brain-based teaching often worry about "doing the right thing" and "meeting all the requirements," they all enjoy the excitement and interest of filling their day with meaningful reading and writing. As one school principal put it, "By the end of three years you will have covered all of the requirements of the district but with a heck of a lot less nail-biting."

Not only are the children learning what is required, but they are also developing a highly positive attitude toward reading and learning in general. They read and write all day and, as both our initial research and twenty years of practice have shown, they are picking up all the skills through this highly extended practice. Perhaps more importantly, they are learning about functional literacy in the same natural way in which they learned about functional oral language. They not only revel in fun stories and interesting books but use reading to learn, to find things out, to enlarge their vocabulary, to follow directions, and to communicate with others. Printed language is becoming a familiar part of their way of communicating and they use it freely. Because children see so many different kinds of written materials, they are very open to trying out new reading materials and tasks and they do so without fear or stress. So if at the beginning of the year you are worrying that skills are developing too slowly, that not enough progress is readily visible, keep your eyes on the children, trust that they are learning all the important things about reading – including decoding skills – and *hang in there!*

Use nursery rhymes to aid emergent reading

■ It seems that many children are no longer learning nursery rhymes at home. In order not to lose that heritage and fun, use nursery rhymes in class as reading material.

■ Print nursery rhymes on large charts (laminate them if possible) and keep them readily accessible. Children will return to them again and again.

■ Use them for unison reading sessions.

■ Encourage memory reading as a first step toward actual reading to give children the feeling that they can read. Once they know the rhyme well, ask for volunteers to "read" and hand the pointer to them.

Hints and particulars

- Have several beautifully illustrated books of nursery rhymes available in the classroom. If you don't have any, the library is sure to have several.
- Set up a nursery rhyme center with the rhymes on charts, figurines, or felt cut-outs for flannel-board fun; murals to serve as backgrounds for artwork and plays; costumes to encourage mime and acting.
- Role-play nursery rhymes.
- Have the rhymes on tape in the listening center.
- Have sets of word cards that match those rhymes you have on charts and encourage children to put the words in sequence. Leave these sets in a readily accessible place so that children have the chance for voluntary practice. (See also suggestions for using pocket charts.)

Use pocket charts for reading practice

Children enjoy playing with word cards and arranging them in the transparent pockets of a pocket chart (pocket charts can be found in most teachers' stores). Here are some suggestions for using pocket charts:

- Start by reading or reciting a familiar poem or nursery rhyme.
- Show the entire poem on a large chart and run your hand along the lines of print as you and the children say the words together.
- If children want to volunteer to "read," offer to help if they wish.
- After reading the poem several times with the children, hand out cards, each showing one word of the poem.
- Tell the children that first you want the title and have them check who has "Polly Put the Kettle On." Put the title at the center top of the chart.
- Then work on the first line: "Who has 'Polly'?" Children will help each other, interact, guess, jump up quickly to place their cards.
- When all the cards are in place, read the poem once more, this time with the children's help.
- To add fun, have the children's names on cards and replace *Polly* or *Jack and Jill* with *Meghan* or *Dave and Joan*.

- Replace other words that occur to you or the children. They derive a lot of fun and practice playing with these name and word cards. They will arrange sentences, turn them around, and keep changing names.

- As in all activities, be aware of the children's attention span. Change to a new activity as soon as they start to fidget, but leave the materials out so that the children have a chance to use them during choosing time.

Children's names afford endless opportunities for practice

Most children take great interest in their names and quickly learn to recognize not only their own names but those of other children as well. At first they simply associate the name tag with its wearer, but very quickly they begin to note similarities – *Dawn* and *David* start the same way; *Brent* and *Eva* have an *e* in their names; *Stephanie* and *Inderdeep* have long names. Here are some ways to use the children's names as practice material:

- Have children wear large name tags the first few weeks of school.

- Make "name hats" from strips of construction paper.

- Use name cards to show where children sit and shift the seating arrangement so children will have to find their names each day.

- Cut out airplanes or cars and print the children's names on them. Create matching drivers or pilots, and have children put them in the right car or plane as a means of taking roll. Begin by matching first names, then shift to matching first names to last. Even kindergarten children can do it. (Parent helpers will help with the cutting and labeling.)

- Make a name book of the children's names – one name per page. Leave it out where children can use it. They will help each other find their own names and those of their friends. Use the name book to pick children for special jobs or treats. Simply flip the book open and have the children call out whose turn it is. Children will play school with the name book, copy letters and names from it, and read it at book time.

- Hold the name book together with rings that open easily so that the children can take out the cards and alphabetize them, sort them into boys and girls, or put them in the order of seating for the day. Grade-one children will do quite elaborate matching jobs and will invent new ways of working with name cards. Let the children play with the name cards or book any way they like. They learn a lot more than simple word recognition from such practice.

Add variety and interest to story time

Keep your selection of story time reading material very flexible and be prepared to shift at a moment's notice if some exciting event suggests that something other than the story you had selected for that day would capture the moment better. *Here are some suggestions for picking books or stories:*

Suit the story or book to the occasion
- Birthdays
- First day of the season – by calendar or weather
- Losing a tooth (tooth fairy book)
- Easter
- Christmas
- Vacation coming
- Going to the dentist
- Being scared
- Getting lost
- The weather – foggy, sunny, stormy
- Going to the hospital
- Taking a trip
- Having relatives visit
- Anything that relates to the children at that moment!

Children love to laugh, and books like *The Stupids Step Out* or *Bonnie McSmithers* will be a success every time. But they will respond as strongly to other sentiments. Reading *The Christmas Kitten* may find you, as well as the children, crying as you experience the sadness of losing a loved pet. The bond between you will be strong and reading will gain yet another dimension. Share the beautiful language of poems you enjoy. The children will sense your pleasure and even if they don't understand the full message, they are likely to find pleasure in the sound and rhythm of beautiful language. Always keep in mind that *you* have to enjoy the reading material. If you think a story is a bore, the story session is bound to be a flop. So read to enjoy!

Physical involvement enhances reading practice

Becoming physically involved with stories and reading draws children to hours of voluntary reading practice. Talking, manipulating, miming, and role-playing are wonderful ways to bring physical movement into learning to read. As you watch the children interact with the books and each other, there will be no question in your mind about the benefits to learning and motivation. Your own observations are backed solidly by brain research that demonstrates the importance of sensory integration and physical movement in learning. Once you provide a few examples of physical interaction with story material, children will soon provide their own variations.

Nadine Westcott's *I Know an Old Lady* is a great favorite with children. To add to their involvement with the reading, Margaret has cut out cardboard to make an "old lady." She is about two feet tall, has wool hair, a pair of wire glasses, and wears a dress made of cotton. Her stomach has a see-through window made of clear plastic that forms a pocket at the back. As the old lady "swallows the spider" the children drop in a spider and it shows up in her stomach. With each verse – spider, fly, cat, bird – the children drop in the appropriate animal. They never tire of either the game or the reading and take turns being reader, "feeder," or watcher during center time.

Story time lends itself to the same physical involvement with reading. When listening to *I Was Walking Down the Road* (by Sarah Barchas) the children love to act out the story using cutouts made of felt. As the little girl walks down the road she sees a toad, picks it up, and puts it in a cage. As the story unfolds the children follow along taking turns picking out the animals and putting them in the little girl's cage. They listen to the rhyming words – *sky-butterfly, rake-snake, log-frog* – and put each animal in the cage. At the end of the story the little girl looks at all the animals in her cage and decides to set them all free; so the children, too, take all of the animals out of the cage. Fun, reading, rhyming, manipulating, and endless voluntary repetition make this reading-cum-action a marvelous practice tool.

Attract children to books and reading

When you become aware of the tremendous power of teacher modeling you will find any number of positive ways to attract children to books and reading. If children perceive that reading is an important, useful, and pleasurable part of your life, they will internalize those attitudes. Actions are far more persuasive than lectures and if you love books and reading you will think of many more ways to attract children to reading than we are listing below.

- Fill your classroom with books and keep adding new ones.
- Include as many of the classics of children's literature as possible.
- Read to and with the children as often as possible.
- Put enthusiasm and feeling into your reading.
- Talk about your favorite books – now and in the past.
- Show genuine interest in the books brought in by children.
- Talk to children individually about the books they are reading.
- Make time available for extra trips to the library.
- Order books and show your excitement and anticipation.
- When book orders arrive, stop everything and join children in reading.
- Tell children about books that have been filmed for TV or movies.
- Have both men and women model reading – the principal, parents, visitors.
- Let children relax in comfort when they read.
- Always make time if a child wants to read to you or discuss a book.
- Involve parents in their children's reading.
- Show interest and delight when a child describes a favorite book.
- Invite authors into the classroom.
- Honor the writing and publishing of your students.
- Spark children's interest in using books to get information.
- Demonstrate the use of cookbooks and other how-to books.
- Encourage children to bring in their own favorite books.
- Enter into the excitement of collecting as many works by a favorite author as possible. (Bill Peet was the great favorite one year.)

Integrating a basal reader into a literature-based classroom

If you are required to use a prescribed basal reader, integrate it with your other reading. We usually wait until later in the year to introduce the basal reader, but you may want to intersperse basal reader stories with your other reading throughout the year. Use unison reading and try to infuse as much life into stories that have limited vocabulary. Don't feel you must use the workbooks or job sheets. Children who are accustomed to reading will handle any of the tasks asked for and your independent readers will move through the series very quickly. Both developing readers and emergent readers may need extra help with texts that at times have somewhat unnatural language patterns.

Working with reading groups

When using unison reading, there is no need to resort to ability grouping. To gather a reading group we simply call on those children who are free to participate at the time we are ready to read. If a child does not look as if s/he is on task, we take that as a signal to call him/her over for reading without any comment about daydreaming or dawdling. Another child may just have returned to the room and may not yet have settled down to the next task, so we call him/her over. Yet another may be in transition from one activity to the next. These children are unlikely to be in the same reading group for more than one day.

Though they may all be at different levels in their reading development, all can follow along with the unison reading. At the beginning of grade one we may read selections from the beginning levels of one of the series that includes children's literature, but we also include a few more advanced pieces to add further interest. At the outset of reading instruction, beginning readers may just listen, emergent readers may start to track print actively, and developing readers will join in here and there to say a few words. If there are independent readers who have learned to read at home or in kindergarten, they will not only read along but volunteer to read individually right from the start. Though there may be wide differences, all of the children will have participated. To assure that each child participated in reading group, Margaret kept track of participants in her reading log and made it a point to call on those who had not yet been included.

With flexible grouping, none of the children are stuck in "beginners' texts." All children listen to the same stories but are free to participate at their own levels. Peer modeling becomes a powerful learning tool and the relaxed atmosphere encourages all children in the group to engage in reading and reading-like behaviors. Beginning readers may take group reading as their starting point for more individual practice. At times they will reread the story or passage covered during reading group later in the day, the following day, and even days later.

Get overly active children settled down for reading time

Particularly at the beginning of the year, children need a lot of modeling of quiet behavior, attentive listening, and patient forbearance. Setting the right climate will get these active children settled into reading without dampening their spirits. Here are some of the ways we have found effective.

- *Quietly* lay down rules about not disturbing others and enforce them. Use a quiet voice and direct eye contact to ask children to quiet down. Give active children jobs:
  - Help to hold up the big book
  - Pass out little books
  - Help their peers with bookmarks
  - Help arrange chairs for reading group
  - Go to the library to pick up books
  - Put away books
  - Do anything else that is genuinely needed
- Ask about their preferences and have them help select reading material. Watch for their special interests and select reading material to fit them. Speak directly to them if they are fidgeting or not attending: Comments like, "Isn't that right, George?" or "Do you think they are afraid, Sandy?" will bring children back to the reading group without scolding or negative remarks.
- Comment on even the slightest improvement in behaving more quietly. When all else fails, raise your normally quiet voice just slightly to ask for more quiet behavior.

- Intersperse very active times with reading sessions and encourage active children to play vigorously to let off steam.
- Keep quiet table work brief and lengthen sessions as children settle down.

- Allow children to move out of their seats. The permission to move about (within reason) eases a lot of tension that can build through enforced inactivity.
- Allow children to stretch out on the floor, under desks, or in comfortable spots during reading and center time.

Working with "reading buddies"

Children like to work with each other and at times learn more from peers than from adults. Having "reading buddies" read to and with kindergarten children or other emergent readers offers learning to the buddies as well as their young partners. Keep these sessions unstructured and don't give the reading buddies a list of do's and don'ts, but simply thank them for their efforts and occasionally offer them a treat as a token of your appreciation.

When the reading buddies enter kindergarten, they immediately settle down with a kindergarten child and a book in some comfortable corner. The two partners take turns choosing reading material and both enjoy the sessions. At times, they reverse roles and the kindergarten children read to their buddies. Though we try to have buddies change partners to give everyone a chance to get the extra personal attention, close personal friendships evolve and buddies will look out for their young friends outside of class too. The enjoyment and dedication of these reading buddies shows itself in little notes they leave in kindergarten if they find that the class is away on a field trip.

A reading buddy system can be set up in several ways. Here is one teacher's description: I found that there needs to be a bit of an age gap between the buddies and their listeners, so I reached an agreement with a second-grade teacher who was willing to have her students come into kindergarten. I scheduled my kindergarten book time to coincide with the second-graders' recess to give the buddies a chance to go into kindergarten without disrupting their schedule. Though giving up recess was quite a sacrifice, some ten children volunteered to act as reading buddies each year. For the afternoon session, the reading buddies had to work out a time-keeping system in order to join their young friends. They maintained time cards showing when they left their classroom and when they returned. One year a group of grade-five boys acted as reading buddies all year. I thanked them, called their parents to tell them how helpful the boys were, and had their names placed on the Service Roll. The same boys returned for another year of reading. The interesting thing is that reading buddies quite regularly are not the top readers but the ones who are struggling. Working with the younger children seems to give them a sense of accomplishment and confidence. Emotional and linguistic intelligence join and grow.

Introduce children to the library

Make arrangements with your school librarian for active use of the library (within established rules) and reach an understanding about visits to the library by groups and individuals. Ask the librarian into your class for a visit. Make it a fun session with story reading, a display of books, and an invitation to the children to come into the library to start building an inner map about the joys a library has to offer.

Then take kindergarten and grade-one children into the library every day to choose books. Model the kind of behavior that is appropriate. Take books down from the shelf and browse through them. Talk to yourself as you decide whether you want that particular book. If the librarian has time to talk to the children, keep these early talks very informal and focused on the fun of reading. Reading or telling a story would be an excellent addition to library time. At the early stage of using the library it is best not to tell the children too much about how a library works. Let them discover what they need to know and make trips to the library exciting explorations. Later on in grade one, or even at the beginning of grade two, the librarian will give the children some instruction on library procedures and rules. But to get them started, it is important just to use the library every day. If your school librarian agrees, have the children take over some of the signing-in-and-out procedures – writing their names on the cards, checking due dates, or whatever else seems appropriate. One teacher remarked that the library never ran as well as when the second-graders were doing a lot of the work.

At some point during each day take the children into the library to return the books they have brought back and to pick up new ones. Encourage them to take a book home every day. Don't worry about books that are not returned on time. Try to make library time as positive an experience as possible.

Once they have become thoroughly familiar with the library, children will not hesitate to go there on their own if they want specific research material – books on boats, snakes, ballet, hockey, whatever. If the local public library is close by or if parents are willing to take them, the children will quickly become regular visitors and will continue to expand their inner library map. By grade two the library will be firmly established as a valuable resource and a great place to get just the right kind of interesting reading material.

Spotting and working with children whose reading is slow to evolve

Children whose reading is slow to emerge generally have a number of shared characteristics. To spot those who will need extra encouragement and help, look for any combination of the following traits:

- They are usually immature in a number of ways.
- They are generally slow to evolve in most learning tasks.
- Their fine muscle development is often poor as yet.
- Their eye-hand coordination may be poor.
- They generally are inattentive listeners.
- Their attention span is usually short.
- They generally are not as verbal as other children.
- It may be hard to keep them interested in news time.
- Sometimes they are hyperactive.
- Many are slow to move; they fiddle with things, don't finish work.
- They are usually somewhat disorganized.
- Often they will be easily upset.
- They will move more slowly through reading stages than other children.
- They may linger longer than other children at the pupa stage.
- They have difficulty creating a pattern with pattern blocks.
- They may want to read the same story again and again.
- They often receive little encouragement at home.

To help these children evolve their reading skills, they need
- To have their eyesight and hearing checked to make sure both are normal.

- To go step by step on *their* terms and at *their* pace.
- To build on successes and personal interests.
- To establish good rapport with the teacher.
- To be shown rather than told how to do tasks.
- To practice with a variety of patterns.
- To hear/read stories with a strong repetitive pattern.
- To have particularly good liaison between home and school.
- A lot of individual attention.
- A lot of praise for small accomplishments.
- A lot of active play and talking time.
- Special interest material to suit them to start them reading.
- Close supervision with table work.
- Feelings of being successful and of making progress.
- A warm, supportive environment where they are accepted as they are.

Spotting and working with children who are ready to read and move ahead

Suzanne came into kindergarten a mature little girl. She was 5 years, 7 months and quite self-confident, very vocal, and happy to be in kindergarten. During morning news time she was always first to take the next step, first to call out initial consonants when invited to help with spelling, and first to recognize the concept of compound words. She never failed to point out when one occurred on the board. She recognized recurring words – *the, today* – and the *ing* ending. Once she picked up the *ed* ending, she commented on it whenever it appeared on the board. She was definitely a leader and there came a time when she had to be told, "Let's have you keep quiet today when we are spelling so we can see what the other children can do."

Suzanne showed herself to be a reader shortly after she entered kindergarten. She began to read the sentences on the board and would also sit in a corner with a book to read. Her mother told us that Suzanne had not been reading at home, but entry into kindergarten seemed to bring everything together for her. By the end of kindergarten she was reading *Little House on the Prairie*. But Suzanne still liked to play and would read only when it suited her. She would read from a new current reading series if her teacher called her over to try out new stories, but it soon became apparent that Suzanne did not like to be interrupted at center time but wanted to read on her own terms. She liked books but wanted the freedom to choose them and the time to read them.

By the time Suzanne entered grade one she was a fluent reader and needed mostly enrichment and more advanced practice. At times she joined a reading group, but generally she preferred to read on her own. She did much enrichment work of her own choosing: making big books, publishing stories, doing research in the library, or teaming up with Maeve, another advanced reader. Suzanne became the official sign maker for the class. She left signs at the door to inform parents "We have gone to ... and will be back later," signs on the hamster cage urging people not to touch it on pain of being bitten. She also created a travelogue of her visit to England, complete with photos, travel brochures, and maps. As a result, she became a model for her peers who wanted to do some of the interesting things they saw her do.

Classroom teaching aids that present details of print

Whenever the children are free to choose activities (at center time or when they have completed work early) they delight in using the games and toys that show letters, blends, and words. Such extra practice reinforces the knowledge gained from writing, participating in news time, and more holistic work with reading. Here are some of the items we have freely available to children:

- Pocket charts with cut-up stories, poems, or nursery rhymes
- Blocks that have letters on them
- Jumping mats with letters on them for playing hopscotch
- Puzzles of all kinds to match or assemble pictures, letters, or words
- Sequencing and matching games with pictures or letters
- Word games and puzzles including card games and board games
- All kinds of phonics games – preferably self-checking – that focus on beginning consonants, ending consonants, vowel sounds, blends, digraphs (these games can be commercially produced, teacher-made, or even child-produced)

If you find a child has difficulty with recognizing letters and their sounds, take some extra time to sit down with him/her and play a few of the games that you feel would be of benefit. Don't turn this time into a test, simply play the game and trust that the child derives solid benefit from it.

Learning about letters

When entering kindergarten most children are familiar with the alphabet because they have watched children's programs on TV. Those who don't know their letters simply are not interested in learning them as yet. Don't worry about them because they will see the letters each day at news time and in games around the classroom. If you are concerned toward the end of kindergarten that a child has not yet learned the letters, give the child some individual attention with games like the lollipop tree.

Margaret finds that for learning letters, children particularly enjoy using the lollipop tree she has in her classroom. It consists of a tree cut out of construction paper with slots for letter lollipops to be taken out and looked at. The lollipops are circles of colored paper stapled to a lollipop stick. Each one has a letter printed on one side of the paper.

To play the lollipop game, children pick one lollipop at a time, see if they can name the letter on it, and if they can, they get to keep it; if they can't, the teacher names the letter, puts the lollipop back on the tree for another try and continues the game. At the end of the session, children count up the number of lollipops they were able to win by giving correct letter names.

Peter didn't know his letters and wasn't interested, so Margaret used the lollipop tree game with him toward the end of kindergarten. He enjoyed playing it and used it many times. Peter's mother, who helped Margaret mark the children's readiness test at the end of term, remarked, "I am amazed at Peter's letter recognition. I didn't know he knew that many. I guess it sort of snuck up on him!"

Letting a child set the pace of learning

Matthew joined a classroom full of children who already knew each other and who loved to read and interact when using books and writing. Matthew enjoyed the unison reading sessions and the freedom to work on his own, but as soon as his teacher so much as approached him with a book under her arm, he froze right up. To give him the space he needed, his teacher merely observed how Matthew was progressing during unison reading and group reading. She also noted how attentive he was during story time. Since his writing evolved quite nicely there was no need to panic. His writing and his reactions to stories and general reading clearly showed that he could relate well to print. He simply had a tremendous fear of being asked to read aloud.

After several months of observing other children come forth readily to read during news time or in reading group, Matthew was reassured that the teacher never made it obligatory to read or speak up. So he took courage and approached the teacher to let her know, "Today I want to read to you." That breakthrough was as exciting to him as it was for his teacher and Matthew retained his courage for other individual work as well.

Leaving the timing and pace-setting up to the child was a crucial factor in dissolving a block created by anxiety and in fostering natural development instead. Trust and careful observations of the learner served the teacher and reassured her that Matthew was making progress, even though he did not wish to do any individual oral reading.

Observing a child break out of the "pupa stage"

Gale L. had immersed her kindergarten children in print all year with varying results. Some started to read early, some toward the end of the year; some merely listened and showed little inclination to read as yet. Jeff was one of the children who gave every indication of not being ready to read for quite a while. Outwardly he showed few behaviors that suggested that his emergent reading was shifting into true reading – tracking print, saying some of the words, engaging in memory or pretend reading. But underneath his placid behavior he was absorbing everything he saw and heard.

Quite unexpectedly, he simply walked up to Gale and announced that he wanted to read to her. And read he did! Not just a few words but a whole book! Jeff's excitement was matched by his teacher's, and that day everybody heard that "Jeff is *reading*!" At gym time Jeff found that he could also skip – something he had not mastered before. At that point he declared, "I can do anything!" and he certainly progressed from that day on in both his reading and his overall development. Giving him the time and encouragement to develop at his pace and in his way suddenly let all the learning come together, and it burst forth like a butterfly that has ended its pupa stage and is ready to fly.

Personal involvement may launch reluctant readers

Personal involvement often becomes the motivator for taking an interest in reading and writing. Inderdeep had shown no inclination to participate in reading until the day he lost his tooth right in class and made the news as a result of it.

As the teacher began to put the news on the board, the children debated whether it should be *fell out* or *came out*. Inderdeep decided on *fell out* and proudly accepted the long pointer to run it along the line of print as he "read" his news item.

Throughout the rest of the day he returned to the board, perhaps a dozen times, telling the teacher he wanted to read his sentence again. Having made the news not only convinced him to read, but also started his attempts to print his name and, in the process, to learn about some of the letters.

When the teacher takes time to respond fully to such teachable moments, there is often a wonderful spurt forward for a previously reluctant reader.

• •

Easter became the impetus for David to begin to read. Upon returning to school after the holiday, David proudly announced that he had seen the Easter bunny. The class shared his excitement, and David made the news that day. For the first time, he did not hesitate to come to the board to "read" his very own story. Like Inderdeep, he continued to come to the board throughout the day and then moved on to further reading. All of his covert learning had been drawn to the surface by that very personal sharing. David has been making progress in reading ever since. Giving him the time to work at his own pace provided a solid foundation for his reading development; taking his personal cue has added the necessary motivation.

Learning to Write, Spell, and Sound Out

4

Learning to write, like learning to read, begins with meaning and then develops more detailed knowledge of the particles of speech. When learning to talk, babies are well aware that speech is a means of communicating. Though they are still babbling, they are intending to convey messages, and they become increasingly accurate in their use of sounds, words, and language. When children work in their own way, their writing development follows the same direction and sequence. The intent to convey a message becomes the driving force behind the tremendous sustained effort required to learn all about letters, sounds, spelling, and the full range of grammatical and stylistic considerations that eventually make for quality written work. As long as children are intent on what it is they want to convey, they will continue to work on upgrading the requisite skills. If the steps forward seem slow at first, remember that learning to speak and read also evolve gradually. Problems, blocks to learning, or refusals to practice generally occur in situations in which children are asked to work on tasks imposed by adults and/or in instances when children are pressured into precise detailed work before they are ready to upgrade their performance. But when children initiate activities of interest to them, problems become challenges, blocks tend to vanish, and attention spans can be considerable.

When teaching children to write, talking comes first

Having something to say is the first step in getting down to writing. Do you remember the agonies of trying to stretch an essay into the

Writing

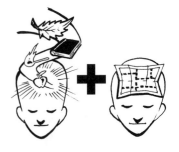

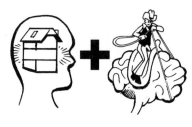

required number of words when you really didn't have anything to say? Children are no different. Some of your students may come to school well accustomed to talking about their daily lives but many have not learned to express themselves with any degree of fluency. Learning the art of conversation to start a flow of open communication is as crucial a part of learning to write as it is of building community. (In chapter 5 we will describe more fully how to build the skills of conversation that enhance the emotional intelligence needed for the give-and-take of effective communication.)

So the first step in preparing children to become writers is to encourage them to talk. Genuine sharing of personal anecdotes about daily events at home makes for a good start. We talk about some of the things we do at home and invite children to do similar sharing. Once such shared experiences as special events, field trips, visitors coming into the classroom, or seeing a film provide common ground for discussion, a lively exchange of opinions, reminiscences, and questions begins to evolve. Stories lend themselves to being retold, role-played, and discussed in terms of the children's own experiences. Planning special events, getting ready to cook or to make things, all offer opportunities for talking, describing, and thinking aloud. If the talk centers around the children's personal experiences and interests, even shy children eventually venture forth and participate. Of course the inclusion of story reading from the very beginning of school does much to enhance the children's knowledge and use of written language.

Immersing children in print fosters emergent writing

Enjoying stories, experiencing the many uses of print, watching the teacher, other adults, and peers produce written messages and seeing all kinds of labels around the classroom ensure that the children accept written language as a natural part of everyday communication. By immersing the children in print they move toward writing in the same manner they move toward speaking and reading. First there is the awareness of written language as a means of communication; then there are playful attempts at pretend writing (making wavy lines or letter-like marks on the paper) or babbling in print (strings of letters not yet formed into words); from there, simple personal compositions and rough approximations of spelling evolve toward accuracy. All of these steps are valuable

parts of emergent writing. But even children who come to school knowing about letters and writing benefit from being surrounded by print and by being encouraged to begin with pretend writing or invented spelling to build their inner maps by writing.

Modeling writing demonstrates how print conveys messages

Just as you can talk to babies or read to youngsters before they can respond in kind, so you can write for your students before they themselves know how to produce printed messages. Just as Mommy assumes that her baby understands far more than s/he can say, so you know that children understand what you are doing even though they themselves do not yet write. We find that if we use written language day-in and day-out the children begin to understand what we write and then begin to imitate our writing activities.

Modeling the many uses of print fosters independence and functional literacy

Starting in kindergarten and throughout the primary grades, we never miss an opportunity to write in class and to accompany such writing with a descriptive monologue. Printing picture captions under the drawings the children produce, making grocery lists for cooking, printing recipes on the board, making notes about the weather on the calendar, and putting up notices at the door are among the first uses the children observe. Name tags become the models for the children's early printing as they label their artwork and begin to exchange name cards with telephone numbers in order to get in touch with their new friends. Even at the very beginning, the writing and modeling they see are not abstract lessons *about* writing or print, but simply the functional uses of written language.

Because the writing is connected with concrete activities or objects, the children have no difficulty in understanding the messages, and they readily enter into composing and printing as the occasion demands. Plans for field trips are made by the entire class and the teacher records the decisions, produces lists of items needed, rosters of partners who are supposed to share, and permission slips to be taken home and returned. Within short order, children who are

beginning to print take over the production of name lists and then monitoring of who has brought back a permission slip and who still needs one. Once the teacher has modeled a writing job several times, children are eager to take over and assume responsibility.

Labels, instructions, and messages are produced on the spot, first by the teacher and then the children. When Raymond the hamster appeared in class, everyone made a welcoming sign and then produced instructions for his feeding and care. Sign making really got under way when Raymond managed to escape, and children wanted help finding him. The entire school was treated to the urgent calls for help produced by the first-graders.

Letter writing may begin with the teacher sitting down saying, "I have to send this note to the principal." Or "I'll write a letter to Mrs. ... to see if she will come and show us her...." Children love to look over the teacher's shoulder as she sits down to compose such messages. Based on the models they have seen they will compose notes asking for permission to attend special events or will produce notices to let parents know where the class has gone. Greeting cards for special events, letters to friends who are in hospital, and even letters of condolence become the subject of writing for children who have observed the writing activities of their teacher or peers.

To add mystery and excitement to writing practice, the teacher will print welcoming messages on the blackboard, put a special notice in the reading corner, or print a child's name as a way of indicating whose turn it is. If most children are still in the emergent writing and reading stage, there will be excited consulting, some guessing, while the teacher is printing, and then the rush of recognition shared by all.

"Experience charts," composed and dictated by the entire class to capture a special event, are printed by the teacher if children have not yet evolved their writing to a point of independence. Here sequencing, joining sentences, and choosing just the right words and phrases begin to model composing and editing that children will use in their personal writing and during news time.

News time models all of the writing skills

News time is probably our most comprehensive way of modeling all of the writing skills. While the teacher leads the way, particularly in kindergarten and in the early months of grade one, peers become

Dear Mrs Reinhard,

    I feel so sorry for you, and I wish your husband didn't die How are you feeling? Are you all right? My Grandpa died too. My Grandma is in a wheel chair. And my couisn died.

             love
             Andrea

Dear Mrs Reinhard

    I am very very sorry that your husband died Last night my eyes were watering I was almost crying. I hope you will come back soon. I'm sure all the kinders are missing you, everyone will be so glad when you are back. Don't feel so sad, everything will be alright soon. I hope! I will if I can come and visit you soon Everythings alright in the kindergarten, I hope you will be alright soon.

           From Jeannie

Letters

When Margaret's husband died quite suddenly, the second graders who had spent the two previous years in her classes opted to write individual letters instead of sending a joint card of condolence. As they worked on expressing their feelings, a hush fell over the room, and each child in his/her own way spoke directly and personally to Margaret in ways few adults would.

increasingly important partners in modeling language, idea generating, spelling, reading, and editing. We describe the *how* of news time in chapter 6; here we are presenting more detail on what the children learn from the daily modeling and practice.

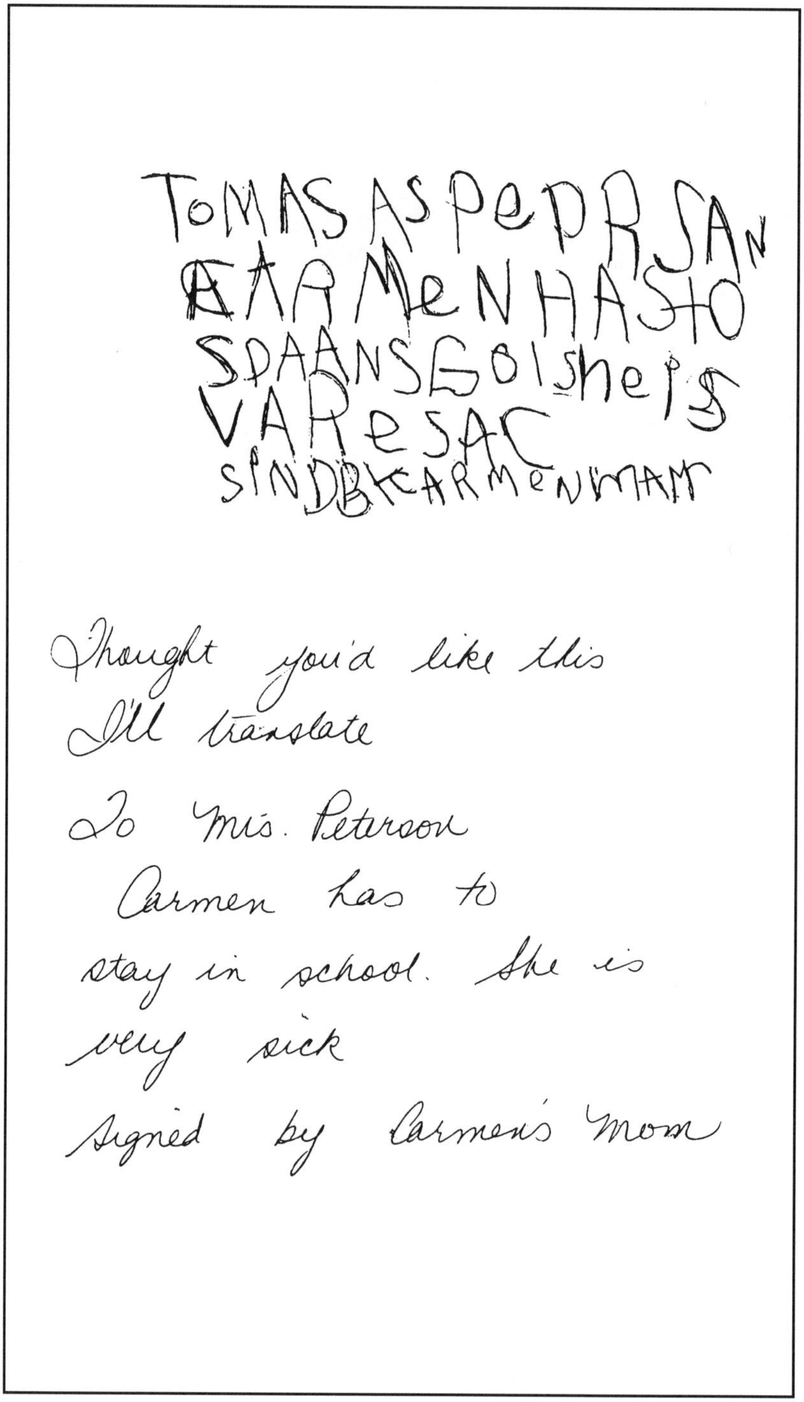

TOMASASPEDRSAN
AARMENHASTO
SPAANSGOIsheIS
VAReSAC
SINDBYCARMENMAM

Thought you'd like this
I'll translate
To Mis. Peterson
Carmen has to
stay in school. She is
very sick
Signed by Carmen's Mom

Then there are important messages to the teacher

Learning about the power of written language becomes an incentive to write. When Carmen decided she needed to stay in at recess, she composed this note. To lend weight to her message she signed it "Carmen's Mom."

**The children's own materials
become the basis for favorite
experience charts**

*Pictures children bring to school
can become the starting point of an
experience chart that remains available
to be admired and read, with or
without the help of an adult.*

*Vocabulary becomes richer and moves
beyond the monosyllables of initial
basal readers.*

*Personal involvement in initiating and
creating the reading material assures
high interest and voluntary practice.*

News time produces language development and sharing

- Sharing messages
- Participating in the discussions
- Taking pleasure in generating ideas
- Developing imagination
- Expressing ideas in coherent sentences
- Speaking up in a group
- Cooperation, taking turns
- Improving diction
- Enriching vocabulary
- Using language to learn, question
- Translating experience and spoken messages into written language

News time introduces the children to all the details of print about which we used to worry a good deal. Every single day, children are seeing, hearing, and using:

Printing, letters and their sounds, punctuation, and more
- Letters, their shapes and sounds
- Spelling and sounding out
- Rules of phonics (repeated often)
- Written words (shown by spaces)
- Parts of words (suffixes, prefixes)
- Compound words (spotted by peers)
- Look-alike, sound-alike words
- Similarities and differences
- Left-right progression of print
- Capitalization and its uses
- Proper use of punctuation
- Complete sentences
- Inference drawing and rule generating based on observing and listening

Composing and editing
- Phrasing messages
- Clarifying, expanding statements
- Proofreading
- Considering style (how it sounds)

- Correcting spelling and style
- Considering coherence – one idea
- Starting to use paragraphs
- Editing to take the audience into account

In addition to demonstrating and drawing attention to all of the details of printing, spelling, and composing, news time also imparts:

Reading and listening

- Reading words and messages
- Observing and listening
- Attending and sitting still
- Eye-voice (pointer) coordination
- Using context and memory
- Using syntax and experience
- Using good intonation and phrasing
- Asking for/giving help

The bonus of news time is that not only is all of this teaching/learning free of stress but it also promotes:

Enjoyment and the motivation to write, spell, and read

- Pleasure of being listened to
- Seeing personal messages in print
- Taking small steps forward
- Accepting trial-and-error learning
- Being co-creators of news
- Feeling excitement of discovery
- Feeling safe in sharing ideas
- Having fun participating

When we abandoned structured lessons in favor of modeling functional writing throughout the day, we wanted to make certain that we were not short-changing the children. Keeping an eye on the list of skills to be taught and comparing that list with what the children were learning convinced us that they not only learned all the required skills but a good deal more. If you are just beginning to shift to holistic teaching, you, too, may derive reassurance from making occasional checks against your Scope and Sequence Chart to see that the children are indeed learning all that is required. You will probably find that the learners' sequence differs from that on the chart. We certainly have. But we also continue to find that when the children are following their sequence, their learning is more solid and pervasive than it was in our days of preplanned exercises.

What is a writing workshop?

The concept of "the writing workshop" no doubt will be familiar to you. Donald Graves' (1983, 1994) approach of encouraging young writers to generate their own ideas and spelling has been applied widely, and many teachers are now aware of the wonderful benefits that accrue from placing students in charge of their own composing and writing. When we made our gradual shift to teaching the learners' way, we did not immediately abandon our former, more structured ways of teaching, but with each passing year observations of children's ways of learning have convinced us that to give them complete control over what they are going to say and how they are going to put the messages on paper produces far more profound learning than our structured exercises of the past. We will be describing our ways of using the Writing Workshop, but if you want additional detail, you will find Lucy Calkins' *The Art of Teaching Writing* (1994) a very comprehensive guide.

Learning to write by writing is probably the most accurate definition of the writing workshop. Children are invited to put down anything they would like and to do it as best they can. Pictures are often the first steps to producing messages, but the lively talk at news time and throughout the day have sparked ideas as well. If children are just beginning to communicate on paper, pretend writing or babbling in letters may be the extent of the written messages, but it is important to realize that these emergent ways of writing are not random scribbles but are intended to convey meaningful messages. As in any other workshop, skills are built gradually and the end products gradually become ever more sophisticated. The key elements of the writing workshop are learning by doing and trusting the children's capacity to evolve their skills.

Of course, the learning-by-doing approach requires feedback that acknowledges and expands the young writers' work, yet still leaves them in control. Talking to children about what they want to write, encouraging them to put down whatever they can, discussing their ideas and their attempts at writing provides the individual, on-the-spot feedback children need. Such feedback can be offered while the children work or through "conferences" scheduled to discuss the work at greater length. When you first introduce the writing workshop these conferences will be brief, but once children's writing has evolved from a few sentences to paragraphs and page upon page of narrative or descriptive writing, interactions in conferences will require a bit more time. In either case, the individualized help in these conferences assures that the children receive exactly the kind of input they need and want at that moment to help them refine all of their writing skills. Not surprisingly, we have found that this personalized teaching, done as and when needed, is absorbed more readily and transferred to other situations more easily than group lessons directed at the entire class.

From the standpoint of classroom management, the independent work inherent in the workshop approach frees the teacher to provide on-the-spot feedback and conferences. As the children's volume of writing increases, more time is allotted to the writing workshop, but it is not necessary to see every child every day. In time, peer conferences provide some of the input made originally by the teacher.

How to get started

Begin by telling the children that each day you and they will spend some time writing and that during this workshop time they can put down anything they like and that anything they are able to produce will be just fine. Assure them that you are interested in their ideas and want to see them written down but know that they can't print or spell very well. Explain that you will help them think of ideas but won't give too much information on spelling because you want them to learn on their own. Shore up their confidence by telling them that you know they will become really good spellers and will do lots and lots of writing. You may need to reinforce that message from time to time with children who worry about their inability to print or spell accurately. One teacher found that the children in her class forgot about their worries when she told them that she used to engage in pretend writing when she was a little girl and was just getting started.

To get the writing session under way, ask the children if they have any ideas for writing. If you started the day with news time, a number of ideas may have come up then, and children will remember to write about their special news of the day. "My grandma is coming to visit." "I lost a tooth." "The wind blew down a tree in our backyard." "I watched wrestling on TV last night." Sharing ideas for writing helps children think of their own, and if you do some sharing of what you are planning to write during workshop time they will show a lively interest in your news. In fact, they will begin to question you to elicit further information just as they have observed you do when you listened to their news.

Messages begin with just a few words

Just as babies will say just a word or two to convey a whole message, so beginning writers at times use a telegraphic style that gives only the key words but is meant to convey more. Kelly read her picture caption, "This is my cat and my dog." Tim said, "This is my Hallowe'en pumpkin."

Peter contented himself for quite a while with simply printing his name. Yet he would dictate full messages such as the one shown here. He continued to be slow at evolving his writing, but by April he had moved along to produce the three sentences that the teacher had set as his minimum daily requirement.

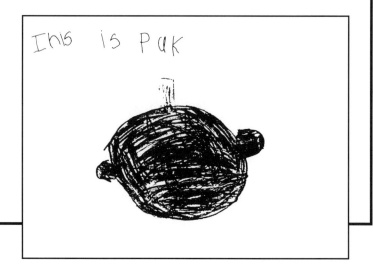

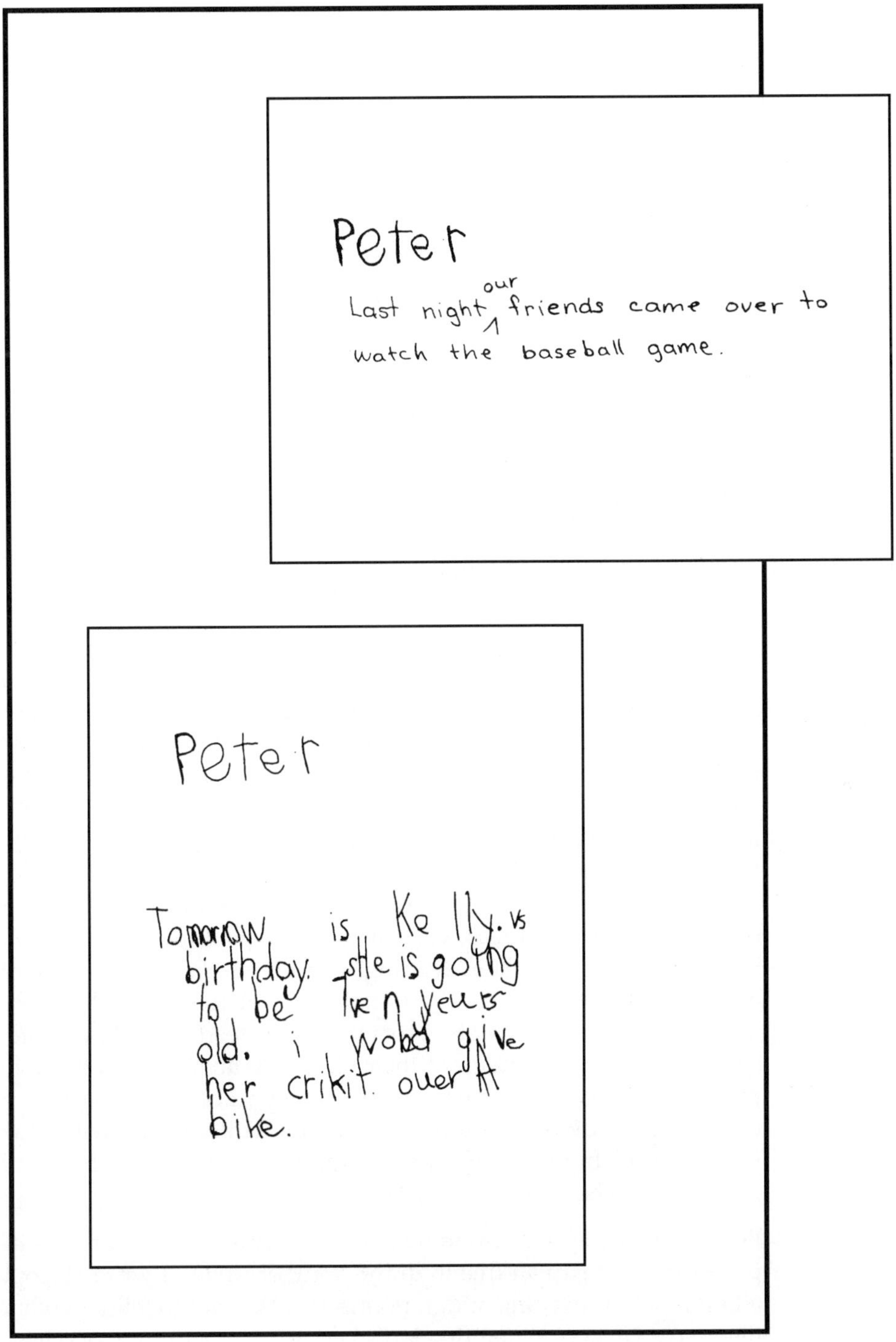

Peter

Last night our friends came over to watch the baseball game.

Peter

Tomorrow is Kelly. is birthday. She is going to be Tren years old. i woba give her crikit. over A bike.

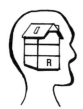

What are you going to write, Mrs. Reinhard?

As Margaret sits down to do her writing for the day, some of the children will crowd around to see what she will be choosing as a topic that day. Singly or as a group they will question her:

QUESTION: *What are you going to write today?*

MARGARET: *I think I'll write about last night when Jamie stuck his head around the corner and shot me with his water pistol.*

QUESTION: *Wow! Did you get wet?*

MARGARET: *You bet I did!*

QUESTION: *What did you do? Did you chase him?*

MARGARET: *No, I just shouted at him.*

QUESTION: *What did you tell him?*

MARGARET (shouts): *Jamie, you stop that! I'll get after you!*

The children delight in that kind of first-hand account of Margaret's interaction with her son and will tell their own home stories in turn.

If you show genuine interest in their thoughts and proposals for writing, few children will be completely at a loss for topics. If they are, they may look around to see what other children are doing and may begin by imitating their news. Hence, at the outset you will probably see a number of similar or even identical sentences. But after copying a few times, even the more timid children will begin to generate their own ideas. One year, going to EXPO was a favorite topic with children who had the opportunity to see the World's Fair. After quite a few repetitions of the same message, their writing evolved from there. Ideas will flow even for children who are still pretend writing, and their "reading" of their messages is often more elaborate than that of children reading what they actually wrote down. If at times children find that they can't read what they wrote, see if you can get a clue from their picture or any letters they have printed. If nothing gives you a hint, you may want to suggest, "Why don't you sit down and think about it for a while? I bet it will come back to you." In most cases it does, and after a while the child will recall what s/he had intended to convey.

Begin the writing workshop by giving the children blank pieces of paper and leave them free to draw, print, or pretend write. Accept all facsimiles of writing and, if necessary, ask them to tell you what they have written. When first launched into the writing workshop, most of them will begin by drawing pictures and if they have not decided in advance what they want to write, the picture often becomes the concrete base on which they build their writing. If you provided captions for their pictures in kindergarten, some of the initial writing may simply describe the picture the child has drawn.

You will note changes in the children's writing from day to day. At first, getting crayons and pencils out may take a while. Children will sit quietly toying with the box of crayons or looking at the blank piece of paper in front of them. Some may talk – to themselves or each other – before making that first mark on the page. Give them time, observe, trust, and hang in there. Eventually they all begin. Accept all attempts, praise steps forward, ask specific questions about the children's messages and pictures: "Is that you and your dog? What's your dog's name?" "Is that a Concord? Did you see it flying by when you were at EXPO?" "How did your dad get that huge fish into the boat?" As you continue to observe, you will be very conscious of their move from gross processing to fine. Pictures, printing, spelling, and messages are rough at first, but as you compare children's early attempts with later work, you will note definite steps forward that you can comment on as you talk to the children, their parents, or your supervisor.

Though you sit down to do your own writing – to be shared later on – you may also want to circulate quietly to chat with the children, asking them about their pictures, acknowledging steps forward, and encouraging them to evolve their own spelling. But resist the urge to spell for them. To demonstrate what we mean, here is a typical exchange between teacher and child:

MARTIN: *How do you spell* my sister?

TEACHER: *Say the words and see if you can hear the sounds.*

MARTIN: *Mmmmy – em.*

TEACHER: *Right. Why don't you put that down?*

MARTIN: (writes M)

TEACHER: *Can you hear any other sound in* my?

MARTIN: (shakes his head)

TEACHER: *O.K. Let's go to the next word. What sounds do you hear in* sister?

MARTIN: *Ssss – ess*

TEACHER: *O.K. Leave a finger space and put down* s.

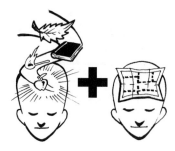

MARTIN: (writes down *S*)

TEACHER: *Can you hear any other sounds in* sister?

MARTIN: *Sisssterrr – ar*

TEACHER: *Good. Put down* r. *Anything else?*

MARTIN: *No.*

TEACHER: *Fine. That is a really good try at spelling* sister.

If *M SR* seems like rather skimpy spelling for *my sister*, remember we are talking about taking first steps. Many children have little or no experience with doing their own spelling and some may have no letter knowledge at first. They may begin to hear the sounds of beginning consonants but may be unsure about the letter names and shapes as yet.

Peter is one such child. He is bright, loves books and stories, but while in kindergarten he showed little interest in learning about letters, doing any writing, or even drawing pictures. He likes to do things slowly and takes his own time to do whatever job is before him. Watching other children get on with their writing, then moving to the various language centers of their choice has stirred him to action. Now he too wants to write. Since he has not developed any letter-sound correspondences and knows only a few letters, his teacher works with him daily asking him what he wants to write that day, helping him develop a repertoire of letters and sounds with which to begin his writing.

To get Peter started with spelling and printing, his teacher asks him to listen for the sounds of the words he wants to write. If he wants to write *mom* he will say *mmmm*, and his teacher responds, "Yes, you are hearing an *m*." At the same time she writes the *m* on a piece of paper to show Peter what it looks like. As a result of the individual attention, Peter is making progress and is beginning to write more readily each day. To help Peter along, he now has a piece of paper showing the alphabet in both capitals and lowercase letters taped to his table. As he begins to write he refers to that reminder. Going into the computer room and playing games became a strong incentive to learn letter names for Peter.

Authors' circle

As children complete their writing they date stamp the sheet and either file it in their personal folder or place it in the "Author

Basket" because they want to share it. Later that day, usually after recess, the teacher asks the children to gather around the "Author's Chair" to share that day's work. As she takes a piece of writing out of the basket, she invites the child to read it and show the picture. Following the teacher's model of being positive, the children say what they enjoy about the content, ask for further clarification, and, as they begin to feel more knowledgeable, make suggestions about revisions or the insertion of punctuation or finger spaces. At times the teacher may share her writing or a page by a favorite author like Bill Peet (see Bibliography) and ask for input from the children. The sessions are fast-paced, highly positive, and charged with excitement and enthusiasm. Children see themselves as authors and begin to think about expanding their writing or considering the reader.

Conferences

Once a week – more frequently if you can make time – meet with each child to talk about a given piece of writing – their choice or yours. Since you are giving them your undivided attention and a willing ear, children love this quiet time with you. We find that some children tell us, "I need a conference," almost from the beginning of writing workshop. Conferences are intended to draw children out, to help them evolve their ideas with open-ended questions, "What else did you do at EXPO?" "Where did you find your cat?" "Who was there with you?" "What happened then?" With the help of your genuine show of interest, children expand their writing from terse statements about concrete things – "I have a cat" – to more process-oriented writing, "My dad came to our house. We went to the friends. We got corn and carrots" (Meghan, September 22). In addition to commenting on the composition, you may also use conference time to give individualized phonics lessons. If the child agrees that s/he wants to see how close s/he came to standard spelling, you will print your version on the child's page or on a sticky paper to leave the child the option to change the printing or leave it as it stands.

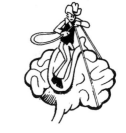

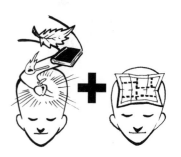

Timothy's writing conference

TEACHER: *Will you come for a writing conference now, please, Timothy?*

TEACHER: *That looks like your dog. And you did a lot of writing. Will you read that to me?*

TIMOTHY: *My dad is coming back tomorrow.*

TEACHER: *I didn't know he was away. How long has he been gone?*

TIMOTHY: *I'm not sure; couple of days, I think,*

TEACHER: *You and your mom must have missed him.*

TIMOTHY: *Yeah. We're going to pick him up at the airport.*

TEACHER: *Boy, that sounds exciting. You could include that in your story tomorrow and tell me more about what happened. Let's take a look at your spelling now. That's really good work, Tim. Do you want to see how close you came to standard spelling?* (Tim nods) *On here or on a sticky paper?*

TIMOTHY: *On here.* (He watches the teacher print the standard version under his own words.)

TEACHER: *See, you started off with a capital* M *for* my. *That's good. Let's put a* y *for* my. *You spelled* Dad *perfectly, but let's put a small* d *at the end of* Dad. *O.K., Tim, when you print* I *alone it is a capital, but in a word we use a small* i. *You spelled* coming *almost perfectly. Let's put an* o *instead of an* a. *Remember your small letters in words.* (Points to capitals in Tim's writing.) Back *has a* ck *at the end – remember the list of* ck *words we had on the board yesterday?*

TIMOTHY: (Looks uncertain but nods his head)

TEACHER: Tomorrow *is a pretty tough word. It's all one word, and this is how we spell it.* (Writes tomorrow.) *And, of course, we have a period at the end of the sentence. Good work, Tim.*

As the year progresses we shift more to eliciting further comments and variety of sentence structure, but make sure to keep the conferences positive and firmly focused on the children's ideas, messages, and ways of expressing themselves. Nothing dries up the flow of writing faster than having it critiqued in a negative way or rewritten so that it no longer resembles the original. Conversely, interest and positive comments coax even the most timid or reluctant writers to come forth with further detail to elaborate on the cryptic notes that characterize some early efforts.

Once the children have thoroughly absorbed your supportive way of commenting on writing and asking for additional information, peer conferences with two to four children can be productive. In time, children will turn to each other more and more, and in grades two and three peer conferences will be important adjuncts to your own work. Having a larger audience and several questioners can spark a new flow of ideas and create a better sense of audience than one-to-one conferences achieve. The realization that their writing will be read by others can become an added incentive to become more descriptive and to spell more accurately.

Editing

When suggested editing takes the form of expanded feedback, children accept it as readily for their writing as they do for talking or reading. Comments that expand on the message, or invite further elaboration or clarification are not threatening or aversive when given in a matter-of-fact way and as genuine suggestions. Children are free to incorporate any changes or leave their writing as is. Suggestions or questions other children proffer invariably address themselves to the content and frequently prompt the writer to revise his/her work to make it more comprehensible or complete. Seeing another child's writing may serve as feedback and trigger editing or self-correcting.

Discussions, modeling of editing during news time, or questions by peers alert children to considerations of clarity and style. As soon as their compositions expand to a line or two, some children begin to test their writing by reading out loud, and start to cross out words or phrases that don't seem to fit. Though such direct editing may look a bit messy, a bold cross-out represents a big step forward in composing. Self-correction moves writing to a new level.

Editing may not show on the piece of writing that was discussed at conference time. Children do not necessarily choose to amend what they have written. But at times a new version of the same message or story will emerge on successive days. Like professional writers, the children try out several ways of saying the same thing. They begin to take their audience into account and become more aware of using the right words and style of writing.

Publishing

Though they love to participate in the "Authors' Circle" to share their writing, the need to write so someone else can read and understand their messages has little importance to children at the outset. Since the aim of the writing workshop is twofold – to elicit children's thoughts and written expression and to move them toward greater precision – publishing a piece of writing becomes the occasion to proofread it carefully and to make all the changes necessary: edit content or style, produce standard spelling and careful printing, and, if necessary, upgrade the illustrations. Conferences that correct and revise the children's work with their cooperation are the first steps toward publishing. Early work may consist of no more than a sentence or two with an accompanying illustration to be shared with other children, taken home, or displayed on the bulletin board. But as the year progresses, the children's writing will evolve into stories, reports, poems, and books.

Genuine interactions and personal involvement stimulate learning

Teacher-learner exchanges foster purposeful writing. By the end of the year, writing and reading have evolved to a high level of proficiency.

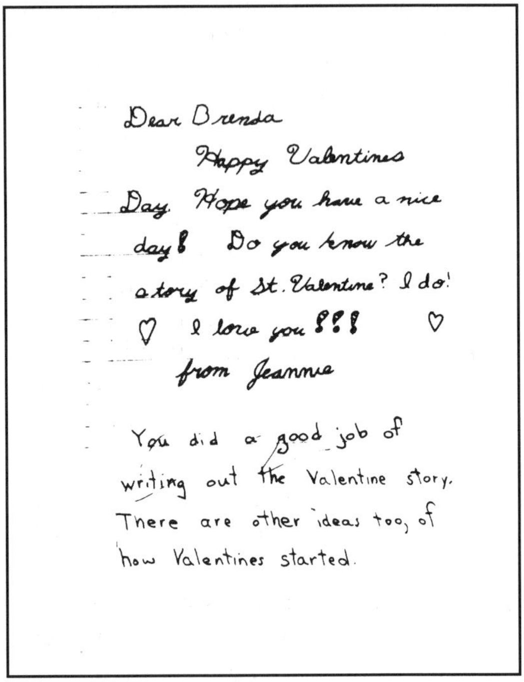

Dear Brenda
Happy Valentines Day. Hope you have a nice day! Do you know the story of St. Valentine? I do!
♡ I love you !!! ♡
from Jeannie

You did a good job of writing out the Valentine story. There are other ideas too, of how Valentines started.

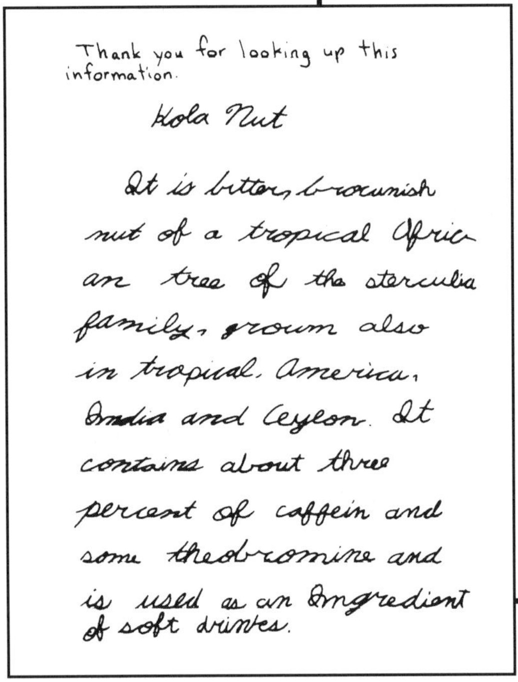

Thank you for looking up this information.

Kola Nut

It is bitter, brownish nut of a tropical African tree of the sterculia family, grown also in tropical America, India and Ceylon. It contains about three percent of caffein and some theobromine and is used as an ingredient of soft drinks.

My Little Sister

Once upon a time there was a little girl called Laurel Laurel was a very good little girl, but alas she didn't have a little sister. Every night she would go outside and wish upon the stars, almost every star in the sky had been wished on by Laurel. One night Laurel

rels father sent her to bed early, because that night Laurels wish came true. The next morning when Laurel woke up she heard a waily - waily noise coming from her mothers bed room she rushed in to her mothers room and there was a cradle by her mother and there in

in her mothers arms was Laurels wish a baby sister! Laurels mother asked Laurel if she wanted to hold her baby sister "Her name is Grace" said her mother. Laurel held her and cuddled her new sister, she was so happy that her wish came true, and that proves that some wishes come true!

If you refer to title pages, names of authors and illustrators as you read books and stories to the children, they will want to produce their own title pages and attractive cover sheets to show their authorship of written work. They will be eager to produce publishable material, and you will find them very receptive to suggestions and comments on composition, sentence structure, spelling, printing, and illustrations.

When children feel they have work that they would like to publish, they put it in the special "Publishing Box" for the teacher's attention. As soon as s/he has time, the teacher sits down with the child to edit the manuscript, change wording, make additions or deletions, and produce standard spelling as needed. When editing is completed to the satisfaction of writer and editor, the teacher or a parent helper will type the finished work, complete with title page and space for illustrations. The child adds any finishing touches that are needed, including a stiff cover to protect the pages. In grades two and three, neat printers may want to hand letter their published works to produce big books or attractive display pages. If a computer is available to the children, encourage them to do the final copy work. At the child's choice, the published book is added to the classroom library, goes home with the author, or becomes a present to a family member or friend. Children generally choose their fantasy stories or research reports for this more elaborate publishing. But the choice is theirs and many pieces of writing remain rough drafts consigned to the writing folder without another look.

Tracking progress

Simply observing how quickly children get down to work, generate ideas, begin to draw, or put pencil to paper will tell you a good deal about progress when you first introduce writing workshop. But collecting their daily work in individual folders will produce a more graphic record of steps forward, lapses, and new moves ahead. Have the children print their names on each piece of writing they produce, ask them to stamp it with a date stamp (provided on your desk) and file it in their personal folder. Keep these folders in a box that is readily accessible to the children. Those who are still in doubt about the spelling of their names soon become accustomed to locate their folders in the box. Having the children do the naming, stamping, and filing on their own is another instance of building their independence and freeing you to work with individuals or small groups.

To preserve a continuous record, keep a special writing notebook for each child. Once a week, ask the children to do their writing workshop in the notebook instead of on loose sheets of paper. In short order you begin to see the week-by-week progress as you scan the books. At the outset, the notebooks should be unlined. Later you may want to shift to paper that is partly blank and partly lined. It is important not to impose constraints of narrow lines on children when they are not yet ready to fit their printing into small spaces. Asking children to fit specific standards before they are ready can affect content, spelling, and creativity as well as printing.

Josh

Josh was doing well in writing workshop, producing messages to fit his pictures and moving closer to standard spelling, but his printing remained very small and cramped. Feeling that he was probably ready, his teacher asked Josh if he could print a little larger. Josh made a try, but the effort to suit the teacher turned his work into mirror writing. For several days, he reversed every letter and printed from right to left. Asking him to change the size of his printing interfered with his natural process and had a detrimental effect.

The cumulative record in their folders and notebooks will give you a more detailed view of each child's progress. Look back now and again to remind yourself how Rosalyn or Brandon began the writing process early in September. The folders can become your guide to individual intervention for children who need extra help with building their skills.

This cumulative record of children's work also becomes a guideline for adjusting individual work assignments. Voluntary participation functions within a framework of minimum work requirements that the teacher sets and upgrades throughout the year. At first, one sentence is just fine; then two or three sentences become the norm; and gradually, as children's ability to write continues to grow, the required amount of written work is adjusted upward to provide a challenge and to fit their growing abilities. Many children opt to write more than the minimum, but all are aware that they may not move to center or choosing time until they have produced their set amount of writing.

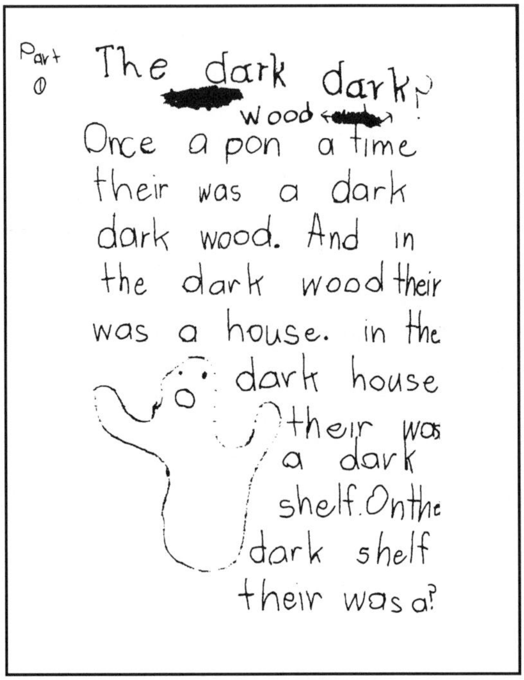

Part
0

The dark dark?
wood

Once a pon a time their was a dark dark wood. And in the dark wood their was a house. in the dark house their was a dark shelf. On the dark shelf their was a?

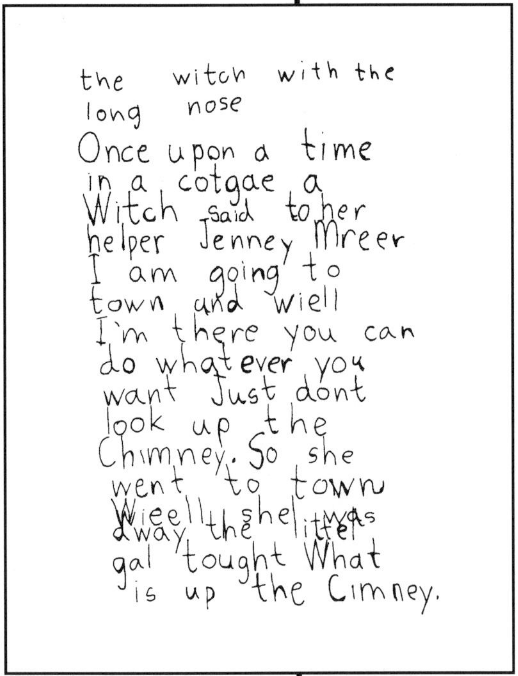

the witch with the long nose

Once upon a time in a cotgae a Witch said to her helper Jenney Mreer I am going to town and wiell I'm there you can do whatever you want Just dont look up the Chimney. So she went to town Wieell she it was away the little gal tought What is up the Cimney.

the magic fiary.
Once upon a time tehre
was a magic fairy her
name was ditsy. She was
the yogest one, all
the other fiarys picked
on her. So she went
away.

the Hunted Hose   Meghan
Once upon a time
there was a
Hunted Hose a gost lived.
in. It. It was a scairy one
when ever anyone went
there it woled scare
It out.
One day a litel
day went Inside
And never came
out. dIS mom.
was woied. She
did the
peles.

Fairy tales become favorite topics for a while

Here are examples of drafts produced by grade-one children during February and March. Published stories are corrected for spelling and punctuation, and the children take great care producing title pages, covers, and illustrations.

Center time promotes writing

Left with a choice of activity after completing their required writing, many children opt to continue writing during center time. If they are working on stories or special projects, they may simply remain at their table to carry on writing. If special events call for invitations or the production of greeting cards, some of the children will use center time to produce the cards. If plays are underway, roles may be written out. If story time has been particularly gripping, some children may decide to create a story of their own modeled on the one they have heard.

The writing center is a popular gathering place and two or three children often work together to do special projects involving a combination of artwork and writing. The supplies in the center invite imaginative work. Here are some of the items that children enjoy and use in the center:

- Colored paper of varying sizes and weights
- Colored pencils, felt pens, and crayons
- Blank greeting cards (samples or inexpensive stock)
- Envelopes of different sizes and shapes
- An old typewriter with a two-colored ribbon
- Bits of art materials to embellish the writing
- Glue and scissors

Children use the writing center to do personal letter writing, and the classroom mailbox becomes the distribution point for in-class notes and greetings.

Writing in grades two and three

Toward the latter part of grade one most children will have shifted from writing two or three sentences during writing workshop to producing quite coherent accounts of activities or special events. Some will already produce excellent stories, poems, and research projects, and publishing expands the accuracy of their work. Grade two builds on the solid practice and expands the children's skills in producing increasingly varied writing. In grade three the children consolidate and refine their composing, editing, and spelling. The freedom to initiate their own topics, to publish or leave material as drafts keeps children excited about their writing. The opportunity to interact, compare notes, read, or listen to each other's writing

*Learning to
Write, Spell, and
Sound Out*

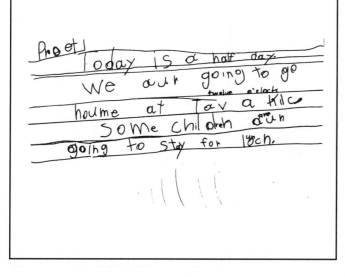

Keeping track of progress

Preet

September:

Preet is an excellent artist and though he was already writing, his drawings became the focus for his early work. Though the message is short, together with the picture, it conveys that Preet saw the Concord flight demonstration at EXPO.

Words are clearly separated by spaces. To aid his printing, he has drawn a line and his four words are almost entirely correct. None of the vowels are missing, but the n *of* went *is left out. Capitals and lowercase letters in the message are used accurately, though Preet prints his own name in all capitals.*

November:

Preet's writing has expanded to a four-sentence paragraph. He no longer uses his artwork as the starting point for writing but describes what is going on in school. There is variety in his sentence structure and the sequence is logical.

Thirteen of his twenty-three words are spelled correctly. The teacher has provided some corrections during a conference (some of the small insertions were made by her), but most of the words are accurate enough to be understood. Capitalization is accurate and most of the consonants are correct. A few vowels are omitted and the are-our *confusion occurs twice. Preet has decided to use lined paper and has drawn his own lines.*

March:

From single paragraphs, Preet has moved to writing fairy tales. He evolves his story over two days and lets the reader know that his tale will continue.

From the standard opening "Once upon a time," his story presents all the elements important to a good story: description, action, suspense, climax, and a happy ending. Vocabulary and sentence structure are more advanced than those in Preet's earlier work and produce a smooth flow.

Of the total 120 words 93 are spelled accurately. Those that are not can be understood based on their phonetic spelling and/ or the context. Capitals and lowercase letters are used accurately and all sentences are set off by periods. Words like saller, pasig, *and* btall *reproduce the sounds of* cellar, passage *and* bottle *quite well.*

Some of the e endings – aroude, doune – suggest that Preet is overgeneralizing the silent e. To form the past tense he uses ed endings in Hotied and foued but changes to t in wikt, no doubt because walked *gives the* d *the sound of* t.

From a four-word picture caption Preet has moved to authoring imaginative stories of considerable length. His reading and writing enhance each other. He enjoys both and practices throughout the day.

① Preet.
Once a upon a time, there was a hotied house. I went in to it. Whne I got in to the hotied house there was a trap door. I fiall doune the trap door. I fiall in to the saller room. I wikt aroude the saller room whne I got out of thiat saller room. I saw a goost.

To be cneoued.

② Preet.
I was sared so I ran throe the goost. Thin I saw a pasig way. I went throe the pasig way. Thene I fqured I was in a room I saw a cvired I opind the cvired and I saw a btall i ppind the btall and I sayv a goost I ran out of that house.

shows them differences in style, topic, and form of writing. If there is special appeal in the poem or story a child has created or the teacher has read, many and varied copies of it will appear. The practice of copying passages from reference books sensitizes children to different writing styles in the same way different types of conversations alerted them to intonation patterns at home. Without specific lessons or even comments about style, children begin to match their writing styles to the topic.

The amount of reading children do and hear produces knowledge of narrative and stimulates imagination. We found that although most of children's writing practice had been centered on creating factual accounts on concrete topics, when we suggested that they "write a story," the children came forth with appropriate beginnings, endings, and stories replete with gold, fairies, and goblins. Animal stories as well as fairy tales featured among the productions. Children had definitely developed a clear idea (an inner map) of what constitutes a "story."

Since children are surrounded by books and printing, there is never a dearth of models to follow as they evolve their writing. Did you ever experience the sinking feeling that you were not at all sure what your teacher, professor, or boss had in mind when asking you to produce a particular piece of writing? Not having a model can be as counter-productive as having little or nothing to say. In the interactive atmosphere of the classroom, models of writing abound. Books, games, other children's writing, the teacher's writing on the board, experience charts, discussions of projects, stories told by visitors, messages, or words displayed around the classroom all become models for printing, spelling, or composing. The great variety of books, their format, style, and topics show clearly that there are many ways of talking or writing about anything under the sun. Because they interact freely with each other, children have models of writing in progress and in finished form readily available. That horrible question "What does she really want?" never arises to interfere with the free flow of writing development.

The practical uses of print are learned as readily through writing as through reading. Boys in particular reveal that the utility of being able to convey and conserve messages is a strong incentive for them to learn. Labeling items, tacking up warnings, "Don't come in here," "Please don't erase the blackboard," "Don't open Chummy's cage

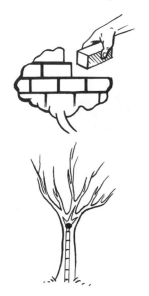

door," and messages to parents or the teacher become very much part of writing practice. Copying a recipe or directions for making something is a favorite way to take school experiences home.

Though special times for writing are part of the daily routine, working on science projects, producing a play, or building things may all involve writing. Self-correction and editing become part of voluntary practice as children actively think about and evaluate their own writing and that of other writers. Being writers, they read with an eye for style and pick up interesting turns of a phrase for their writing and talking. Vocabulary, syntax, and sentence complexity evolve as the children's self-initiated writing expands.

Though functioning at a more advanced level, writing in grades two and three grows from the same activities that we have described: news time, writing workshop, center time, incidental writing, projects, and all the functional writing associated with the daily activities in class. Like reading, it pervades the day and becomes a natural extension of oral communication.

Learning to spell by spelling

Writing requires knowledge of letters and their sounds

Observing children learn has taught us to keep the *focus on meaning when children learn to read and to provide detailed information about letters, sounds, and spelling when they learn to write.* When reading, the children can draw upon context, pictures, memory, knowledge of language and its syntax to aid comprehension. But when it comes to writing, they need specific details in order to produce messages. So we talk about letters and their sounds at the time when the children need that information. The children concentrate intensely on learning about sounds as they write, and they readily transfer what they learn to their reading.

Though writing, too, focuses on producing messages and conveying meaning, it requires greater attention to letters and their sounds than reading does. Modeling again becomes a natural way of introducing children to the intricacies of written language. Show the children how you are converting spoken words into printed ones. As you print their names, caption their pictures, put messages on the board, say the letters aloud, then read the word and finally the entire phrase or sentence. Encourage children to talk along, to help with spelling, and to call out familiar features – silent *e*'s,

Mandy
We will roll the eggs
three times a day.
This weekend Kelly K. will
take the eggs home
On the towanty-frstday
the chicks will hach!

Mandy
Wojcik

We are going to have
our Mexican Feista on
March 5th My Dod's
birthday is on the same
day as our Mexican
Feista. Aod my Ganny is
coming on March 10th so
is my ugpahca!

Three chicks hatched
today. My class got to
see the blood Vessels.
Mrs. Reinhard helped
one chick hatch.
The chicks are cute.

Special projects generate writing

Hatching chicks

While the eggs are in the incubator, children keep track of progress in their personal writing. Some produce full-scale reports, replete with technical terms like embryo *and* blood vessels.

Getting ready for the Mexican Fiesta

Social studies that culminate in special events spark a lot of writing.

Dear Mrs rienhard Brad
my crayons are all gone
I need your crayons to have
thankyou

Dear Mrs. Reinhart I
Thankyou for using your craons
Becase I used myn at Hallooween
I Love you

Dear Mrs. Reinhart

Thank-you for lending me your black crayon
I needed your black because at Halloween,
we had a pece of paper and then we colours
bright colours and then we used our black
over top very hard and then we took our
ruler and scrached it and made pictuers if you
know what I mean. from Katrina

Dear Mrs. Reinhard

I appreciate you for letting
me use your black crayon
but I am going to bring a
black crayon back. Thank you.

from Jacquelin Inness.

*Cooperation between
grades produces writing*

*Second-graders borrow
some crayons*

*Writing notes of thanks is
excellent writing practice
and maintains a pleasant
connection between children
and their former teacher.*

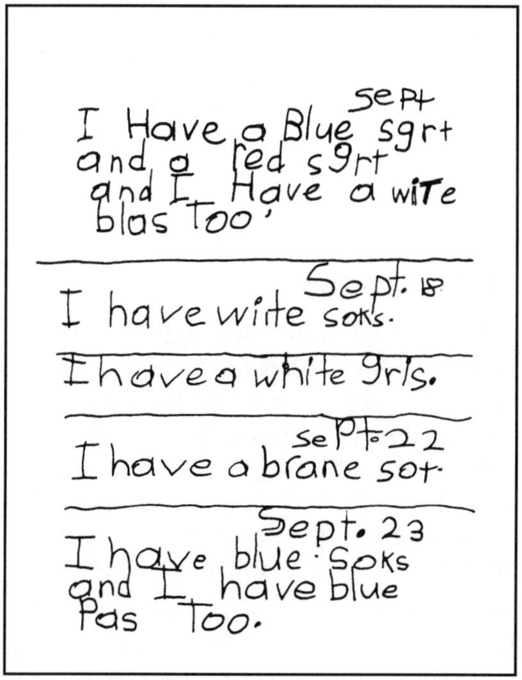

Sept

I Have a Blue sgrt
and a red sgrt
and I Have a wiTe
blas too'

Sept. 18

I have wite soks.

I have a white grls.

Sept 22

I have a brane sot.

Sept. 23

I have blue soks
and I have blue
pas too.

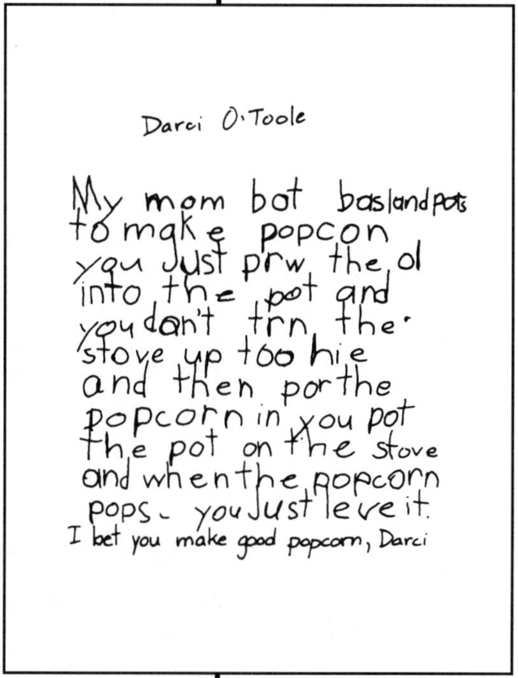

Darci O.Toole

My mom bot baslandpts
to make popcon
you Just prw the ol
into the pot and
you dan't trn the
stove up too hie
and then por the
popcorn in you pot
the pot on the stove
and when the popcorn
pops. you Just leve it.
I bet you make good popcorn, Darci

*Second-graders make big
strides in their writing*

capitals, *ing* endings. As you model printing and spelling, comment on spelling patterns – *th, ow, ph, ght* – and on sound-alike words – *to, too,* and *two; for* and *four.* Peer modeling, reading familiar texts, playing with letter games, and printing the children's names on their artwork augment the modeling you do, and from an early point in the school year you will have a good chorus of voices "helping you spell."

But modeling is just the beginning. Though children become quite adept at spelling orally, their spelling, like their talking, evolves on the basis of active practice and self-programming of rules. To shift their attention from the meaning of words to their sounds, model careful diction and invite children to put down the sounds they hear as they begin to write their first messages. When you see the intensity with which they say the words to themselves as they begin to write, you will come to trust that the children will progress in their spelling. The daily practice of working at converting words into sounds and letters will foster steps forward and definite stages of spelling development. Because the children themselves are generating these patterns, the learning is more profound and more transferrable to other tasks than the memorization of individual spelling words, and you will find it exciting to watch the stages of spelling unfold.

Stages of spelling development

When learning to talk, children move through a sequence of babbling, one-word sentences, two- and three-word sentences, self-programming of simple rules that do not necessarily conform to adult norms, overgeneralizations of acquired rules, and finally the adoption of more precise speech. All along the way, they are talking to convey messages. Even though their speech is imperfect, they mean to communicate. When given the chance to initiate and invent spelling, children move through a very similar sequence:

- Babbling in print (strings of letters not yet formed into words)
- One-letter spelling
- Two- and three-letter spelling
- Self-programming of simple rules (some conventional, others not)
- Overgeneralizing acquired rules or patterns (phonetic spelling, transfer of spelling patterns of known words to unknown ones)
- Adopting more complete, more standard spelling

***Reversals do not dyslexia
make***

*In October Meghan and
Mandy continue to reverse
letters even though their
composing and spelling have
progressed well. Given time,
models of correct printing,
and lots of writing practice,
they continue to improve their
printing until it is free of
reversals. The development
from gross processing to fine
discrimination shows itself in
the improvement of their
handwriting as well as their
composing.*

As in learning to talk, children mean to communicate even with their earliest attempts at spelling or writing. They talk while engaging in pretend writing and, in kindergarten, will ask us to read what they have just written. Though it may be hard to accept – in light of the general aim of school teaching to produce accurate forms of writing – this babbling in print is as important to spelling development as oral babbling is to language development. If babies can be trusted to move from babbling to more precise speech, so school children can be trusted to move from babbling in print to more precise spelling. Children *want to advance* and as they practice and build their knowledge of letters they begin to apply it. Surrounding them with print as well as modeling writing and spelling every day at the blackboard and in writing conferences assure that they have the information they need.

Self-initiated spelling emerges in a predictable sequence

Comparing the children's spelling with records of initial talking, we have noticed that the omissions they make when beginning to spell are as systematic as those when learning to talk. In both cases children select for attention words or word units that carry most meaning. When talking, their one- and two-word sentences contain nouns, verbs, and sometimes adjectives. When spelling, consonants carry the load. Seen in context, *blls, hlday*, and *jantr* are as readily deciphered as *balls, holiday,* and *janitor,* as baby's early *groggy* or *nana* are recognized as *doggy* and *grandma.* When we began to give children the room to guide their own learning, it became important for us to recognize this parallel between the two developments to reassure ourselves that the children were actually progressing in a quite systematic way.

Like the baby beginning to talk, beginning spellers are content to let single letters stand for entire words. One-letter spellings – R = *are*, U = *you*, or B = *be*, M = *am* – appear in spelling and creative writing during the early phase of their writing. During oral spelling at news time, children usually start by giving beginning consonants only. Final consonants generally emerge next and median consonants follow. Blends like *bi, fl, br,* digraphs like *ch, sh,* or *th* and endings such as *ing* or *ed* follow next. Words used frequently soon become established as complete units, and children will spell *today, the, we, have,* and the like in a single breath. But in trying to sound out unfamiliar words, vowels and their sounds are last to become solidly established. Even our best spellers and readers will continue to guess vowel sounds for some time. When starting to write, children traverse the same sequence they followed in oral spelling. Even children who have developed quite a repertoire of oral spellings generally revert to two- and three-letter spelling, primarily using consonants, before evolving more conventional spelling patterns in their written work. It seems that they do not yet transfer what they "know" in one context to another one. In each case they need to move through the process of generating their own rules if the knowledge is to be truly theirs.

Children generate their own rules of spelling

Children's self-programming of simple rules generally consists of spelling phonetically. It took us a while to recognize some of their efforts, but once it became clear that the children were using *what they actually heard*, we began to realize that our own thinking about sounds had been influenced by our knowledge of spelling, while the children use their acute hearing and try to represent the sounds they perceive. Suggesting *d* as the beginning consonant for *there* or median consonant for *mother* is quite understandable. But *ch* for *train* and *trophy* is more of a challenge. If you listen closely when saying these words in a colloquial way you will hear the *ch* sound. Many of the vowel omissions are simply a matter of trying to spell a word the way it is said. We are no longer *sprised* at some of the more common phonetic spellings but continue to learn more about the highly acute hearing children bring to "sounding out." (See examples of children's writing.)

Overgeneralizations of acquired patterns or spellings are next to emerge. Here, too, children's spelling work demonstrates that they are building on what they know. They try to formulate rules to help them meet new situations just as they do when learning to talk. Knowing about the spelling of *today* and *say*, they may offer spellings like *laydy* or *waying*. Sometimes *s* will appear in place of a *c*, and *anywear* or *two many* gives evidence of knowledge of sound-alike words. Along more sophisticated lines, rules for making long vowel sounds may show up in *mele* or *chane*. Once you get in the habit of asking yourself how children come up with their spellings, you will find many more examples like these. Accept them as signposts of children's progress, and enjoy the detective work of

figuring out the derivation of a particularly interesting answer. Often the children themselves will provide the answer if you ask.

As in learning to talk, differences in children's development will be vast. Some children progress rapidly and internalize new patterns after just one or two tries. Others need weeks, and even months of practice. The important thing to remember is that the kind of internal programming the children do when learning to spell by spelling will give them a far more solid foundation for moving along than the ability to parrot back rules we provide ready-made in worksheets or exercises. We abandoned phonics exercises when our research evidence convinced us that children did not generalize the work to their reading or writing. We find that individualized phonics lessons that give each child what s/he needs at that precise moment – when writing or spelling – are much more effective than whole-class phonics lessons.

Children need to evolve at their own pace and in their own way

We abandoned the practice of having children copy written messages as a beginning move toward writing when we became convinced that despite the practice, children did not apply what they learned in their own compositions until and unless they were ready to do so and they initiated that move. No matter how many times we showed and told them that the end of a sentence needed a period, children would not put periods at the end of their own sentences, even though they quite readily repeated during news time that that was the thing to do.

They may copy words provided on the board when writing about shared experience, but once they focus on their own thoughts and composition, *frog*, though copied from the board several times, becomes *fg* if that spelling is more in tune with their own level of spelling development. Just as you may be able to get a baby to say a word with greater accuracy only to relapse into the usual way of talking, so young spellers need to move through definite stages and at *their* pace to truly internalize spelling rules. If this sounds dubious, observe the children in your class and note how they may be quite able to copy words but will revert to their own way of spelling when "playing" at writing.

"Levels of knowing"

Based on these observations and the fact that quite good oral spellers will revert to their own invented spelling in their writing, we have come to think of these seeming discrepancies as *levels of knowing*. On one level a child "knows" how to spell *today*; on another, or perhaps in another context, s/he does not. As Piaget (1955) has shown so clearly, children will not necessarily "transfer" what they know in one setting to another. Concrete learning needs to guide each new development. Observing how children move through the same stages in written spelling as they have traversed in oral spelling has convinced us of the accuracy of his findings. Rote learning is another instance that demonstrates *levels of knowing* in action: Brandon may have been quite proficient at printing his name at the top of the page, but when he wrote about himself, his name became *Brdn* or even just *Bdn*. Until his overall spelling development had progressed to the inclusion of vowels, he continued to use the consonant-only version of his name. Self-programming of rules and concrete practice allowed more accurate spelling to emerge when Brandon was ready to move to a new level of knowing.

Spelling generates self-programming of phonologic awareness

*Learning to
sound out*

As the children work at generating "invented spelling," they are also beginning to generate awareness of phonology. Since writing takes up much of the children's day, practice in spelling and sounding out has become more pervasive, more active, and more effective than it was when worksheets governed our structured phonics lessons. The fact is that the integration of work on letters and sounds with practical applications in writing makes for solid learning, learning that encourages the kind of voluntary practice that has worked so effectively in the home to self-program language. Practice embedded in meaningful work is eagerly pursued and bears no resemblance to structured phonics lessons that bored some children, served a few accurately, and overwhelmed others.

Group sessions such as news time give children a chance to practice both hearing and seeing the application of spelling or sounding out. If not yet ready to speak up, some children will rehearse silently. As

Levels of knowing

Brandon

On one level Brandon knows how to print his name; on another, he reverts to showing consonants only. He reads his two picture captions: "Brandon made a house" and "Brandon has a pumpkin." Though the two are right next to each other, Brandon perceives the labeling of his work as separate from the writing. Once he made the breakthrough and his writing shifted from strings of letters to words, the two levels of knowing merged, and Brandon appeared in the body of writing as well as at the top of the page.

she sees a child quietly forming letters or words, Margaret may quiet down the eager spellers to give someone else a chance: "Just a minute, let's give David a chance to spell all by himself" or "How would you like to come up to help me spell this one?" or simply, "That's right, go ahead and say it out loud."

Because children ask for and receive information as and when they need it, individual work on sounding out becomes particularly effective. On-the-spot lessons in phonologic awareness answer specific spelling questions connected with children's own writing and individualize the learning. Children readily transfer such learning to new words. Our group lessons about phonics rules with all their exceptions – though memorized carefully – showed no such ready transfer.

Though the children do not receive instruction in "sounding out" in connection with reading, they readily apply the knowledge they have gained through writing to the decoding of unfamiliar words. Visitors to the classroom have expressed their amazement at the persistence, willingness to try, and at times great ease with which children will approach difficult words and reading passages. Through their day-to-day practice in spelling, children not only develop knowledge of letter/sound correspondences, spelling patterns, and punctuation, but they also transfer that knowledge quite freely to their reading.

Like reading, spelling and sounding out move from global patterns to finer discrimination of detail. But even at the initial stage, children will show tremendous concentration and effort as they work at sounding out words to generate spelling. Some of the children will engage in the same descriptive monologue their teacher modeled while writing. As a result, their knowledge of spelling and sounding out is reinforced by several senses. They see, say, hear, and feel the letters, words, and sounds as they proceed. They become confident spellers and are willing to try to sound out even the difficult words facing them in a story. Encouraging them to evolve their spelling from their early crude invention has transformed the structured phonics lessons of yore into a natural developmental progression toward accuracy in both *spelling and sounding out*.

Phonics games

*Phonics games become lively fun
when children are left free to play
them together or alone and, at times,
according to their own rules. The good
feelings engendered by the fun
of playing produce learning
without stress or anxiety.*

Fostering writing development

Sharing ideas, discussing what has been written, listening attentively, giving encouragement and advice on spelling and printing keep the young writers moving along. Peer modeling becomes a strong source of information for those who are hesitant. You will find considerable copying among children. Accept it as a part of the natural way in which children learn; they will progress to more individual work. In the meantime they often find it easier to relate to peers and their work than to an adult's oral direction.

**Hints and
particulars**

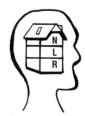

Talking is a vital part of composing and sorting out ideas. If you model speaking quietly and remind them to do likewise, children will learn to keep their voices low. If their tables are pushed together closely, there is every opportunity to share pictures, messages, and spelling, and during the writing workshop there is a constant chatter in low voices as children talk to themselves and to each other.

Give some personal attention to children who obviously need extra help and encouragement to draw them out, though you may not need to do so every day. But you will be listening daily to children sharing their writing during Authors' Circle and can use that time as well as individual conferences to satisfy the children's need to be heard.

To give special encouragement you might comment on such things as:

- Content of the writing
- Your interest in the message
- Novelty of the work
- Choice of words
- Willingness to try
- Volume of printing and composing
- Complexity of sentences
- Beauty of language
- Originality of thought
- Improvement of printing
- Fewer inversions of letters
- Good illustrations
- Staying on task
- Forward steps in spelling
- Interest in the topic

- Good editing
- Choice of words
- Accuracy of description
- Any forward step that you can detect in the child's writing

Margaret Reinhard's way of teaching children to print

Like the other basics, printing is best learned through modeling and practice. Margaret models good printing in kindergarten during news time at the blackboard and when writing captions under the children's pictures. She offers no formal lessons on printing during kindergarten, but if children ask her how to "make letters" she demonstrates at the blackboard and invites them to practice.

In September she starts to teach letters to grade-one children – not during writing time but in separate sessions. Using the blackboard she shows how to form the letters and then has the children practice moving their hands through the air in large movements to develop their global motor skills. Next she has them practice printing on unlined paper beginning with circles and sticks then moving to forming letters. After that, she introduces baselines, then wide lines, and finally regulation paper. The move from gross processing to fine has full play in this progression and children who do not have good control over their fine motor skills have ample time to practice on unlined paper before moving to the constraints of small print and accuracy of form.

Margaret does not insist on accuracy of skills at this point. Children do the best they can, and it takes all of September – sometimes part of October – to go over all of the letters. The learning assistance teacher, a parent helper, or visitors to the class will give help to children who need it, as Margaret does not review printing lessons for the whole class. Instead she will work with individual children and small groups who need extra practice or instruction.

Though Margaret demonstrates the Maclean's method of printing, she leaves the children free to develop their individual styles. She will show how to hold the pencil correctly, but if children have difficulty following her example, are left-handed, or particularly inclined to use the pencil their own way, she gives them a great deal of freedom in this matter and simply focuses on upgrading their printing. One of her bright kindergarten children gripped the pencil in her left fist and did not move from that way of holding it. But Jenny's printing flowed beautifully, evolved into very attractive cursive writing, and later into excellent calligraphy. In printing as in all learning, safety to move from gross processing to fine produces excellent results. Left to work their way, children evolve their skills to the best of their ability.

Looking at children's handwriting

Since we have shifted to the writing workshop (see page 130) and give children full latitude to evolve their invented spelling, we may eventually shift to abandoning formal printing lessons and trust that the children will learn enough from the general modeling. But for the moment the brief afternoon sessions on printing are still part of our early fall teaching schedule.

When looking at children's handwriting it becomes important to separate practice in printing or straightforward copying from writing and composing. Each year we find neat little printers lapse into quite poor performance when shifting from copying to composing. If you think of your own handwriting when producing rough drafts of written work, there will be little cause to worry. When composing, the attention of the writer is focused on the creative task at hand. Neatness of handwriting takes second place. It is a matter of focusing on one thing at a time.

When introducing the writing workshop we want to encourage children to focus fully on composing. We give them unlined paper so that they do not have to worry about staying within lines, being neat and tidy, or printing according to the rules. After all, practice in printing and practice in composing are two separate activities. Both will progress but will move much better when kept apart. If it seems unacceptable or risky to allow crude printing during the composing stage, stop to consider the horrendous task facing children if we asked them to print neatly, spell accurately, compose productively, and be creative all at the same time. Could you do it?

Once children begin to edit and publish their writing, the time has come to produce clean copies of written work. But once again, composing and printing are separate tasks. Rough copies are produced first, revised in conference, and then copied as neatly as possible.

Printing aids and dictionaries

Once they have gained experience in writing and sounding out, children learn to look not only for human aid but to printed sources of help as well. Books, experience charts, special aids around the classroom all become models of spelling for children. If most of the children plan to write about a special event or topic, the entire class may participate by calling out beach-, fire-station-, or Christmas-themed words. The blackboard will be filled with these special words to be used as reminders while children write. While copying such words or sentences from the board, some of the children will engage in the same descriptive monologue their teacher modeled while writing. As a result, their knowledge of spelling and sounding out is reinforced by several senses. They see, say, hear, and feel the letters, words, and sounds as they proceed.

Once children shift to more formal spelling and composing, their dictionary becomes a further model of spelling for them. Like a rite of passage, receiving a personal dictionary marks an important step forward in the children's development and is perceived as such by most. Seeing one of their peers graduate to a personal dictionary becomes an incentive to shift to more independent writing for many. The dictionaries provide spelling words and extra space to add further words of the child's choice as s/he progresses. The dictionary is simply an exercise book with a list of commonly used words arranged in alphabetical order on individual pages, with lots of space for further additions. Having watched their teacher consult a standard dictionary, children will often turn to the right page to find or add a word before they ask for help. They are developing independence and the type of questioning that asks for confirmation of their own hypotheses – "Does that take a capital letter?" "Does *hammer* have two *m*'s?" "Does that begin with a *d* or a *t*?"

These printed aids to spelling and writing merely reinforce the children's own spelling development. The intensity with which they focus upon inventing their own spelling as they evolve their writing can not be equalled by any external input. But accurate models of written language aid the process of self-programming.

What do you do when children are slow?

Spelling, writing, and printing present teachers with the opportunity to track each child's move from gross processing to fine discrimination. But it still took us some time to stop worrying about individual children. When Christine entered school, she was slow to respond to lessons; she lacked confidence, and she had a pronounced stutter. Her reading developed slowly and her written work was full of letter reversals, right-to-left progressions, omissions of letters, and over-the-line printing. So we worried about her progress until one day she announced, "I like to read, because I do it *so well!*" With that we relaxed. Sure enough, Christine progressed slowly but steadily on all fronts. Her reading became more fluent and accurate, reversals diminished and then disappeared, and her printing improved. She definitely was not dyslexic, but her early work only roughly approximated standard spelling and printing. Observing her progress was somewhat of a turning point for us. We learned to trust in face of strong evidence to the contrary. Christine also taught us that if a child whose abilities seemed so limited at first could feel confident about her skills and then proceed to merit that confidence, surely instruction was moving in the right direction. Her confidence never flagged and the added bonus to shore up our confidence was that when she read, Christine did not stutter!

Peter will amble into class, take his time getting settled, spend twice as long as anyone else to get ready to do anything, and sit through the entire writing workshop producing no more than his name and perhaps a letter or two. Cajoling and pushing only got him and the teacher upset and irritable. With Peter and children like him we have found that it doesn't help to nag or scold. Once we make it clear that it is his responsibility to produce the required amount of work, then it is also up to him to get the work done. If he chooses to sit through center time dawdling at his writing, that is his option. If he stays late to finish up his work, again, it is his option. Each day, by one means or another, Peter gets his work done. If we nagged, scolded, or tried too much to encourage or help, we would be taking away his initiative. What we want to do is empower children to work their way and if that way is slow, then slow it must be.

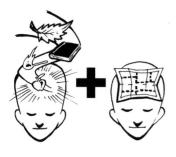

News time offers unlimited teaching opportunities

While printing news on the board the opportunities for on-the-spot mini-lessons are unlimited. Aside from "thinking aloud" as you print letters, words, and sentences, here are some examples of things you can bring to the children's attention through comments or side notes on the board:

- Sound-alike words – *to, too, two; there, their; see, sea*
- Words they confuse easily – *are* and *our*
- Silent letters of all types
- Compound words
- Spelling rules
- Capitalization
- Punctuation
- Spelling patterns – *read, tea, lead; look, took, food; why, what*
- Word endings – *ing, ed, tion*
- Differences between a hard and soft *c*
- Questions of style and coherence
- Paragraph unity
- Anything that seems interesting or worthy of note

Once you have pointed to certain features of print several times, the children will begin to call out what they notice about the words and phrases on the board. They are actively involved in watching for interesting features of print, spelling, or style.

How to foster spelling development

Since writing is such an important part of the day, children practice spelling quite intensively. Here are some ways to help them evolve their spelling:

- Model writing at every conceivable opportunity to show that talk written down is composed of letters and words.
- Talk about sounds and letters as you write.
- Show children how to print and spell their names and ask them to label all of their artwork and writing.
- Invite children to help you spell while you write messages or news.
- Encourage all efforts at spelling, even those that are incorrect as yet – "Good try," "That's almost it."

- Be sure to comment positively on generalizations that are good approximations though incorrect spelling, such as using *s* for soft *c, ee* when the word is spelled *ea*, confusing sound-alike words like *there-their, are-our*. It is important to reinforce those moves in the right direction to build children's knowledge and confidence.
- Leave each child as much time as necessary to move through the stages of invented spelling.
- Resist the temptation to give children the spelling of words while they are working in writing workshop. Let *them* build their knowledge gradually.
- Reassure children that they are moving in the right direction.
- Model accurate spelling at conference time and comment on every forward step the child has taken in that piece of work. Provide examples of sound-alike words as you write and invite children to do the same.
- Comment on rules and spelling patterns as you write for children or talk to them about their writing: "That needs a silent *e*." "This is one of the question words with the *wh*." "Two *o*'s sound like *u*."
- Acknowledge that in everyday speech many vowel sounds are omitted. "*Surprised* sure sounds like *sprised*, but the standard spelling has some extra letters." (Then say the word very distinctly.)

Fun projects that spark writing

To expand writing, offer extra opportunities and fun projects that invite yet more practice:

- Have a mailbox in your classroom and empty it once a week to distribute the mail. Children love to write to each other, to you, to their parents or grandparents.
- If you have a computer available, get a basic wordprocessing program like Writing Centre, ClarisWorks, or Once Upon a Time to give children the chance to compose and print out their messages on the computer.
- Tack up a fresh sheet of poster paper each day to serve as a bulletin board and invite children to use it any way they want. Begin by putting down a message or funny quip and then stand back to let the children do their own writing. You will

find that everyone gets in on the fun, even those who are still babbling in print.

- Invite children to create a "Rainy Day Book" to talk about all the things they can do when they have to stay inside.
- Cut out different shapes of paper and staple them into books to be used for special stories – a castle for fairy tales, a chick for the report on chick hatching, a pumpkin for Halloween stories.
- Encourage children to use the blackboard to draw and write.
- Make an old typewriter available for the children's use.

"Feeling" the letters

Since consonants are first to emerge in children's efforts at spelling and sounding out, one effective way to create greater awareness of letters is to make children aware of the feel of consonants as they say them. When you enunciate clearly and emphatically, letters like *m, l, p, t* produce very definite sensations. Lips, tongue, teeth, and palate actively form these consonants, and when you watch children who are concentrating with all their being on "sounding out" a word, you will notice their mouths working energetically.

Though "sounding out" is the standard way of talking about working with letter-sound correspondences, when it comes to spelling, the suggestion of "feeling" the letters in the mouth makes a great deal of sense. Somehow, touching of lips for an *m* or the tongue touching the palate for an *l* make sounds more concrete and easy to discern. Talking about the *th* sound in terms of having the tongue peek out between the teeth is much more memorable than any other drill we ever tried.

Asking the children what a word feels like in the mouth produces some very intense efforts at working out spellings. The approach has the added benefit of inviting careful and precise diction.

With a bit of practice you may even be able to work the more distinct vowels into the pattern of feeling the sound. Since an *o* can be produced by forming the mouth into a round, *o*-shaped opening, that can be a good place to start.

Have fun with encouraging children "to feel the words" and watch them be creative. But do keep in mind that with their acute hearing, children will still be guided by the actual sounds of spoken language they hear, not by our idealized version based on our knowledge of spelling.

Adapting Teaching to the Children's Way of Learning

5

If you think of the countless learning tasks you have accomplished during your lifetime, chances are that the vast majority of them moved from whole jobs to a discrimination of skills, and from initial gross performance of the entire task to greater refinement. You learned to talk by talking, walk by walking, drive by driving, and cook by cooking. Try to think of learning that moved from the introduction of isolated skills and a requirement to perfect those skills before you were allowed to move on, and you come up with school or other institutional learning, such as reading, math, playing the piano. Now compare the efforts, feelings, and outcomes of the two types of learning and ask yourself how much of the carefully structured school learning you actually integrated, still remember, and use compared to the learning you accomplished by *doing* the job to be learned. Imagine also what it would be like to be required to learn cooking by mastering the skills of stirring in an empty pot, handling knives without anything to cut or scrape, or being asked to classify accurately each move that goes into riding a bicycle or driving a car before being allowed to use those vehicles. Would you have persisted in learning and would that type of practice or knowledge have helped your performance?

You may argue that the skills you learned on your own were not very complex. But speaking a language certainly is, and in the not-too-distant past virtually all crafts and skills were learned through apprenticeships. Craftsmen, artists, lawyers, merchants, nurses all learned on the job. They learned the attitudes, social behaviors, ethics, and customs as well as the skills they needed. Looking at the

cathedrals, works of art, or fine furniture of Europe, or reading the poetry and scholarly works of the past can hardly suggest that such learning was ineffective. The young apprentices moved in an environment of real work, gradually acquiring and then refining the skills they needed to become journeymen and then masters.

The whole range of research – from how the brain works and constructs knowledge to emotional and multiple intelligences – affirms that that kind of reality-based learning flows effectively, often effortlessly, and has greater staying power than the very best drill-for-skill education has to offer. The effectiveness rests on personal involvement, hands-on learning, and the absorption of attitudes and values from models and the entire setting of the work. Complex skills and abstract principles are internalized in the context of meaningful interactions that affirm the learners' willingness and ability to learn.

To move closer to our own topic, think of the countless children who learn to read and write at home. Often they are the ones who become avid readers and excellent spellers and writers. We have found that if we make reading and writing materials as readily available in the classroom as talking is at home, children will learn to read by reading, to write by writing, and to spell by spelling. In fact, they not only learn the requisite skills but gain experience in the full range of uses of print and develop highly positive attitudes toward reading and writing. When the learners are allowed to let their own brain determine how to go about doing a job, learning moves along more smoothly and with less stress, and self-programming makes the brain function very effectively.

Those convinced that children must learn skills *before* they can read have challenged us many times. "How can you learn to read by reading when you don't know how?" The answer lies in proceeding the same way parents do in the home, immersing the child in language and basing all teaching of reading and writing on communication meaningful to the child. After all, children know a great deal about language and about the world around them. If you build on that knowledge instead of proceeding as though written language were something totally new, they will readily absorb information about print. Their *right* – holistic-receptive – brain comes into play when learning to read by reading. But the *left* – feature-analyzer – brain is there to give full support as details of print come in for discussion and use in writing.

However, we too had our doubts and worries at the start and only gradually shifted to learning to read by reading. Once we had satisfied ourselves that no matter what the teacher did, children still tried to learn their own way, we decided that learning would be most effective if we built on *their ways* of learning and adapted the effective home-teaching-learning to school. The three principal ways in which parents teach are:

- *Modeling* (demonstrating) the behaviors children are expected to learn – talking, listening, getting along
- Allowing children to *practice* to their hearts' content
- Providing *feedback* that acknowledges the meaning of what the child has said and expands the as-yet-imperfect language into correct form

At first it was quite a challenge to adapt modeling, practice, and feedback to teaching thirty or more children without losing control of the class or abandoning standards of performance. We found that, unlike parents who seem to know intuitively how to teach language, we needed to proceed gradually and to try out what worked. All along the way we observed the children closely to see how they responded to our modeling and feedback. Their positive reactions and productive learning – more than anything else – have shored up our confidence about the soundness of teaching the learners' way. In the meantime, our own work was confirmed and reinforced, first by other researchers who referred to language learning as a basis and closely observed learners (Harste et al. 1984) and then by the burgeoning research on how the brain works. Not surprisingly, the effective language teaching by parents in the home closely fits normal brain functioning as described by researchers (see chapter 1). They emphasize the importance of setting learning into a meaningful context, giving learners every opportunity to practice actively, and creating a learning environment that is non-threatening. Learning by imitating models definitely is part of brain-based learning. But in school, as at home, learning involves more than academic skills and children respond well to all kinds of modeling.

Modeling social behaviors

The truth of the old saying that children do as you do and not as you say has certainly been borne out by our observations. If we model calm, cheerful behavior and meet the minor and not-so-minor crises

**Children learn
from models**

in the classroom with a relaxed, matter-of-fact manner and quiet voice, children pick up on such modeling. The tensions and anxieties of entering school, facing new people and unfamiliar tasks, ease quickly when the teacher is calm and cheerful. Looking back at the end of the year we have a hard time remembering what behavior problems arose early on.

Kathy comes to the rescue

When Kathy observed that 2-year-old Shawna – visiting the first-grade classroom with her mother – had hurt herself and was crying, she quietly left her seat, picked up a box filled with colorful blocks to show to Shawna. Within seconds Shawna had dried her tears, and Kathy returned to her writing. Calm was restored without fuss and without either mother or teacher intervening. Kathy was simply following the teacher's model of interacting.

If you are just beginning your teaching career you may find it difficult to be a model of calm during your first year. But for your own sake as well as that of the children in your care it will pay to cultivate ways of being calm and relaxed. Take some time each day just for you, go for walks, listen to your favorite music, relax in a hot tub, follow your favorite hobby or sport, or find other ways that will physically relax you. The children in your care have had five or six years of practice reading the moods of adults and will readily spot the subtleties of your feelings. They will pick up tensions you feel and act them out. Your calm moods and cheerfulness will also be reflected.

While it is a good idea to state some of the rules of conduct early in the year, children don't necessarily understand or follow oral instructions. A far more effective way of inculcating the behaviors you want is to be consistent in demonstrating them in action. Listen attentively and acknowledge feelings. Comments like, "You are really excited this morning," "You are kind of scared," or "You really miss your mom," reassure the children that you see and hear them and know about their feelings. At the same time, if you maintain a matter-of-fact attitude you will not be giving undue attention to crying or unruly behaviors.

Modeling cooperation, helpfulness, and the sharing of interests enhance the positive non-threatening climate in the classroom. Children will emulate such behavior just as readily as they do our favorite hands-on-the-hip stance or tone of voice. They love to play teacher and their helpfulness (or lack of it) clearly mirrors what they perceive us to be doing. If you ever want to get a sense of how you come across to the children, just observe closely what they do and say when they play at being teacher. It can be very heartening to hear them mimic, "I know you will be interested in this book because it's about...." But particularly in the early days of our observations in class we were often chastened by the children's mimicry of our own inflexibility.

If the children behave in ways we find disruptive or unacceptable, we ask ourselves if there may be anything in our own behavior – raising our voices unduly, interrupting speakers, not listening carefully – that models such behavior for the children. Then we try to model consistently what it is we do want, be that quietness, attentiveness, cooperation, or enthusiasm.

Morning meeting is the perfect forum for modeling effective communication

At home, children are used to small gatherings and one-to-one interactions with adults. Coming into a classroom full of strangers and only one adult to share among them offers a whole new challenge. So in building the "climate of delight" Margaret makes modeling positive, effective communication her top priority from the beginning and throughout the year. Gathering the children around her for story time and personal sharing set the tone as she quietly talks to the children and listens attentively to what they are willing to share. The informality of sitting on the floor being free to interact with each other – in quiet voices – and to speak without first having to raise a hand to gain the floor give morning meeting the feel of a large family gathering. Feelings as well as information are shared, and as Margaret models sensitive, empathic responses when children voice their excitement, worry, or sadness about happenings at home or in the school, children soon emulate her ways and even the shyest among the students eventually come forth.

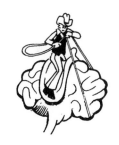

Modeling the art of conversation builds emotional intelligence

The calm and respect Margaret exudes as she listens and interacts with the children assures that morning meeting does not turn into a shouting match to gain attention. As the children perceive that what they have to say is important to the teacher and of interest to the

other children, they feel assured that they will be heard. On that basis, they learn to take turns, to use quiet voices as they make comments to each other, and to become attentive listeners like their teacher. The entire session is a powerful model of emotional intelligence in action.

Reflecting on the importance of open communication among the entire class, Margaret sees morning meeting as a way of teaching the children the art of conversation – an open give-and-take in sharing information. Modeling what it is she needs to inculcate, Margaret becomes totally absorbed in what the children say to her and to each other, making eye contact, turning toward the speaker, allowing her face to reflect the feelings that are implicit in what is said. Her inviting smile or leaning forward toward a speaker gives the clear signal, "I am ready to hear you fully." A gentle hand signal lets those eager to interrupt know that as soon as she is finished listening, she will give the next speaker her undivided attention.

At the same time, as in adult conversations, children are also free to turn to each other to have a quiet side conversation. Having established the need to use soft voices, children soon follow Margaret's example of speaking softly and listening attentively. There is an ebb and flow of interaction and, strange as it may seem, the very freedom to communicate freely and interact without the teacher controlling the children's movement, makes for excellent discipline and a climate of harmony. As morning meeting shifts into news time, children are ready to collaborate effectively to generate the news of the day and provide "help" to the teacher with spelling and editing. Academic learning and the development of emotional intelligence are growing together in harmony.

Becoming a model of learning

In the traditional classroom we model far more teaching behaviors than learning behaviors. We show that we know answers rather than how we find them. We talk more than we listen, and we present problems rather than solve them. To give children a chance to emulate learning behaviors we work at being learners in the classroom. Listening and observing closely are keys to learning. We continue to find that observing children closely and listening to learners attentively tell us more about what each child needs at a given point than prepared lesson plans or guide books. Talking with children conveys more than paper and pencil tests. The bonus is that young learners thrive on the genuine attention they receive and, in turn, develop their powers of listening and observing. They become quite adept at following what we model in the way of listening and attending.

The art of questioning to explore something more fully is best conveyed by genuine enquiry behaviors. All too often questions asked by teachers are pseudo-questions or tests. They already know the answer but want to find if the students know the answers too. Helping children with research projects, asking probing questions of visitors who are giving special demonstrations or talks, preparing for field trips, musing or thinking aloud, using the dictionary or encyclopedia to find answers, using the library, all help to demonstrate how we as adults question and explore. The bonus for us is that we continue to learn along with the children. We do, that is, if we genuinely look for further information. Working with children in conferences or during news time is perhaps the best model of enquiry behavior of them all. Children readily begin to question one another to elicit further information or detail that will enhance a story.

Trial and error is a highly important part of natural learning. We often learn more from our mistakes because they cause us to reconsider, to pause, and to try another approach. We make certain that the learners in our care observe that we, too, make mistakes, false starts, backtrack, reconsider a course of action, and correct or adjust an approach to a problem, all without worrying about having been wrong. Here again, a calm, matter-of-fact attitude toward "trying again" models persistence as well as trial-and-error learning. "Well, I guess that didn't work. Maybe we could try to put this together this way. Let's see what happens."

Modeling curiosity and discovery techniques pay genuine dividends to all concerned. We find that our own learning is enriched when we model discovery behaviors. Comments like, "I would like to find out more about that," "Maybe ... knows, let's ask her," "Let's check to see what we can find out in the library," demonstrate that we, too, are still eager to learn more and are curious about all kinds of topics. In all of these instances we make certain not to fake or exaggerate interest. (Children readily spot insincere behavior and learn to emulate that as well.)

Discussions of the relative merits of stories or the correctness of information model critical thinking. Our own comments and expressions of interest, doubt, or evaluation show children how to be active participants in their learning rather than passive receivers of knowledge handed down from on high. If we give thoughtful critiques of books or stories, children learn that we do not accept all print uncritically or with equal interest. Discussions of what sounds best or fits together well when working on writing projects suggests that editing is a natural part of composing. In order to encourage children to develop their own critical faculties, it is highly important to accept their ideas and opinions. No doubt you will remember how you felt when your literature teacher told you that your interpretation of a poem or short story was "wrong." So value all input.

Reading has many uses

Reading aloud is, of course, the most obvious way to model reading. Hamming it up adds fun and the children learn about intonation and fluent reading. But the principal aim is to demonstrate that reading is enjoyable, makes sense, and can be shared repeatedly. Instead of teaching reading skills in isolation, we are demonstrating that literacy is a desirable goal. Children who have not experienced the fun of reading at home may be hearing fluent reading and book language for the first time. Modeling fluent reading introduces story lines, conventions of poetry, and the language of books. The mysteries of unfamiliar expressions or uses of language add interest and excitement for the children.

Reading has as many uses as talking. We have come to see almost our entire teaching day as a continuous workshop in literacy. Just as parents at home accompany many activities with talk, so we take every opportunity to use written language as part of ongoing activities. Signs, labels, name tags, directions, recipes, newsletters, maps for field trips, letters to and from home or to pen pals, journals, diaries, research projects, film or picture captions, reminders to do things, experience charts, games, and dictionaries are among the many ways of weaving the use of written language into the activities of the day and demonstrating to the children that written language is as natural a part of everyday communication as speech. Their inner maps of reading expand day by day.

Integrating social studies and science

When we study Mexico or Holland, we compare Mexican or Dutch family life with ours and intersperse what we learn throughout the day. Children decide what they want to find out about these countries and gather materials to be placed in special centers. They may bring things from home, borrow books from the library, cut articles out of newspapers or magazines, and make costumes for the special ethnic lunch that culminates their study. As they move along, they read about these countries, write stories or poems, follow recipes at cooking time, and practice songs or dances to be performed at the special lunch. Science projects such as hatching chicks or growing beans are integrated in the same way. There is no special time set aside solely for science; instead the children gather research material, draw pictures, write about and discuss what is happening. Story time may be taken up by books about chicks or seeds, and during center time children inspect the eggs or chicks, measure the growth of the bean plants, and then record any new information they have gleaned.

Unison reading of books and stories lends itself well to modeling reading. During these sessions, as with story time, we model fluent reading, good intonation, and the art of predicting what comes next. Tracking what we read with a hand, pointer, or bookmark, we indicate that print is read from left to right and from the top of the page to the bottom.

No matter how many participate, story reading is for enjoyment and comprehension. (Decoding skills are best demonstrated at the time children need them in order to write or spell unfamiliar words.) Like adults, children respond well to literature that relates to their interests or experience. Our initial prompting – "Have you ever seen a dog like that?" "What would your mom say if you tried that at home?" "You have seen a big ship like that, haven't you?" – is quickly picked up, and the children's spontaneous comments or questions about the reading reveal their comprehension far better than answers to prepared questions about what Jane or Spot did and who said what.

Book time is a fine opportunity for us to model selecting and enjoying our own favorite reading material. Children are intrigued by our choices of reading material and will ask about them, try to decipher titles, or look at pictures of magazine articles. Interesting bits of information, a funny quip, or a beautiful poem reinforce the pleasant feeling of sharing reading with others. We are well past selling children short by attitudes or comments about not being ready for this or that reading material. Sharing quite advanced material can be deeply satisfying for all involved and certainly enhances the climate of cooperation in the classroom.

Daniel and the dinosaurs

On Wednesday, Daniel spends center time poring over his library book, *Prehistoric Monsters* (Hongkong: Mandarin Publishing, 1979). Though it is obviously intended for youngsters in the intermediate grades, Daniel is enjoying the pictures and works at deciphering their captions. Other children join him, and Daniel takes great pride in displaying his knowledge about ceratosaurus and other carnivorous monsters. He explains that the woolly mammoth is now extinct and readily finds information in the book to back up his statements. The fact that he cannot read most of the rest of the text does not detract from his enjoyment of the book or the learning he derives from his struggle with those interesting names.

Other children are sure to pick up on such interest and dinosaurs may become a theme for reading, writing, research, and discussion for a number of days.

The importance of reading is best conveyed by giving it prominence in the curriculum. We encourage children to order inexpensive books through a publisher's book club, and on the day the books arrive, everything else comes to a halt. That box of personal treasures is more exciting and important than any other learning. Reading becomes truly interactive as everyone shares stories, riddles, or pictures. Spontaneity, flexibility, and love of reading become part of learning without us saying anything about motivation, attitudes, or attention spans. The excitement of reading new stories teaches the joys of literacy far better than the best lessons in phonics or guided reading. The interest and enthusiasm of teacher and peers are excellent models, especially for children who have no books at home.

Writing and spelling lend themselves well to modeling

Converting spoken messages that the children dictate into print is one of the first ways we model writing. Discussions of the news culminate in sentence-writing at the blackboard. Captions for the children's pictures, language experience charts of special events, and messages of various kinds are ways in which we model writing, printing, and spelling from the beginning of kindergarten. As with reading, we do not worry whether the children are ready to write as yet but simply show how we are converting talk into print.

Thinking aloud is an easy way to model composing and editing: "I wonder what would be the best way to start our story?" "Maybe we could put these two sentences together to make this sound more interesting." "Oh, now that we have put these sentences together we don't need a period here. Let me take that out." Such a monologue generally turns into a discussion and idea exchange as the children voice their opinions on what should be included and how the text can be revised.

In the writing workshop children will be guided by many models. At first the quieter children benefit from listening to the lively exchange of ideas before everyone settles down to write. David's "I watched wrestling on TV last night and then my dad and I wrestled," produces four different pictures and sentences about watching wrestling. That same morning several children decide to elaborate on their plans for Thanksgiving – the news-time topic – while Chris opts for the fairy tale opening he heard during story time: "Once upon a time there was a prince and..." Sharing writing, using books and reference materials, learning poems, stories, and songs all act as models for the children's writing. But most important of all is the model of genuine enquiry behavior as you and the children ask the young authors to tell you more, to clarify what happened, and to expand on how they felt.

Spelling lends itself well to a descriptive monologue, but don't overdo it. Though initially it helps to intone every letter as you put it on the board – t-o-d-a-y, *today* – the children will soon want to chime in, and after a while only the more difficult or interesting words need oral spelling or commentary. Once you have modeled a running commentary on compound words, periods at the end of sentences, sound-alike words, and apostrophes, the children will take over and will call out, "There's a silent letter in *wrestling*," "We've got two kinds of *to* on the board – *two* and *to*," "*Thanksgiving* is a compound word."

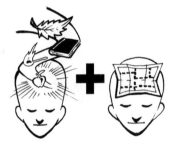

Models of writing and accurate spelling serve as useful guides, but just as the baby at home responds with babbling and then one-word utterances to Mommy's or Daddy's talking, so young spellers use the accurate models as their point of departure and evolve their own spelling from there. If the children fail to use the readily available models around the classroom and omit vowels from much of their early writing – producing *rd* instead of *red, ml* instead of *mail* – do not worry, but recognize such work as an early spelling stage and another example of levels of knowing. So, *hang in there* and watch the next stages emerge.

Models are many and varied

At the beginning of school, the teacher will be the children's principal model. But visitors, parent helpers, the custodian, anyone who comes into the classroom will read or write to and with the children. We – as female teachers – make sure that male visitors read and talk with the children about books and stories as often as possible to make it clear that men, too, are avid readers. During years when a lot of our parents are non-English speakers we encourage them to come in to help in class with anything they feel they want to do – artwork, printing, or making things. Models don't have to be fluent as yet. In fact, it helps to give children an opportunity to see that adults, too, are still learning.

Peer modeling evolves as naturally as it does at home. Children watch and copy each other and often find it easier to learn from a peer than from an adult. We encourage interaction and sharing and the children become helpful rather than competitive. Observing others participate in oral reading, spelling, special projects, or the production of plays encourages more timid children to take part as well. The power of such modeling revealed itself when a young reader gave a perfect rendition of the British accent his reading buddy, Sarah, had modeled when reading to him.

Materials in the classroom become models as well. Our classrooms are well stocked with books of all sizes and descriptions. Walls are adorned with experience charts, the children's artwork, and handy reference charts about colors, numbers, letters, or important words the children may need on a given day. When children read as widely as possible, they gain confidence and proficiency not only in reading, but in writing as well. In their research projects about whales, eagles, or hockey they may begin by copying information and picture captions from the reference books, but gradually they turn to paraphrasing and then independent composition. Those interested in sports at times mimic the reportorial style of sportscasters. Walt Disney material or fairy tales become models for creative fantasy writing and, with a bit of encouragement, the children begin to create their own poetry, first staying close to the models they have read or heard, but becoming ever more creative in the development of their own style.

Along with style, critical abilities evolve in the classroom where many models of writing are freely available. The rich vocabulary and syntax of good children's literature and the organized

*Models are many and
varied*

*In an environment largely
dominated by women, it
becomes important to have
men model reading for the
children. Most men will enter
into the job with joy and
verve, leaving no doubt in the
children's minds that males
enjoy and use reading.*

structures of expository prose in reference texts enrich the children's
speaking and thinking skills. Children will notice and comment
upon the stilted style and impoverished content of some of the basal
readers and generally opt for more advanced reading material at
choosing time.

Attitudes, interests, and values are learned – not taught

English teachers will tell you that their goals are to inculcate an
appreciation of literature and the ability to write and speak
coherently. As reading teachers we share those goals and are well
aware of the difficulties of making them explicit and desirable to
young students. At home, children absorb attitudes and values
from those around them. Most of what they learn remains implicit
but nonetheless powerful and pervasive. As we model reading and
writing and show our attitudes and feelings freely in our
interactions with the young learners in our classes, we find that the
same absorption of implicit values and attitudes works at school.
Children perceive and internalize our enthusiasm for books, stories,
poems, writing, and learning new things. They absorb courtesy,
cooperation, and interactive learning the same way.

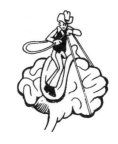

Holidays; Hoildays, Holidays
Long holidays
Short holidays
Big fat loud holidays
Little skinny quiet holidays
Those are just a few.
Thankful holidays
Giving holidays
Great big happy holidays
Tinny small sad holidays
Crying holidays too.
Old holidays
New holidays
Don't forget midd' holidays
Last of all, best of all
I like chankuh.

Poetry

Poetry fashioned after a model stimulates writing and, later on, forays into more individual poetry.

Once children have developed a liking for this type of imaginative work, their fantasy provides the necessary input for creative writing.

Grade-two work builds on these early foundations. At school and at home, young poets delight in sharing their work with an appreciative audience.

The Snake Pome.

A snake went behind me
A snake went in frant of me
I think hes gona eat me
I think hes gona eat me
If only I had an egg
I'm sure he would go for it
instead of me me me.
Maybe he would go for the egg
and maybe he would go for me
instead of the egg.
(I just made it up.)

Illustrated and written
by Shelly Young.

Following a model is more than copying

If all this modeling sounds like just so much copying without any effort on the part of the followers, remember that the most difficult learning children accomplish – learning their mother tongue – is based on listening to others talk, picking out familiar patterns, and imitating those parts that are manageable at the time. Think of your own efforts at learning a foreign language and the difficulties you may have had in segmenting that flow of language you heard into recognizable words. Recall how hard it was to get your tongue around sounds that flow freely from even a 4-year-old French or Chinese child. Could you remember or work out how to spell words? Did it help to listen to native speakers and to have lots of examples of easy-to-read texts at the start? Did you begin your writing and speaking by following closely whatever examples you had? Did you move on from there to more independent work? Children certainly do. Time and again we observe that children's use of models – spoken or written – is their first step toward evolving their own ways of using print. Based on the models they find around the classroom and at home, they move through definite stages of reading, writing, and spelling. Once you learn to recognize these stages and develop the trust that children will indeed move onward and upward, modeling will seem as natural in class as it is at home.

Practice may make perfect, but the question becomes, practice in what and for what? In sports, coaches insist on daily workouts. Music requires sustained practice if the learner is to become proficient. But the two have traditionally used different approaches to practice. In sports, young athletes actually play ball, swim, sprint, or do gymnastics, working on warm-ups, strength-building, and the polishing of skills in the context of the overall activities. In music, much practice is devoted to working with scales and the theory of music. Traditionally, far less time has been devoted to playing or enjoying music. To be sure, students of the piano or violin learn to play, but if restricted to too much detail work they may not develop the enthusiasm or versatility to infuse their performance with life or joy. Voluntary practice for the sheer joy of it, so often seen in sports, may be confined to a small minority of music students. Yet popular music and dancing stir as much enthusiasm as sports. Could the difference lie in the way we require

Practice makes perfect

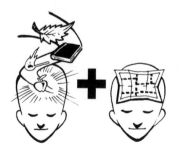

learners to practice? Sports begin with the total activity and make the polishing of component skills subservient to it. When music begins with perfecting the components, the parts-to-whole approach may not engender the enthusiasm needed for consistent practice. In fact, the approach may block learners from progressing to enjoyment, voluntary practice, and proficiency. Unfortunately, reading and writing have long been in the parts-to-whole category. Children who work at phonics drills, worksheets, and lists of sight words, may fail to capture the excitement of reading and creating their own writing that urges them on.

Once we turned to modeling fluent reading, and skill building became a support system, practice expanded tremendously. Story time introduced children to written language, and unison reading invited one and all to participate. With book time established as part of each school day, children immediately began to practice handling books and thinking in terms of reading. Though at the outset there may have been some picture reading and pretend reading, children soon shifted to memory reading and from there to actually deciphering familiar – and then unfamiliar – text. We have come to value these early global ways of practicing as the very foundation of literacy. This kind of practice fuels that all-important motivation for working on upgrading reading skills and removes the anxiety or frustration that can be part of trying to learn letters and their sounds.

Since all books, games, and reading materials in our classroom are freely available to children, they readily choose reading and reading games at choosing time and abandon toys or manipulative games in favor of reading. Taking a look around the first-grade room as early in the year as October, we may find more than a third of the students settled down to independent reading with books of their choice. Given the freedom to choose, children practice what they need or want at each stage of development and abandon as boring that which no longer serves them.

Writing, spelling, and printing, too, are practiced more intensively and effectively because children are working on producing their own messages and much of writing is voluntary. During news sharing time all of the children participate, eagerly suggesting sentences and spelling.

Voluntary or self-initiated practice leads to a number of crucial benefits. Attention spans expand and production increases tremendously. Mistakes or false starts are steps to further learning rather than impediments. Since they are interested in their own projects, children will try again, find a different approach, or muse about new ways of solving a problem when they have come to an impasse. The fact that we do not set time limits for the completion of child-initiated projects allows for their full development.

In addition to skills, confidence is built as a result of extended practice. The importance of confidence and its transfer value was brought home to us when Candace overcame her struggles and doubts about reading by dint of confidence gained on the ski slope. On Friday she was still struggling with reading and voicing her frustration about being unable to read unfamiliar words or stories. The following Monday she returned to school aglow with her ability to ski and do it well. That feeling of success carried over to her reading. She simply picked up a book and began to read! She had broken out of the cocoon of the pupa stage and all the knowledge she had gathered over the previous weeks converged to let her read.

The kinds of voluntary practice that children choose also become valuable indicators of their needs and progress. Without interfering in their activities we note who is playing what games, reading books, writing, drawing, or using the blackboard. Trust in a child's ability or desire to progress maybe taxed at times, but the sudden spurt forward often comes after such sustained voluntary practice. A child who has read the same book or story twenty or thirty times will suddenly come up and say, "Today I want to read a new book." More often than not, from that day forward the child progresses rapidly. Through lengthy practice with the same material, skills, confidence, and language patterns were internalized to a point where the *learner* knew that the time had come to move on.

Independence guides voluntary practice

Voluntary practice flourishes because the children are accustomed to doing independent work. Beginning on day one of class we shift responsibility for initiating work to the children. At first there are small jobs such as tidying their desks, picking up after themselves during center time, and getting books for themselves for book time. But as the year progresses the children initiate more and more of their learning. They know that during center time they are free to

pick any language arts material or activity they choose. They learn to turn on tape recorders, switch on viewing screens for stories-in-pictures, and ask permission to go to the school library to get books or research material for a project. Within the guidelines we have established at the beginning of the year, we leave children free to move about the classroom, use the blackboard or any other aid available, and trust that the children will be careful not to damage equipment or books. The cooperative climate definitely pays off, and children freely help one another to set up easels, find books and art materials.

Visitors to our classroom note the self-reliant ways of the children. The day before Thanksgiving, Sandy Sherman, the librarian, came in with a complaint. "I am redundant!" he said with a look of consternation on his face. "I sent your kids into the computer room and by the time I got there, all of them were busy. They turned on the equipment and simply got going on their own!"

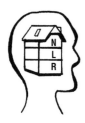

As we observe children at work, we find that practice time has expanded to hours. More important, the quality of practice has improved dramatically. The animation with which children practice literacy skills rivals that of sports fans and music lovers. Practice has become far more than rote repetition or mere time on task. It is the practical application of useful, enjoyable reading and writing on topics of the children's own choosing. In that context, practice does indeed make perfect.

Feedback confirms and expands learning

Feedback completes the three-way system of learning from models. Practice can itself become part of feedback. Some things work, others don't. Checking your work against a dictionary can serve as a form of feedback. But in school, the teacher becomes a highly important source of feedback that extends well beyond the simple correction of errors or acknowledgment of right answers.

A look at transcripts of our early observations reveals that the children did not necessarily absorb what we intended to teach. The taped discussions of children trying to answer questions about reading passages were particularly striking.

(Question on blackboard: Why did John have to get up?)

TRACY: (whispering) *... get up.. Why did John have to get up?*

JANICE: *...have . . . have* (she is looking for a sentence that answers the question in her basal reader)

TRACY: *He had to get up to go to school.*

JANICE: No. *You can't have* had *there cause that's not what Mrs. Reinhard said.*

TRACY: *John had to go to school. Had, yes.*

GORDON: *Did the teacher say we could use* he? *He had? Well, if it's wrong it won't be my fault.*

The children obviously had the idea that what counted was to answer exactly as the teacher had put it during earlier oral practice. Content, their own knowledge, variety of style, or correctness of their own perception or opinion did not seem to count. Errors of form received the focus of attention rather than content or communication. Predictably, there was little enthusiasm for writing. The children's work improved in accuracy but they learned little about composing written messages and using print to communicate.

Comparing our own findings with transcripts of young children's language learning revealed that feedback given by parents is quite different from what we were doing in school. When responding to the baby's efforts at talking, the focus of the parents rests squarely on meaning. In addition, parents take the whole situation into account and assume that the baby intends to convey a complete message. The excited shout, "Dadda, dadda!" when Daddy is not in view prompts Mommy to come to the window to have her confirm, "You're right: Daddy is coming home." If little Bobby is rushing up to Daddy waving a bleeding finger wailing, "Hurt, hurt!" Daddy is unlikely to respond, "Say that in a complete sentence." Chances are he will scoop Bobby into his arms, saying, "Oh dear, you got hurt." In each case the feedback given by parents responds to the content of the message and at the same time expands the incomplete form into a complete sentence. The exchange is positive and invites the child to expand not only the content but the form of the communication as well.

Since parents obviously achieve good results with this kind of feedback, we have shifted more and more to giving feedback that acknowledges what the children are saying (or intending to convey) and helping them to upgrade their early inaccurate work by

expanding it. Individual writing conferences are prime examples of such focus on content. In discussing the children's writing, we place the greatest emphasis on the message they wish to convey. Our questions address themselves to the content and are intended to help the writer expand it further. Corrections of spelling, grammar, style, or layout take second place and become important only as writing is readied for publication. The children learn quite clearly that their messages are valued and of interest to others. At the same time they begin to perceive that if outsiders are to be able to read such writing, then it must become more accurate in spelling and overall format. As in learning to talk at home, the desire to be understood becomes the motivator to upgrade form as well as content.

Examples of feedback teacher may provide in response to children's work

CHILD: looks at picture, reads: *"We play ball."*

Book: *We play catch.*

TEACHER: *Good reading! We play catch.*

Child's spelling shows *BLAK BARE*

TEACHER: *That's exactly what* bear *sounds like. You have all the right letters. That* E *tells that* A *to say its name, and if we turn the two letters around we have standard spelling.* Blak *sounds right too; we just need an extra* C.

CHILD: writes caption under drawing: *THIS IS PUK*, then reads, *This is my pumpkin.*

TEACHER: *It sure is! That is a beautiful picture of your pumpkin.* (May write correct form under child's version if child asks for standard spelling.)

In using expanded feedback remember that just as at home, a child may need to receive the same feedback many times before internalizing it. As you insert missing punctuation or letters for the umpteenth time, trust that the desire to become more accurate is there and will show itself in time. When the children continue to use immature forms of grammar, simply respond as a parent would at home and observe that eventually the unorthodox forms of grammar disappear.

A positive way of giving oral feedback

CHILD: *Mrs. Reinhard, we goed to the circus last night!*

MARG: *You went to the circus; how exciting!*

CHILD: *I don't have no crayons.*

MARG: *Oh dear, you have no crayons today. Take another look.*

CHILD: *I brung my lunch today.*

MARG: *Good for you. You brought your lunch.*

When giving feedback for reading, we have abandoned our practice of requiring word-for-word accuracy in the children's oral reading and keep the focus on meaning instead. We make no comment about substitutions, omissions, or rearrangement of word order, secure in the knowledge that fluent reading is a matter of overall meaning more than the precise reproduction of words. If too much is missed, we reread a passage, provide a missing word, or add some explanatory comments to elucidate what a word might mean.

Reading for meaning

BOOK: *There is my hat.*

MARKO: *This is my hat.*

BOOK: *There is my belt.*

MARKO: *This is my belt.*

(No comment needed)

Using picture cues to aid reading

BOOK: *Would you rather have supper in a castle?*

JAMIE: *Would you rather have dinner in a castle?*

MARG: (No comment)

BOOK: *Or tea on the river?*

JAMIE: *Or tea on the boat?*

MARG: *Or tea on the river ... hmmm.*

Commenting in a matter-of-fact voice, "That doesn't make sense," often produces spontaneous self-correction as the child stops to look back at the lines just read, but personal knowledge or lack of it often takes precedence over feedback and children will not correct their rendition.

BOOK: *Under the old elm tree*

CHILD: *Under the old oak tree*

MARG: *Hmmm... under the old elm tree*

CHILD: (No response)

(Several other children read oak tree and fail to respond to feedback. They know about oaks but not about elms.)

If such lack of accuracy seems to invite sloppy habits or absence of attention to detail, you will note, as we have many times, that once the children progress to fluent reading they will, in fact, correct you if you are making minor errors in your reading.

Feedback children give to their teacher

BOOK: *The little, little bird…*

MARG: *The little bird…*

MANDY: *The little, little bird*

MARG: *The little, little bird*

(Modeling herself after her teacher, Mandy gives the expanded feedback in a quiet, matter-of-fact voice.)

Along similar lines, if we encourage children to discuss their reading materials – instead of going over guided reading questions – they provide us with feedback about their reactions to stories, their own experience, and how it relates to their reading. These spontaneous reactions often give us the chance to build on the children's interests or encourage research projects. They also tell us very clearly that children are reading for meaning and are understanding the stories they hear or read.

Spelling lends itself particularly well to positive and expanded feedback. Children feel free to help with spelling at the blackboard because there is no penalty for wrong guesses. If they suggest *u* as the vowel for spelling *new*, we comment, "It sure sounds like *u*, but here we need *e* and *w* to spell *new*."

If the children supply *c* and *r* for *camera*, we put down these letters and leave spaces to fill in the rest. The fact that some letters are missing does not detract from the right answers provided. We simply expand on what is provided and comment positively on guesses that are good approximations. The message children get from such feedback is that their ideas have merit and, if possible, will be incorporated. Imagine the feelings stirred in a young child who correctly suggested *r* as part of *camera*, had it rejected (on the unstated ground that something else comes first), and then saw that *r* appear on the board a minute later. Children will focus on what they know and on what they perceive to be important. Sequence may not be on their mind at the time.

During news time with its focus on communication, everyone has a chance to make suggestions regardless of sequence. Feedback becomes a matter of sorting, pulling together, and consolidating information offered by the children. Once their contributions have been acknowledged, children don't mind having them edited, shifted to another place, or even omitted. They are quite open to suggestions but they also learn to disagree with the teacher on matters of style or preference. They do so in the same conversational way they have observed the teacher use when she is commenting on their work.

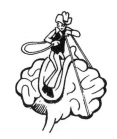

Jesse edits the newsletter

MARG: *What shall we put on the board as our news for today?*

LISA: *Next week will be Thanksgiving.*

MARG: *That's a good idea.* (Writes sentence on board with children's help in spelling words) *What else shall we say?*

MANDY: *Everybody will be eating turkey.*

MARG: *Is that really true?*

KIDS: *Yeah, everybody!*

MARG: *I don't know. It seems to me some people won't eat turkey.*

HEATHER: *We could say, "Some people will be eating turkey."*

MARG: *Right. How does that sound?*

KIDS: *Yeah.*

MARG: (Writes sentence on board) *Can you think of anything else?*

TIM: *I'm going to visit my granny.*

KIDS: *Me too. I'm visiting my uncle. My aunt is coming over.*

MARG: *Is everybody going visiting?*

KIDS: *No, just some people.*

MARG: *O.K. Shall we put, "Some people will be visiting their families."*

KIDS: *Yeah, not everybody.*

MARG: *But then we'll have* some *at the beginning again. I don't think that sounds too good. I wouldn't use that again.*

JESSE: *I would. Sounds fine to me.*

After some debate Jesse's view prevailed and the sentences on the board that morning read: *Next week will be Thanksgiving. Some people will be eating turkey. Some people will be visiting their families.*

Building on strengths and offering expanded feedback eliminates the negativity attached to evaluation that we noted during our early research. Children seemed far more anxious about their mistakes. Now they generally accept feedback and corrections without signs of upset or anxiety. They are quite sure that we are interested in their answers (not in their ability to second guess ours). As a result they are open to expand their learning and to engage in trial-and-error explorations of unfamiliar tasks. Overall achievement and quality of work have actually improved rather than declined under this gentle way of dealing with errors.

To give feedback you have to be a good observer

Feedback has the further benefit of focusing attention squarely on the children and what they are doing at the time. If Teresa is not speaking up but is moving her lips, you encourage her to "say it out loud." If David hesitates over reading a child's name he has just drawn out of the stack of name cards, you note his looking around, wait, ask him to look at the beginning letter, and watch him beam with pride as he comes up with the right answer. If at the same time you notice that the other children are eager to help David out, you hold them in check without dampening their enthusiasm with a quiet, "Just a minute. Give David a chance. He is thinking about it." They not only respect that request but join the rejoicing about David's success. Children thrive on the close attention you give them and since you are modeling careful listening and attending all day long, they too become better listeners.

Giving feedback that acknowledges and expands the children's work shifts the focus away from teaching outcomes – right or wrong answers – to observing and noting children's behaviors. In fact, you become a detective or researcher in your class, and the tedium of counting mistakes or drilling children in the use of particles of speech is converted into absorbing fact finding that will hold your interest. You also signal to the children that you are keenly interested in them and their work. We find that as our observation skills sharpen, we are rewarded by seeing clearly how individual children grow.

Timing is a crucial element if feedback is to be effective

Timing and a light touch are the keys to success in giving feedback. Parents give expanded feedback right at the moment the child is acting or talking. In class we try to do the same, capturing the moment when a child is genuinely interested in a topic or needs an answer or explanation. As long as the suggestions remain just casual comments rather than disguised requests, children will often respond with interest or even enthusiasm to comments like: "That might make a fun play," "Do you want to take a look in the library to see what else you can find about that?" or "How are we going to get Weenie Witch's witch costume off and turn her into a fairy right in the middle of the play?" (They solved that problem all by themselves.)

In our early observations we noted that when we were too concerned with the right/wrong answers the children were giving, we tended to move too quickly from one child to the next. Often we would see a child silently mouthing what appeared to be the right answer just after the teacher had turned to the next child with, "What kind of letter do we need here?" or "Is this a long or short *a*?" Now we make certain that children have ample time to give a response when we ask questions. At the same time, we do not linger too long and thereby put the child on the spot. The answer is to develop a feel for how long to wait, when to supply an answer, and when to curb the overly eager responders to give a more timid child the opportunity to give a response.

These "manuscripts" are included for you to have a quiet chuckle over. Adrian was reading at gr. 4 level according to tests (adult level as far as I could see!) but ~~however~~ socially, emotionally & physically he was no more than a 3 year old — a fascinating child.

Careful observations note strengths and help the teacher trust the learner to grow

A teacher sent this note together with the test results and examples of a young boy's work. The teacher, who was using the learners' way, readily noted the discrepancy between measured levels of performance and actual ability. She also recognized that a child of 6 may be an outstanding reader but still function at a much lower level in motor skills, writing, and social development.

Feb 11 -Jeff
feb 12 Tracy

But He
wos not
like The

and He
can't fix
himself

other

Docter

He kept
on falling
down

He is
geting
hurt.

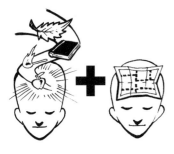

Proper timing captures those important teachable moments when learners are truly open to receive and integrate information. When reading an interesting story the children's focus is on meaning, and waiting too long to supply an unfamiliar word would interrupt the flow of the story. Within the context of a story children readily pick up such difficult words as *rhinoceros, proclamation,* or *beautiful*. When writing, though also concerned with meaning, the children need the sounds of letters and their combinations in order to put their messages on paper. As they try to work out how *yesterday* or *beautiful* might be spelled, they are very open to on-the-spot phonics or spelling lessons.

Working with third-graders, one teacher we know finds that timing can become the main force in beginning or concluding projects. As soon as interest shows signs of flagging, she shifts, ends a project, or puts it aside for the moment. Because children know that reports or research jobs won't necessarily be carried to the bitter end, they are eager to try new assignments and will show remarkable attention spans when searching for or compiling information on subjects of interest to them: their school, sports, their family, or special customs connected with different cultures or seasons. Timing your suggestions to build on the children's concerns can be the key to powerful learning for children just as it is for adults.

Timing demands flexibility

If timing and taking your cues from children are to function well, you will have to be willing to alter your plans and teaching schedules to fit the children. Though there are definite routines and predictable daily work periods, neither the timetable nor the lesson of the day are cast in stone. The arrival of an unexpected visitor, some exciting event at school or at home, the chicks beginning to hatch, an invitation to come to an interesting store, or a field trip may all occasion shifts in the daily routine that benefit everyone. The children will have their full attention riveted on the newcomer, the discussions, or plans that suddenly arise. If you watch closely you may note the greatest strides forward for some children at such unusual times. As even timid children forget to hold back, the entire class enters wholeheartedly into discussions, reading, or writing.

From the standpoint of teaching, it is always easier to move with the flow of interest. Trying to stem a tide of excitement by introducing lessons on arithmetic or printing is bound to lead to frustration.

When to abandon your favorite fairy tale

On Wednesday morning, Margaret was all set to read one of her favorite fairy tales, but the children seemed restless and not inclined to sit still to listen. Feeling that the children needed some physical movement before settling down, she invited a visitor to the class to lead the children in some stretching. Everyone jumped up and in no time the children were reaching high, high into the air to pluck some fruit from imaginary trees. Excitement ran high as apricots, plums, and peaches appeared in the children's hands, were sniffed, tasted, and shown around. Realizing that the intent had been to help the children quiet down, the visitor suggested that they look quietly underneath those imaginary trees to find and pick up a tiny ant. The children readily found what they were bending down for and carefully carried their ants to their seats on the carpet.

They had a marvelous time looking after their tiny captives and two boys got into a tussle over putting the ants down each other's shirts. Knowing the signs, Margaret abandoned the planned reading, invited the children to write instead, and stood back to watch the burst of energy express itself in pictures and writing.

Later in the day she found time to fit in her fairy tale. By that time the children were ready to listen attentively and both they and Margaret enjoyed the reading. Timing and watching the children gave both teacher and children what they needed and wanted.

If such changes in plan sound disruptive or too indulgent on the part of the teacher, think back to the tedium of following to the letter the lesson plans prescribed in the old basal readers. The beauty of taking your cues from the children and being flexible about lesson plans is that teaching takes on new excitement and interest. When you come to school, you never know what the day may hold. The children feel the same way and are eager to come to school and to learn. The benefits of fitting your teaching to their ways of learning accrue to them as well as to you.

Genuine interactions become the best models for learning

*Hints and
particulars*

The kindergarten children find a mysterious friend

One morning the kindergarten children noticed a beautiful painting on the easel in the corner of the classroom. The easel is always set up and ready for any budding artist, but the painting had not been there the night before. That night we left a note thanking the mysterious painter for the picture and said how much we liked it.

The next day there was another painting and a little note telling us something about the artist. The mysterious painter turned out to be the night custodian. All that year we wrote back and forth. He told us about his family and the children told him about things that were important to them. On Friday we always left him a snack and on Monday morning there would be a note thanking us for the treat. We kept our note exchange going all year but we never met our mysterious friend.

Such an exchange becomes a wonderful model of the joys of communicating in writing with someone you can't meet in person.

If the teacher takes the lead, children will share

Having the teacher share her home experience can become a fun model for the children's sharing. While teaching kindergarten, Margaret's home became a playground to a family of field mice who refused to be dislodged. Each morning the children rushed in to see the latest installment of the saga on the blackboard: a mouse scrambling up the stairway; the dog Trico greeting Margaret with a long tail hanging out of its mouth and its own doggy tail wagging; a trap moving about the room as one of the mice dragged it along by its tail; Margaret jumping up on a chair as a pair of mice scurried by! Even the custodian joined the fun and, like the children, kept asking, "Is that really true?"

Children respond with their own descriptions and learn to express themselves more openly both orally and in writing.

Modeling enquiry behavior pays good dividends in learning

When the teacher learns about eagles, so do the children

One long weekend in spring Margaret visited friends whose home is located near the nesting grounds of a pair of bald eagles. She spent the weekend observing the great birds fly back and forth building their nest, chattering all the while. Her hosts told her all they had learned about eagles from watching them over the years. Watching and listening really whetted Margaret's curiosity and when she returned to school, she told the children all she had learned and of her intent to learn more. As her research in the school library and the public library progressed, she kept the children informed of everything she learned. Sensing her excitement they contributed to her store of information by bringing in pictures, articles, and their own drawing and writing. Over a period of months a large collection of research material accumulated, and Margaret and the class learned a great deal about eagles. The children obviously remembered this project well. Two years later, one of Margaret's students dropped by to present her with the latest find from a wildlife magazine.

No science module or structured lesson complete with questions could have taught as much as the sustained search for new material generated by Margaret's genuine interest and excitement. Modeling curiosity and enquiry captured the children's imagination and they, too, became searchers for knowledge.

Sustained practice enriches learning

From small beginnings whole villages grow

A simple activity such as making little houses out of squares of paper can lead to a major project and lots of practice in many skill areas. In one classroom the production of a few little paper houses extended into the creation of an entire village spread out in one corner of the classroom. First the children set the houses along a street, then someone suggested it would be nice to live near a lake. The project evolved from there as the children added churches, gas stations, apartment houses, a fire hall, and shopping center.

The children discussed whether they wanted to live in the city or the lake country and these discussions led into exploring issues of pollution and services such as garbage removal that are or are not available in the different settings. From there, children moved to considering what jobs they would or would not like to have in the future.

Once little toy cars (brought from home) were added, road signs and house numbers made number work part of the village project. Most of the ideas came from the children. The project might have continued much longer if space had not become a problem and the custodians had not begun to object. But in the meantime everyone derived a lot of learning and fun.

Such continuity of practice is important. Think of your own creative efforts and how annoying it can be when you have to stop in the middle of something just when ideas are flowing well. Children are no different. If they are involved in a project they have tremendous attention spans. They groan if the recess bell rings to interrupt them and they don't want to leave. Whenever possible we allow children to work continuously on a job that is important to them. They quickly catch up on other work they may miss as a result of involvement with a project.

Practice imparts many and varied benefits

Choosing time produces solid skill practice

Interesting practice material and genuine options to freely pursue activities generate productivity in both reading and writing. In the past, the reward of completing work early has often been assigned busy work. But when children have plenty of alternatives open to them, they frequently opt to do creative work that stretches their skills.

Poetry offers room for practice in many skills

A variety of imaginative practice with the same material gives children the opportunity to "overlearn" and internalize language patterns, spelling patterns, and story lines of poems. One teacher prints popular poems on large charts, laminates them, and then lets children use them singly or in groups. When first introducing a new poem, the teacher reads it to the class; next, children begin to join in; and after that the teacher or children may use the laminated chart to mark in rhyming words, spelling patterns, words of special interest, or whatever children choose to note about the poem. In the process of reading, rereading, and marking up the poem, all children learn it by heart and get the feeling that they can read. Poems used in this way were the first bits of coherent English learned by a non-English-speaking child in this class.

Extended practice produces "overlearning" and builds skills

Adult standards of boredom don't necessarily apply to children. When a teacher found that she had forgotten to change the record-cum-book in the listening center for three weeks, she noticed that not only were children still listening to it, but had also learned the songs included in the story and were singing them. They obviously continued to derive pleasure and benefit from this voluntary practice.

Careful observations are part of giving feedback

Activity time affords opportunities to note children's overall development

Along with literacy development, children's overall development will give you important indications about strides forward and special needs. *Here are some suggestions for activities or behaviors to look for:*

Note which children will work in groups or alone at centers

- Do some children gravitate more toward action and manipulation? Are some inclined to work more independently?
- Note how block structures children build early in kindergarten are quite simple but become more elaborate as they progress through the year.
- Observe how children move from solitary play to working in groups; how planning and cooperation become more noticeable in interactions.
- Keep track of the noise level and, if necessary, remind children that they may be disturbing those who wish to read or write more quietly.
- Keep track of children's shift from playing with toys and blocks to looking at books or games involving letters.
- Note whether a child is slow in academic work only or whether it is a more pervasive pattern of behavior.

Fitting the learners' way to the curriculum

How to take your cues from the children to adjust the lesson plans or curriculum

- Know your curriculum but adjust it to fit the children's interests, pace, and sequence of learning. Instead of following a set sequence, teach to suit the moment – the light-and-shadows unit would fit in well around Groundhog Day; the young animals unit at times when children are excited about the arrival of puppies, kittens, or a foal, when fish in the school aquarium multiply, or chicks hatch in your class incubator.
- When doing spelling at the blackboard, note which letters or parts of words children will volunteer. If they primarily give

consonants and your lesson book stresses short vowels, postpone work on vowels until later and reinforce the children's ability to recognize consonants. Keep right on mentioning vowel rules as you spell, but don't insist on the children's applying them until they have moved through their consonant-recognition phase of spelling.

- If a child is in grade one but still requires kindergarten type of work – manipulation, developing oral facility – make sure that s/he gets it. Forget the grade one curriculum for the moment and watch him/her unfold. When the student is ready, s/he will let you know in words and actions that now s/he is prepared to do what everyone else in class is doing.

- When children are busily on task reading or writing, don't watch the clock and decide at 10:45 sharp it is time to .... Instead, let them continue for a while longer to take full advantage of the constructive energy.

- Let the children share their interests or expertise and turn their knowledge into lessons in science or social studies. When 6-year-old Ben took over the class to expound on his knowledge about spiders, the entire class, including the teacher, became involved in an exciting research project that took up a good part of the day. After that, children brought in books, articles, and personal information to enhance what Ben had taught. Everyone learned more than would have been gleaned from a structured lesson. Spontaneity and personal interest fueled the learning inspired by Ben.

Day-to-Day Classroom Management Fits the Children's Way of Learning

6

While parents create the right language-learning climate for their children, they do not relinquish control of their entire home. Neither will you relinquish control of the overall classroom when teaching the learners' way. At the beginning of the year, you establish firm guidelines for behavior and set rules about noise, orderliness, getting along together, and doing assigned work. As you enforce these rules quietly but firmly throughout the year, you also establish a routine that becomes familiar and predictable to children and gives them an overall framework within which to work.

As the children develop a spirit of cooperation and begin to reveal or acquire specific skills, start to encourage individual children and small groups to assume more responsibility for their learning. Steps forward may be small at first: hanging up coats, getting settled, speaking up during news time, selecting books, or choosing a center activity. As the year progresses, children will venture forth more readily. Going to the library, getting listening stations operating, moving through the cooking center, or organizing a small reading group around a big book will become part of their independent activities.

Flexibility of scheduling is a natural part of classroom management. As you observe your students at work, you will shift the timing or introduction of lessons to suit the moment. Instead of following a set sequence or timetable prescribed by a guidebook or skillpac, you will note those children who are ready to move ahead and those

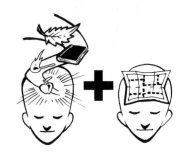

who still need practice to build skills. You will also find yourself allowing extra time to give children a chance to complete a project, cutting short an activity when children start to fidget, or modifying a lesson to make room for sharing a play or the arrival of a shipment of books.

The most important change in classroom management involves offering skill teaching in the context of meaningful communication. If you introduce as many uses of reading and writing as you can possibly think of and will simply comment on skills or component parts of language while writing, children can enter into these activities immediately. They are so familiar with the use of language as a means of communication that they will not be confused or anxious about learning to read and write. Many of them will quickly follow your model of looking at components of print while watching you write. These children become peer models for their classmates and will greatly ease your workload.

Since you are beginning with story reading, message writing, following directions or recipes, picture captions and labels, children are not in doubt about the purpose or utility of their work. As a result, you soon find more and more of the children ready and eager to select their own learning tasks during center time when they are given a choice of activities. The set routine of the day quickly becomes the familiar framework within which children move from one task to the next without waiting for specific instructions for their every move. As the year advances, classroom management becomes more and more a shared responsibility between you and the learners.

Of course, classroom management depends upon the very special combination of people involved. Be sure to be as true to your own personality, background, and preferred modes of interacting as possible. Use your special intelligences to the fullest, be they music, reading, arts, crafts, physical education, or drama. Children are keen observers and excellent intuitive judges of character. They will react in kind to your interest, enthusiasm, relaxed joy, or to your boredom, irritation, and repressed anger. So, as much as possible, include in your teaching day as many activities or materials that are fun or interesting to you.

At the same time, consider also the interests, intelligences, personalities, backgrounds, and levels of maturity of the children.

You will want to adjust the overall activities to the particular children and while your general approach to teaching will remain the same, each year you will want to shift emphasis in activities to accommodate the children's needs. If you have a class in which two-thirds or more of the children are very active, you may want to increase the amount of physical activity to give those children plenty of outlets for active movement. On the other hand, you may want to enlarge on story-reading time to draw these children to more quiet listening with interesting stories that invite participation or active involvement.

We are providing descriptions of typical days in kindergarten, grades one and two to give you examples of how some teachers have managed their classrooms. Take these descriptions as broad guidelines and evolve your own teaching day to suit your personal needs, the interests of the children, and the requirements of your school district. If you keep the overall curriculum requirements at the back of your mind and take your cues from the children's every move forward, you will find that classroom management becomes increasingly relaxed, less stressful, and more effective. Children engaged in work that is meaningful to *them* will remain busily on task and, though perhaps a bit noisy, will find little time to create discipline problems.

As the year unfolds

For teacher and children alike, the transition to more and more independent learning evolves gradually. Children coming to school for the first time, whether in kindergarten or grade one, have not had the experience of being with so many other children. They may not be used to oral instructions and few are accustomed to sitting still for any length of time. Books and games may be unfamiliar and routines of organizing learning materials have yet to be established, If some of the children have attended kindergarten before entering grade one, they may become peer models, particularly if they have been in a constructivist classroom and are accustomed to taking responsibility for initiating activities. Still, there needs to be time for setting the tone, establishing rules of behavior, and letting freedom and safety to learn evolve gradually.

Of necessity, the beginning of the year calls for more teacher-directed activities. The all-important modeling of courteous behavior does much to get children settled. To demonstrate that learning will be interesting and exciting, story time and games or

active work with materials allowing for physical movement take up much more time than later in the year. "Choosing time" (children pursue activities of their choice; the teacher works with individual children) is introduced slowly once children demonstrate that they have accepted responsibility for the routine daily activities: hanging up coats, getting settled for sharing, keeping tables and materials reasonably orderly, finding games and activities during choosing time, putting materials away after using them, cleaning up spills or scraps of art materials, moving to the next activity without having to be reminded. Knowing how to handle materials, what not to do, how to share, and how to put things away all need to be learned and accepted by the children. Attention spans may be short and the teacher needs to keep alert to feelings of unrest or signs of acting out.

Physical activity and the permission to move about absorb extra energy and make learning fun. Hyperactivity or emotional outbursts brought on by enforced inactivity either do not arise or quickly disappear if there is movement and fun.

Activities involving the entire class are much more frequent during the early part of the year than later on. During story time and unison reading the teacher notes who is following along, who joins in during refrains, tracks print from left to right, shows signs of knowing names of letters, or uses pictures to help with recognizing words. On the basis of these early observations s/he encourages children to take more and more initiative in their choice of reading materials and in center activities.

Problems at the beginning of the year may stem from children being unaccustomed to following oral directions, working cooperatively in a group, or getting their learning materials organized. Many children come to school with limited vocabularies, and they may lack experience talking about their needs, fears, or joys. A lot of discussion during which the teacher sets a relaxed tone and more outspoken children model lively oral exchanges can quickly loosen the tongues of timid children. Children who are too shy or afraid to say, "I need help," or "I don't know what to do," soon learn to relax and speak up if the teacher proves to be quietly helpful. Noting tears, looks of puzzlement or distress, s/he simply demonstrates again what needs to be done or comments, "Here's what you need," or "Here's how to do this." Help given in a matter-of-fact way sees unruly children settle down as well. The teacher's confidence in the children's ability to do their work gives them the courage to try new tasks, to carry on, or to ask for help as needed.

Peer modeling begins early in the year if the teacher encourages helpful behavior and sharing. Since they are free to move around the room, children are not limited to interacting only with the children seated beside them. In one case, two boys had become close friends in kindergarten and continued to work together in grade one. Troy was much slower to mature than his friend and made it a practice to copy his buddy closely. As a result, he practiced far more extensively than if he had been left on his own and made great strides forward. Troy's learning gradually shifted to more independent work but following his friend's example gave him the right start. Such work with peers is a valuable part of peer modeling, and the talking children do usually refers to the work at hand or returns to it after brief digressions.

Self-initiated learning and special projects become more prevalent as children move from large-group to small-group activities and from copying others to composing their own writing. More experienced readers and writers lead the way and, as others follow their example, the teacher is freed more and more to work with individuals and small groups.

The children's interests and their rate of development determine the growth in sophistication of reading and writing projects. Books, general reading materials, artwork, and writing become more complex as the year progresses. At the same time, attention spans lengthen and both reading and writing are pursued independently and for longer periods at a time.

The children's personal and skill development mirror the changes in overall classroom management. Social behaviors shift from dependence to independence, from hanging onto Mom at the door to working and playing easily with other children or talking freely with the teacher. They move from shyness to being outgoing and confident with adults and children alike. Artistic talents move from simple cut-and-paste jobs to creativity and a flair for unique artwork. Control over fine muscles is evidenced in improved printing and, in turn, evolves into greater ease with composition. Mind and body have a way of growing together. At their own unique pace, individual children shift from recognizing or saying a few words or refrains to reading with fluency and expression. Composing skills emerge from early rough work. Even children who come to school speaking no English at all become talkative. It took Paul all of kindergarten to say a word here and there, but once

he started talking, there was no holding him back. Like his parents at home, at times the teacher wished for less progress, because it became nearly impossible to keep him quiet.

But learning is not a straight-line progression. Like physical growth and brain development, learning is marked by spurts forward and quiet periods. We have discerned distinct stages of progress throughout the year and they are described in preceding chapters. Close observations of learners in your class are sure to reveal similar moves forward, then pauses or slight regressions before the next move. If progress seems slow at the beginning of the year or at intervals during the year, *hang in there and trust*. In the long run – some sooner, some later, some very late – *all* of the children will become readers, writers, researchers, and quite proficient spellers. They will know how to use reading and writing for learning and pleasure and will use their skills at home as well as at school.

Kindergarten – the foundation of literacy

The unhurried atmosphere of kindergarten offers an ideal climate to teach in ways that build on the children's natural language learning. There is, after all, no requirement to *teach* reading and writing to kindergarten children. As a result, learning is left to evolve in its own way as the children are surrounded by books, stories, and all types of written materials. Though the school day is limited to two or three hours, children move toward literacy as surely as they move toward talking if the environment offers plenty of models to follow, encourages practice, and provides feedback that makes learning safe and enjoyable.

For us, kindergarten became the testing ground of developing literacy skills through modeling, practice, and feedback. Once we added fluent reading, story time, and writing to kindergarten activities, children began to evolve their interest in reading, writing, and story telling. Well before they could read, they had internalized book language, memorized stories and nursery rhymes, and had begun to anticipate what might happen in stories or how a line or story could end, be changed, or acted out. Several learned to read before entering grade one. All internalized the foundation of literacy – enjoyment of books and stories and an understanding of the functions of written language. Whether readers or pretend readers, by the end of the year most of them saw themselves as readers and were ready to move ahead on the basis of that self-image.

The kindergarten day in brief

Time lines are simply approximations and may vary from day to day.

- **Teacher greets children** at the door and listens to their individual news.
- **Getting settled for the day** – Children move to tables, find their name cards. (10 minutes)
- **News time** – Children share their news. Teacher helps children decide what sentences to put on the board. S/he models thinking aloud, spelling, printing, punctuation, and reading. Children begin to spell and read. (30 minutes)
- **Activity time** – Physical movement indoors or out: games, music, singing, and the like. (20 minutes)
- **Story time** – Teacher reads to the children – big books, stories, poems, newspaper clippings, anything they enjoy. Some children begin to chime in. (15 minutes)
- **Table work** to develop fine motor skills – Teacher or a helper will label the children's artwork or write captions for their pictures from the children's dictation. (15 minutes)
- **Writing workshop** – Children communicate through pictures but soon begin pretend writing or adding strings of letters to their pictures. Gradually they move into invented spelling as they share ideas. (15 minutes – less at the beginning of the year)
- **Center time** – Children have free choice of centers or activities. Many children simply play but gradually they gravitate toward reading and writing activities during this time. (20 minutes)
- **Activity time** – Playground play, walks, moving games indoors. (15 minutes)
- **Summarizing the day** – Talking over the events of the day helps the children remember and describe what they learned. (10 minutes)
- **Additional story time** may be interspersed at different points in the day, as may music, movement, cooking, special events, seasonal fun, or artwork.

Please note that both the activities and times are open to change. Especially in kindergarten, but in grades one and two as well, flexibility and spontaneity are essentials of teaching. When special needs arise or children's interests or discussions present special "teachable moments," then the regular daily routine gives way to a special lesson or activity.

A typical day in kindergarten

Starting the day

Exchanging greetings and news as the children enter the room begins the day. Many important bits of information are passed along as the children hang up their coats and get ready for their day at school. In this informal setting even shy children will volunteer a few words before moving to their seats. Almost from the beginning of the year the children recognize their own names printed on large cards and used as place cards to show them where they will sit that day. To give them a chance to sit with different children and to have the fun of finding their name card, the teacher shifts the seating arrangement each day, but on Fridays the children choose where they want to sit.

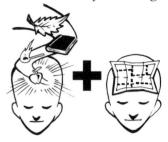

*Morning meeting sets the tone and news time introduces letters,
printing, and spelling*

At morning meeting children gather around the teacher and
continue to share their news. Attentive listening and a bit of
prompting by the teacher help children decide what bits of news
should go on the board that day. In early September the teacher will
spell each word as s/he writes it on the blackboard, and s/he also
begins to comment on sounds, rules of punctuation, and
capitalization. At the same time the teacher invites children to help
with spelling the words. Children who have had reading experience
at home will readily speak up and offer suggestions. Thus news
time becomes a fine opportunity to note children's previous
experience with reading and writing, and the teacher can build on
those home-grown skills right away. Less experienced readers like
to follow the example of their peers and soon most of the children
speak up to offer suggestions for spelling, although quite rough
approximations at first. In fact, in kindergarten, children might call
out any letter at first, or even numbers or made-up letters. They all
want to participate and soon their suggestions become more
accurate as they listen to familiar words and spellings again and
again. Trust in the children's ability and desire to become more
accurate is a key factor, and accepting all input with a comment
about "a good try" makes these initial attempts at entering the
world of spelling safe.

As spelling approximations become more accurate, the teacher
might comment, "Yes, *car* could start with a *k* because that's what it
sounds like, but in this case we need a *c* as the beginning letter." One
kindergarten child surprised her mother by telling her that *ceiling*
starts with a soft *c*. Such comments cease to be surprising to the
teacher who quietly mentions all these rules as s/he prints words
that exemplify them on the board. As s/he repeats them often
enough in the course of writing news, the children pick them up
quite naturally and easily.

News time also fosters reading

While putting the children's news items on the board, the teacher
not only names each letter as s/he prints it but also repeats the
word, then a phrase, and finally the entire sentence. Many of the
children begin to talk along as the teacher goes over the sentence
and runs his/her hand along the line of print. Watching for children

who speak up or silently rehearse the words without actually saying them aloud, the teacher invites volunteers to come to the board to read a sentence. Knowing that they will receive help if they get stuck, children quite readily volunteer to read, memory read, or talk along with the teacher. News time is one of the concrete ways in which the teacher demonstrates very graphically to the children that reading, writing, and spelling are all very closely connected and are intended to make sense. News expands from one sentence to two and three, and children participate ever more freely as the year unfolds.

Children need to move physically

Taking his/her cue from the children's attention span, the teacher ends news time once the children become restless. As soon as interest flags and the children start to fidget, s/he shifts to another activity. The teacher generally alternates quiet work with more vigorous physical activities. Jumping games, clapping, singing, moving to music, singing along with a record or musical instrument, and playing with toys indoors or out give children opportunities to move freely.

Writing workshop encourages all efforts

Writing workshop (see chapter 4) invites children to put messages on paper. At first, they may largely focus on pictures, pretend writing, or strings of random letters, but even at this early stage their intent is to communicate.

Story time is for enjoyment

During story time, children sit on the carpet around the teacher, stretch out comfortably, sit on the teacher's lap, or lean against him/her to see better. As s/he reads, the teacher holds the book so that children can see the pictures and note when the pages are turned. Story time is enlivened by a wide choice of reading material and children soon ask to have favorites reread. Guessing what will happen next – Is the boy going to get caught? Who else is going to enter the story? – adds suspense to some of the reading and tells the teacher how well children are following and comprehending the reading.

Table work focuses on manipulative skills

Table work, intended to develop fine motor skills, follows. As children work at the usual kindergarten art projects of cutting, pasting, and stitching things together, the teacher uses the opportunity to talk about the work and to encourage both the expansion of the children's vocabulary and their imagination. S/he suggests additions or expansions of work begun and introduces paper-and-pencil work. Labeling children's work, writing captions under pictures, or printing a message in a card a child has produced, again demonstrate how print can be used to convey messages.

Center time affords opportunity for writing as well as play

Center time offers children a wide choice. Many opt for toys, the playhouse, sand table, or carpentry bench during most of the year, but books, art supplies, the record player, games and blocks bearing letters and numbers, and puzzles showing not only pictures but written captions all serve as pleasant ways of practicing and becoming familiar with written language and its parts. All of the centers encourage interaction, lively talk, and physical movement.

Book time begins early in the year

Brief though it is, book time begins early in the year. Encouraged by the teacher to select a good supply of books to hold their interest, children settle down to look at pictures, recognize old favorites, pretend to read, or try to recall what they heard at story time. Sharing among each other is half the fun and there is a constant buzz of excited whispers as children exchange books, show pictures, or recite a familiar line or refrain. "Reading Buddies" from grade two may join the kindergarten children for individual reading during this period or later in the day. But generally the children simply "read" on their own. As with other activities, their attention span determines the length of book time. Once the noise level rises and the children become restless the teacher ends the session. Enjoyment, not endurance, is the goal.

The children's ways of interacting with their reading materials during book time tell a great deal about their reading development. At the beginning of the year, some children may use the books they have selected to build houses, stack them in different ways, or

otherwise manipulate them. A good number of children will leaf through the books looking at the pictures, but quite a few begin to go through the stories quite systematically. Pretend reading and memory reading come to the fore, and a careful look at those who sit quietly, noting how their eyes track print or their mouths form words will reveal children who are actually reading.

Just as at home, children have favorite stories and books. In our kindergarten, Bill Martin's *Brown Bear, Brown Bear* is without doubt the all-time favorite throughout the year. Other books by Bill Martin run a close second. The children also enjoy big books made for them by older children and they will pore over pictures drawn and colored by the older students. By the end of the year, books they have produced themselves are also very popular. You will soon find which books the children in your class love best. Encourage them to choose whatever they like. If they pick too advanced material in the library, let them find out by themselves. They may enjoy the pictures regardless of the reading level; if they seem to linger on material that seems too simple, offer wider choices, but do not insist that the children must read them; if you want to present a more elaborate story, read and enjoy it with them.

Book time is not silent. If children want a bit of quiet, they withdraw to a remote corner of the room to settle down with a number of books. But most of them enjoy the discussions and sharing of both pictures and text. The teacher, too, sits down to read a book of

Sharing interesting books encourages the first steps toward literacy

Kindergarten children soon begin to focus their interest on books and choose to turn to them during center time. Note the "Name Book" ready to be consulted on the blackboard tray.

his/her choice. Though s/he may be interrupted now and again to help a child with reading a word or passage, s/he models absorbed reading, and the children at times come over to ask about it.

More physical activity provides a change of pace

After sitting still, the children need a change of pace. Play on the adventure playground, a walk around the block, a race, playing in the snow make room for vigorous action. Indoors, singing, moving to music, and clapping games add a lively time on rainy days.

Story time draws children together once more

The day ends with yet another story as children gather around the teacher.

Looking back over the day

Before going home, the children and the teacher talk over what happened that day. That reminder of the day's activities and favorite books accompany children home to encourage parents to read to and with their children. Sharing the books and the summary of the day's work help to link home and school and make it clear that school is a safe and interesting place for children and parents alike.

What has changed?

Kindergarten has always been more relaxed and open than grade one. But we find that children now build a more solid foundation for literacy than ever before. The most important change has been one of looking at the learners in a different way. Originally kindergarten was largely a time to help children make the transition from home to school and to help them mature both physically and socially. Now there is the added dimension of having the children see and experience themselves as budding readers and writers and the teacher thinking of them as effective literacy learners.

The quality and quantity of printed material and books available in the classroom has increased dramatically. Like the parent at home, the teacher communicates with the children whether or not they are ready to respond in kind. Morning meeting teaches the art of conversation and opens two-way communication. Story time and writing for and with the children have become part of everyday interactions in class. As children dictate news or experience charts

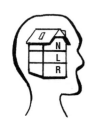

and then read them back, they begin to gather a store of sight words. As they play with name tags, they learn about initial consonants, remembering that *Doreen* and *Diane* both have a *D* at the beginning of their names.

The children's view of themselves has changed. Since their memory reading, pretend reading, and attempts at spelling or printing are encouraged and accepted, they see themselves as readers and writers. Their confidence urges them on to upgrade their skills and fosters lots of volunteer practice. In their own playful way they internalize what they need to know about printed messages to lay a solid foundation for more precise knowledge and then full literacy. They are doing the initial global work and are getting ready for more detailed follow-up.

Independence is one of the hallmarks of teaching the learners' way and throughout the year the teacher gradually turns more and more of the responsibility for learning over to the children. When they enter school, some cling to Mommy, some have trouble hanging up coats or getting learning materials organized. Building on strengths and encouraging every step forward, the teacher demonstrates his/her trust in the children's ability to "do it themselves" by standing back and giving children room to gradually refine initial gross attempts at new skills. Peer modeling becomes a powerful force to help shy or immature children progress. As the teacher comments positively on steps forward children take in becoming more organized, beginning to copy print, volunteering to read, or helping to spell, other children observe and try to emulate such behaviors.

Allowing children to initiate much of their learning makes for safety and absence of stress. As a rule, the children themselves will ask to be shown how to print, read, or do artwork. We observed that the desire to move beyond memory reading, to get to know words, letters, and print urges children on more surely than any worksheet did in the days of our structured lessons. Asking children to "circle all the *b* words" toward the end of kindergarten did not produce much enthusiasm, but story reading and book time do.

Models of enriched language produce tangible benefits

If models of written language are plentiful and rich, even kindergarten and play-school children will generate interesting, coherent stories and dictate them to the teacher. Though the impoverished language of traditional basal readers discounts it, children at age 5 have the capacity for expressive language and imaginative storytelling. Models and a willing scribe are all they need. The following story dictated by a 5-year-old demonstrates the sense of story the child has developed. Even though he does not yet read or write, he is moving toward literacy through storytelling and fluency of thought and language.

SCARY EYE

"EEEEEEK- 0000" said Scary Eye. He walked to the big giant's house who is his friend and he wanted some gold. Scary Eye didn't want any pirates to get the gold so he buried it on an island. He floated in the air to the island where his friend the giant popped the balloon and he couldn't get off the island. His friend sailed without him and left poor Scary Eyes all by himself – boo-hoo boo-hoo. A pirate came out of a haystack. "What is the matter with you, Scary Eye?" "I am shipwrecked on this island." The pirate said, "I am too."

"So what shall we do?"

"Let's live here together Scary Eye. I have a scary eye too," said the pirate.

The End

What are the benefits?

Enjoyment of books and reading, a more relaxed atmosphere, more fun, and good communication are the benefits for teacher and children alike. The absence of pressure lets reading and writing emerge freely. At the end of the year a number of the children may actually read and another group will be almost there. The safety-to-learn has allowed all of the children the opportunity to evolve at their own rate and some may still be quite content to play with toys and leave the glory of reading to their peers. Taking an attitude of detachment, the teacher will simply note that a given child has not yet matured physically, socially, or emotionally to a point of delving into the intricacies of print. As a result, learning to read remains free of problems or stress and is full of excitement. Though some

children may not yet read, they have absorbed many of the conventions of print and will enter grade one well prepared to read and write.

The primary grades

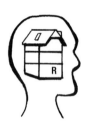

Throughout this book we stress spontaneity, the willingness to abandon plans and move with teachable moments. Here, we are presenting skeleton outlines of typical primary days. Though we watch children closely to note special needs or opportunities for teaching, we do plan lessons, set routines, and use them as a general framework for teaching and covering the required curriculum. Children feel secure with a predictable routine and look forward to favorite activities. They quickly learn what is expected of them in the way of required work and when, where, and how they are free to select activities. They thrive on the freedom to engage in special projects and love the flexibility of time spans within each activity. But the predictable daily routine lends stability and comfort. It's fun and exciting to plunge into projects or sally forth on field trips; yet it always feels good to come home to the familiar day.

Grade one

The grade-one day in brief

Time lines are rough guides only.

- **Morning meeting and discussion** – Teacher listens attentively to encourage children to talk. (5 minutes – more as year progresses)
- **News time** – Children dictate sentences to be printed on the board. They help with spelling and editing. Teacher reads sentences, children do unison reading of sentences then volunteer for individual reading. Later in the year, teacher erases a few selected words to create a cloze test. Volunteers fill in blanks. (10 to 15 minutes)
- **Story time** – Teacher reads to and with the children. Big books aid unison reading. (Time depends on length of story.)
- **Writing workshop** – Children write their own messages and illustrate them if they wish. They use invented spelling and create their own stories. Teacher sees individual children in "writing conferences" to help with

composition and spelling. Children share what they wrote, date stamp and file their work. (15 to 30 minutes or longer later in the year)

- **Center time is choosing time**. Once children have completed their writing they are free to choose language activities – reading, writing, artwork, centers, working on special projects. (10 to 15 minutes)
- **Reading groups run concurrently with center time.** Teacher calls no more than five children together to read. Unison reading is followed by individual reading on a voluntary basis. Children return to activities of their choice once they have finished reading. (10 to 15 minutes)
- **Recess** (15 minutes)
- **Authors' circle** brings children together to share that day's written work. Comments made by teacher or peers give positive feedback and suggestions. (5 to 10 minutes)
- **Book time** gives children a chance to select several books and settle down with them anywhere they like. The period begins with 5 minutes early in the year and extends gradually to 30 minutes or more. Sharing time is part of the fun.
- **Arithmetic** – Teacher works with small groups and hands-on materials. Arithmetic center enhances practice. (10 to 20 minutes)
- **Story time or special projects** if time permits
- **Lunch**
- **Story time** opens the afternoon and invites participation on the part of the children. (10 to 15 minutes)
- **Flexible time** varies depending on the day of the week and time of the year. It includes social studies, science, music, physical education, films, artwork, field trips, library work, French lessons, project day, invention day, puppet shows, Friday cooking and snack. (Time for individual activities varies)
- **Summary of the day's work** is done jointly by teacher and children. They go over the activities to discuss what worked well, what could be improved, and what should happen next day.

A typical day in grade one

MORNING

Morning meeting opens the day with informal talk

Until coming to school, children have communicated primarily by talking. Their ability to understand and use language forms the basis of much of their learning. To build on the abilities they bring with them, the day begins with sharing time and discussion. Children will readily talk about their personal experience – "I lost a tooth." "My brother got a dog." "I'm going fishing with my dad." "Last night I saw lightning." Such sharing affords the teacher a fine opportunity to model attentive listening and demonstrate questioning that will help children to expand their vocabulary and their ability to describe events more fully.

At the beginning of the year, children will crowd around the teacher, lean against him/her or even slip onto his/her lap. They are learning that school is a safe place to speak up and even shy children will begin to share with a bit of encouragement from the teacher. "Do you want to tell us about your weekend?" "Would you like to tell the other children about ...?" Sharing and discussions not only afford excellent opportunities to note children's verbal abilities, their social skills, and willingness to speak up or participate, but also provide the context to set guidelines for cooperation. A few quiet words about waiting for a turn, using an "indoor voice," and being considerate of others go a long way toward setting the tone of interactions in class. Here, too, attentive listening on the part of the teacher will serve as a fine model for children.

Newsletter time shifts discussion into the use of written language

Sharing time shifts into newsletter time and moves the discussion to more general topics of interest to all children. If children continue to give personal news, the teacher comments, "That would make a good sentence for your writing work." If no general news is offered, the teacher may do a bit of prompting early in the year suggesting simple topics such as news about upcoming events, visitors who are coming to the classroom, special projects underway, plans for field trips, or how many more days until.... But as the children gain experience they take over more fully and expand both the topics and complexity of their sentences. As they gather on the carpet by the blackboard, they become the initiators of writing and learning.

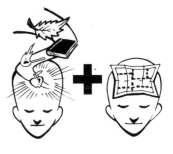

Newsletter work demonstrates composing, printing, and spelling

During newsletter time the teacher demonstrates printing, spelling, and editing. S/he "thinks aloud" for the children as s/he prints letters, words, and phrases on the board. "Here we need a capital letter because it's the beginning of the sentence." "Then we need a silent *e* at the end." "That *c* in *race* is a soft *c*. It sounds just like an *s*." Comments like that repeated daily as the news goes on the board soon encourage the children to spot examples of what the teacher has been saying. They begin to help the teacher spell, and remarks about the spelling of words often turn into a discussion of why something is spelled a particular way or what other words are spelled like it. Here, too, the repetition of the same comments and examples makes for learning that is free of stress. Children see and hear words day-in-and-day-out and they are encouraged to note and comment upon regularities and novelties in spelling. If the teacher accepts children's comments positively, news time becomes an open discussion and children feel free to speak up without being called on. In fact, they delight in pointing out that "*today* is a compound word; there are two *the*s in that sentence; there is a silent *g* in *night*." They are learning the details of print in the context of overall message writing as both the teacher and peers comment on the words or letters on the blackboard.

Editing becomes part of news time once children have had some experience combining sentences, removing repetitions, and inserting explanatory comments. With some prompting, children begin to think in terms of paragraph unity and suggest that topics be separated by extra space on the blackboard.

Once most children have gained familiarity with dictating and oral spelling, a modified *cloze test* concludes news time. The teacher erases a few of the more predictable words and children eagerly volunteer to come to the board to fill in the gaps thus created. Excitement and attention are high as the children at the board print and spell the missing words.

Reading becomes part of news time

Since news is for sharing, the teacher reads the words, phrases, and then the sentences s/he has printed on the board. S/he runs her hand along the lines of print as s/he reads to call attention to the words and the left-right progression of print. Next s/he invites the children to read along, and usually a good chorus of voices responds. Some children may simply follow the lines of print with their eyes or mouth the words, but now and again they will put in a word. Finally, individual children get a chance to volunteer to read a sentence or more of their choice. They come to the board and as they read – with or without help from teacher or peers – they run a pointer along the words and lines of print. Several children in succession may read the same line and that permission to repeat what has already been done gives the more timid children the courage to follow the leader. Generally, eager volunteers are waving their hands trying to entice the one at the board to pass along the pointer for a turn.

The teacher gauges the length of time to spend on newsletter activities. S/he watches the children's interest, level of participation, and their physical reactions. As long as children sit still and attend, s/he continues; once they start fidgeting and looking around for something more interesting to do, s/he shifts to a new activity. But the lines of print remain on the board to give everyone who wants it a chance to read the news.

Writing time

To underscore that writing, like reading, is meant to make sense, writing time begins with discussion of what to write. The children are completely free in their choice of topics and, not surprisingly, will generally opt to write about themselves, their friends, or family. At the beginning of the year, pictures and one or two sentences as captions are the product of some fifteen minutes of table work. But as the year progresses, longer accounts, fewer pictures, and, finally, imaginative stories replace the early work. Chapter 4 describes writing activities more fully and offers suggestions for many ways of introducing children to writing. After years of handing more and more control for learning over to the children, we find that following the Writers' Workshop approach is most productive for children. For more detailed information refer to books by Donald Graves and Lucy McCormick Calkins listed in the bibliography.

Writing workshop generates ideas and invented spelling

Discussion, peer interaction, the desire to convey messages, and the willingness to pretend are all parts of getting started. If the teacher is demonstrating printing and producing news each day, even children who come to school with little or no knowledge of letters internalize the idea that strings of letters constitute words and messages. At the beginning of the year many may be simply "babbling in print," but just as the baby means to convey messages, so these early strings of letters are the children's ways of pretend writing. They are important first steps in moving ever closer to conventional spelling. "Reading" these messages and holding regular conferences during which the teacher may print the child's message and/or correct spelling, demonstrate to the children how to move their own writing closer to conventional ways, and how to expand their writing. Quality and quantity of writing grow from a few strings of letters to sentences and then pages of writing.

Center time or choosing time

Once children have completed their writing, they are free to choose their next activity. Some simply continue to write – alone or with a partner, others move to centers, pick a language game, or curl up with a book. The fact that children will often pick the very thing they need to practice shores up the teacher's trust in the children's ability and willingness to learn. But here is the teacher's opportunity to select a game and suggest to the child that they play it together in order to provide practice in a given skill (say, recognition of consonants) in a safe, enjoyable way. Sharing of games or projects among children makes ample room for peer modeling and certainly enhances the pleasure of learning for children and teacher alike. If the noise level becomes too high, the teacher reminds the children to be considerate of others, and the sharing continues in somewhat more subdued tones. Being free to move around the classroom, to sit on the floor, or work at the blackboard helps to provide some of the physical movement so essential to young children's development.

Grade-one centers include the same reading, writing, and art centers described for kindergarten (see *Hints and Particulars* at the end of this chapter). Listening stations, a filmstrip story reader, and library book table fill out the reading materials. Permanent centers are generally set up and stocked by the teacher. Writing and art supplies are replenished; books, filmstrips and audio tapes, or records are changed to suit the children's needs; and special games or materials are put out to encourage practice needed by children at different stages. Centers are not static. They evolve throughout the year and continue to stimulate interest and skill development.

Integrating listening, talking, and reading helps beginning readers

Listening to stories and becoming entranced by them can be a first step in learning book language and reading.

Excitement, movement, feelings – and sharing – draw the children into participating with body, mind, and imagination.

Reading along while listening becomes the next step.

Interesting stories that change throughout the year draw the children to the listening-reading center for voluntary practice. The opportunity to hear the same story many times while following along in the accompanying book can produce the same type of "overlearning" that leads to learning to read at home when favorite stories are read again and again.

Creating special interest and seasonal centers is very much a joint effort. Children initiate, contribute to, and interact with these centers freely. Tables or shelves are filled with objects collected, books from home or the library, children's writing and artwork, dioramas created by individuals or groups of children. All invite thoughtful discussion, reading, writing, and excitement.

Reading groups

As they are moving to center time, the teacher calls groups of four to six children together for reading. Enjoyable books with predictable patterns (such as Bill Martin's *Sounds of Home*) help young readers succeed. Unison reading with the teacher taking the lead makes ability grouping unnecessary. Everyone can follow along and track print with eyes, bookmarks, and voice. Individual reading at the end of the group session is voluntary and children who do not wish to read aloud that day are free to move out of the small circle.

Story time

Story time is a flexible part of the morning. At times the teacher begins the day with a story, at others s/he fits it into center time or before the writing workshop. In fact, sometimes story time may come along two and even three times a day. But whenever it is, the story or book of the day stays within easy reach of the children so that they can peruse it at their leisure.

Recess

Authors' circle enhances both reading and writing

Sharing the writing they have done earlier promotes a sense of audience and opens the way to peer editing and lively discussions. Positive comments and questions or suggestions expand children's composition and spelling.

Book time gets everyone to look at books and print

Book time begins early in September with just a few minutes but gradually extends to longer and longer periods. Children select several books from the shelves and book bins around the room and settle down to look at the pictures, read, or pretend to read,

depending on their level of development and the books they picked. The teacher, too, selects reading material and settles down to enjoy it. Though it is generally a quiet time, children will do some sharing as they go along. Once the children become restless, the teacher ends the session and those who wish have a chance to share some of their reading with the whole class.

Arithmetic work ends the morning

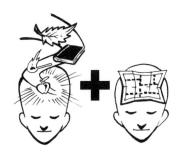

Work with numbers ends the morning. Here, too, manipulative work and concrete objects help learners to develop their skills their way. Hands-on practice and small-group activities help to individualize instruction and an arithmetic center augments personal learning. As in reading and writing, skill practice flourishes in the context of meaningful activities – science projects, games, cooking, making things.

AFTERNOON

Story time

Story reading and informal discussion usually open the afternoon. The teacher reads a story, short book, poems, or anything of interest to the children. The ensuing discussion may lead to the production of a play or puppet show, library research, and/ or special projects, attempts at writing poetry, or the production of books or artwork.

Social studies or science projects

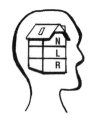

Social studies, health units, and science projects usually fit into the afternoon hours. Ample use is made of reading and writing activities as children research topics and record their observations of science projects carried on in the classroom. Visitors to the classroom who talk about their work or hobbies, bring in books, equipment, or special pets spark further research. the production of artwork, and special reports.

Physical education, music, French lessons, art, and more

Afternoons also accommodate all the special lessons taught either by the teacher or a specialist. Visits to the library, the school computer center, cooking, field trips, puppet shows, and plays fit more readily into the afternoons, but may be interspersed during the morning as well.

Summarizing the day's work

At the end of the day children and teacher take a few moments to recall the day's activities. Discussions of what they did lead to plans for the next day or speculations on how a job could be done differently. Imagination is sparked and children go home, ready to talk about what happened in school.

Invention day

One afternoon a week the children's creativity is given full rein. Children take the lead and create whatever they want. The teacher simply supplies them with strips of paper of different sizes or colors, with bits of cloth, or other scraps that lend themselves to imaginative work, and the children do the rest. Talking, sharing, peer modeling, and here and there a bit of input from the teacher spark the creation of hats, waterwheels, puppets, airplanes, or dioramas. At first children simply label what they have created, but as the year progresses, they write about the functions of their invention, how they made it, what they like about it, and how they might improve it.

Grade two

The grade-two day in brief

- **Morning meeting and exchange of books read at home.** (5 to 10 minutes)
- **Calendar** – Discussion, math concepts, patterns. (5 minutes)
- **Board work** – Teacher writes paragraphs based on children's dictation. News time is part of this activity but writing broadens to include poetry, reports, and general creative writing. Emphasis rests more on composition, sentence variety, and coherence of message than on spelling. Discussion and brainstorming lead children into individual writing. Words needed for projects are put on the board. (20 minutes)
- **Writing workshop** – Children write own stories, diaries, poems, reports, produce big books, or compose letters to pen pals.
- **Reading groups** – Small groups of four to six children read silently with teacher.

- **Center time** – Children choose center activity once they have completed writing and reading. (60 minutes for all three activities together)
- **Recess** (15 minutes)
- **Arithmetic** – Hands-on and manipulative work with concrete materials continue to aid children's math work. (20 to 30 minutes)
- **Story time** – Concludes the morning. (Time varies depending on that day's activities)
- **Lunch**
- **Authors' circle** – Writers share that day's work and receive input from teacher and peers. (10 to 15 minutes)
- **Book time** – Children and teacher read silently for 20 minutes (longer later in the year), share in pairs for 10 minutes, then volunteers share a story, play, poem, or chapter with the entire group.
- **Flexible period** – Discussions of special projects, catching up on work, spontaneous activities, field trips, visits from resource people, special lessons in social studies, sciences, physical education, French, music, and the like. (Time varies according to activity)
- **Choosing time** – Closes the day. Children choose an activity or center. Teacher gives help as needed or requested. This is a period during which the teacher can make certain that required topics are covered and adequate time is spent on content teaching. Reading, writing, research, and spelling are integrated with all of the work. (40 minutes, more if projects demand extra time)
- **Summarizing the day** – Everyone gets a chance to think over that day's work, to voice opinions, and to make suggestions. (5 to 10 minutes)

A typical day in grade two

Modeling, practice, and feedback guide learning in grade two as they did at the lower levels. Trust in the learners' ability to progress makes learning safe and productive. As the children are free to apply their own ways of learning, they develop new skills without stress or anxiety. Overall organization of grade two does not differ materially from grade one. Reading becomes more sophisticated;

writing evolves to more elaborate structures and greater accuracy of spelling.

MORNING

Morning meeting

The communication skills children have built throughout kindergarten and grade one enhance their language abilities and continue to be foundations for further learning. At the beginning of the day, children return and exchange books they have taken home. Comments about interesting passages, brief descriptions or critiques capture the interest of would-be readers. Feelings about the reading material and evaluations of the writings of favorite authors gradually replace the more egocentric talk that characterized much of grade one discussions. During this informal sharing the teacher or a child may read a poem, story, or a few pages from an interesting book. These five or ten minutes of informal talk give the children a chance to settle into the routine of the day and the teacher the opportunity to note some special interests or concerns of the children.

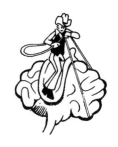

Calendar talk

Discussing the calendar takes only a few minutes but is an opportunity to talk and think in terms of numbers. In September the children produce a calendar for the entire year with special illustrations and notations and each child receives a personal copy. The fact that they produced the calendar adds to the usual discussions about special events coming up, how many days till...., how many Sundays, and the like.

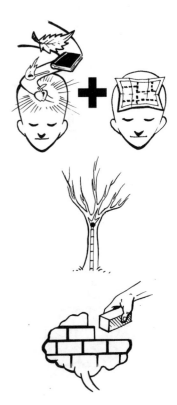

Board work expands to paragraphs and upgrades spelling

As in grade one, the teacher prints on the board following the children's dictation. At his/her prompting and modeling, individual sentences gain in length and complexity. Practice with editing their own work during writing conferences makes itself felt and children begin to suggest that two sentences could be combined, that repetitions sound monotonous, and that more precise words are needed. As the dictation increases in length, coherent paragraphs emerge, and the children will comment on what does or does not fit into that morning's message.

Group brainstorming helps to generate ideas for blackboard news and for personal writing later on. Word banks, ideas for projects and books are the side benefits of sharing and discussion at this point. Since the teacher is willing to entertain all suggestions, children become increasingly confident and willing to volunteer ideas. Knowing about editing, they are quite ready to include or exclude their offerings.

Children continue to help with spelling as the teacher writes on the board, at times making intentional mistakes to open discussion on sound-alike words that some children continue to misspell. But at this point the teacher will put highly familiar words on the board without comment and ask for help only with the more interesting or unfamiliar words.

Writing workshop

Drawing on the earlier brainstorming, on stories read, or on ideas generated in discussions, children settle down to a full hour of independent writing. While some of them may decide to undertake a group project such as the production of a book or research project, there is generally a great variety of writing. Children may write stories, compose poems, make diary entries, draft letters to pen pals, or expand on the news of the day. Word banks and dictionaries become aids to spelling, and conferences with peers or the teacher expand the editing process and move drafts to publishable work.

Authors' circle

The expanded writing and publishing makes the authors' circle even more interesting and productive. Style as well as content will come under review as children share and discuss their writing.

Small-group reading

While the children are busy with their writing, the teacher will call small groups of no more than six children together for reading practice. At the beginning of the year some of these sessions may include unison reading, but as more and more children shift to silent reading, group reading simply becomes a time at which the teacher is available as a resource person and listener. As in grade one, oral reading is voluntary and a number of children will simply read a passage and then return to their writing. Discussions of the story and watching the children's eyes, hands, or voices track print give the teacher ample evidence of reading progress.

Some of the children find opportunities for extra reading practice by acting as *reading buddies* to kindergarten children. For fifteen minutes a day – either during writing time or later in the day, children will go into the kindergarten room to read to a child and talk about the stories. Reading buddies keep track of their going, coming back, and the time spent on a regular timekeeping chart that shows times, dates, and names.

Center or choosing time

Once children have completed their writing and group reading work, they are free to choose any language activity. Many opt to extend their writing time further, others read, listen to taped readings, use games from the centers or do artwork to embellish their writing. As during the rest of the day, sharing and quiet discussions among children form important parts of learning.

Arithmetic

After recess, group lessons, work with concrete materials, and the arithmetic center combine to inculcate number skills. Hands-on materials encourage children to play with arithmetic blocks, to make patterns, to discuss number problems, and to add voluntary practice to the required table work in arithmetic. Moving from concrete manipulation of materials to more abstract concepts works as effectively in grade two as it did in grade one and is just as important at this stage.

Story time

Gathering together for a story concludes the morning. Material slightly more advanced than that read by the average child in class expands children's vocabulary and listening. Enjoyment mingles with the mystery of beautiful, though unfamiliar, language. Suspense is created by reading a chapter a day from a book too lengthy to be shared in one sitting. As at home, this gentle challenge extends the children's reach toward more advanced reading material. As opportunities present themselves, story time may also be interspersed at other times of the day. Having advanced to more sophisticated reading offers greater scope to the possibilities and joys of story reading.

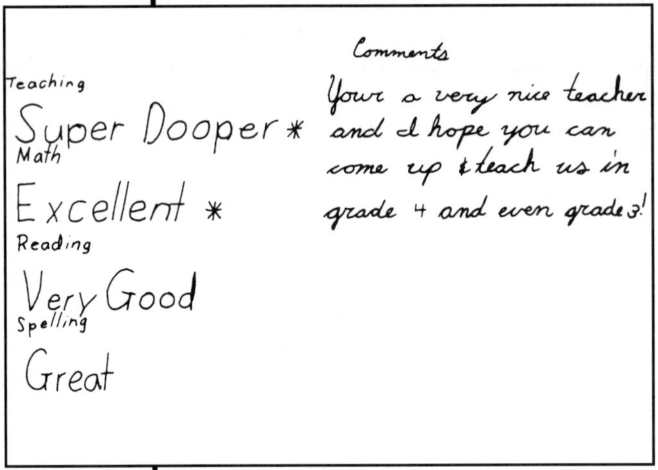

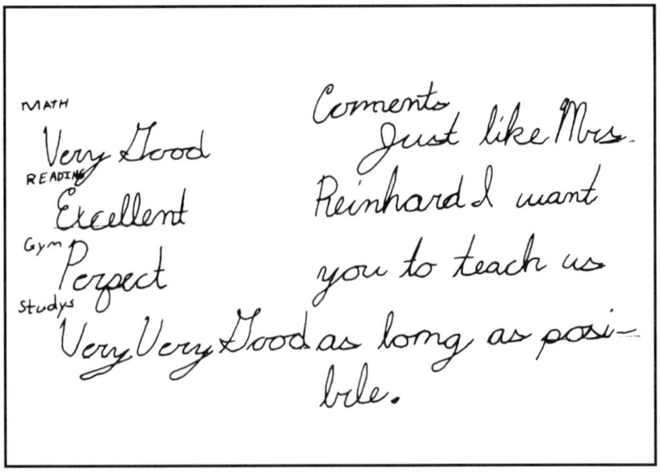

Teaching

Super Dooper *

Math

Excellent *

Reading

Very Good

Spelling

Great

Comments

Your a very nice teacher and I hope you can come up & teach us in grade 4 and even grade 5!

MATH

Very Good

READING

Excellent

Gym

Perpect

Studys

Very Very Good

Comments Just like Mrs. Reinhard I want you to teach us as long as posi-ble.

Grade two expands children's creative writing

Fun projects such as giving the teacher a report card underscore the mutuality of learning and growth in class.

*Day-to-Day Classroom
Management Fits
the Children's Way
of Learning*

**A special center on West Coast
First Nations people**

*stimulates reading and sharing. Maps,
illustrations, and text become part of
the joint reading,*

discussions,

and quiet time.

*These grade-two children make full use
of the special reading corners and
special centers. Interest in the topic and
the inviting environment ensure that
practice in reading and writing
abound.*

AFTERNOON

Book time

As in grade one, book time begins with a short period early in the year and gradually extends to twenty minutes or more. Both children and teacher silently read the books or stories they have selected. Instead of sharing with the entire group, children pair up or form small groups to exchange their ideas. If a particularly interesting passage has captured their imagination, one or two children may wish to present a brief account to the entire class.

Flex time

The flexible period that follows book time integrates research, writing, social studies, science, or anything else on the agenda. Each day takes a different focus as children work on projects, attend music lessons, physical education, French classes, go on field trips, create plays, or engage in special activities that suit the season or their special needs.

Choosing time

Another period of free choice concludes the day. As children pursue activities of their choice, the teacher works with individual children to help them plan or expand their projects and sharpen specific skills. Productivity and enjoyment attest to the value of these sessions.

Summarizing the day's work

Talking over the day's work draws attention to accomplishments and work to come. By listening to the children's view of the day's work, the teacher gets feedback on how the children perceived the activities. Together they plan or discuss what is to follow next day.

Hints and particulars

How do you get children settled into the classroom?

When Tomi entered kindergarten he cried, hung on to his mother, and acted as if he would never settle into the daily routine. Every change in the room or routine would throw him into hysterics. His mother agreed that it would be best to help Tomi get over his anxieties and instead of hovering in the background she would leave him at the door sobbing his heart out.

The solution was for the teacher to remain calm, cool, firm, yet sympathetic. Without babying Tomi, she demonstrated to him that she trusted him to fit in. He quickly learned that she expected him to do the same things the other children did. At every turn she would say in a matter-of-fact voice, "Yes, Tomi is going to go to centers now;" or "He'll be fine in a moment;" or "Don't worry, Tomi is just a little upset." Such comments helped not only Tomi, but reassured the other children (who are apt to start crying if they see someone else cry).

In Tomi's case his interest in his stomach was a great help. Throughout kindergarten and grade one Tomi's self-portraits were almost all stomach. Offering him a little snack now and again had a very soothing effect. Somehow, looking forward to a treat of raisins helped Tomi settle down to most tasks. Gradually he accepted that school was not so terrifying and, following the teacher's modeling, the other children helped to reassure Tomi along the way.

By the end of his first two years in school, he had gained all the confidence in the world. He went up on stage at school assembly to receive an award. From a timid, teary little boy who was afraid of everything, Tomi turned into a smiling, happy, confident child. Ignoring his crying at the beginning of school and providing a safe and interesting classroom had the right effect.

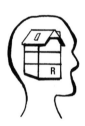

Kindergarten centers

Centers that stay in place all year
- Reading center – books of all kinds that change regularly
- Writing center – paper, crayons, colored pens, maybe an old typewriter
- Listening center – tapes and books for listening and looking
- Art center – easel, finger paints, materials of all kinds
- Arithmetic center – manipulative materials, unifix cubes, number cards
- Toy box and blocks – including blocks with letters or numbers
- Playhouse – anything you can gather, including dress-up clothes
- Sand table – may be filled with sand or rice
- Games corner – educational games of all types, commercial or home-made

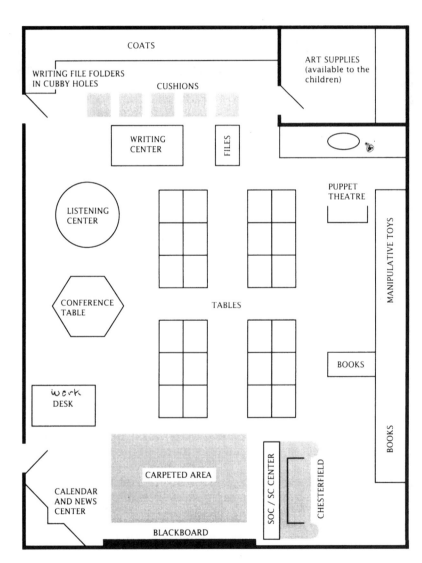

Sample classroom layout

In this classroom the teacher allocated every available space for children's activities. She was able to use the storage room as her "teacher area."

8 M x 10 M

- Workbench – hammers, nails, tools of all kind (may need to be closed for quiet time)

Changing centers - some initiated by the teacher, some by children
- Store – empty packages and cans plus a cash register to make change
- Cooking center – set up by the teacher or a helper for special treats
- Space center – stocked with books and toys of the children's choice
- Kite center – kites made by the children or brought from home
- Halloween center – pumpkins, costumes, and items brought by the children
- Christmas center – filled with decorations of the children's making
- Easter center – bunnies and eggs colored by the children
- Seasonal centers – filled with materials collected outdoors by children
- Hospital center – (sparked by information provided by a child returning from hospital) stocked with bandages, white coats, splints, empty syringes (without needles), medicine bottles, and toy thermometers
- Post office – toward the end of the year, children send and receive mail at the post office offering sticky labels as stamps, toy money for buying them, and a mail box to receive letters

Encouraging them to create, stock, and replenish centers enhances the children's sense of self-reliance and sparks interest. Surprises created by the teacher keep center time lively and instructive. No doubt children in your class will develop their own ideas for centers.

Activities that foster language and literacy development in kindergarten

Planning and facilitating initiated mostly by the teacher
- News time – children dictate sentences and help with spelling
- Story time – reading to and with the children
- Book time – expanding from a few minutes to longer periods
- Choral or unison reading of familiar stories or poems
- Puppet shows and plays produced by children

- Encouraging children to speak up and having lots and lots of discussions
- Having books and other reading materials readily available
- Providing captions for the children's artwork based on their dictation
- Writing on the blackboard – encouraging children to use it freely
- Posting printed labels all around the classroom
- Making reading and writing fun and free of stress

Working and practicing done by the children

- Listening to recorded stories while looking at books
- Sequencing pictures, words, letters
- Pretend-reading or memory reading of familiar stories or nursery rhymes
- Playing with letters made of paper, plastic, or on blocks
- Working with language games
- Learning to print – own name, letters
- Working with reading buddies
- Watching peers begin to read and write
- Inventing/dictating stories and picture captions
- Acting out familiar stories or poems
- Learning poems and nursery rhymes
- Singing songs and following words on a chart
- Using pocket charts to play with word cards cut from familiar poems
- Listening/talking to resource people who come into the classroom
- Cooking – using printed directions and recipe cards
- Playing store – reading labels and brand names
- Drawing pictures, beginning to write

Moving Toward Multi-Age Classrooms

7

Children mature at different rates. They bring diverse backgrounds, intelligences, and experience with them when they enter school. As teachers we know that some children will need a great deal of overall maturing before they are ready to evolve their fine motor skills and with this evolution the ability to print, manipulate implements, and deal with the requirements of school work. We are also aware of the children who come to school familiar with reading, writing, and listening to stories. Some of them already read; others are printing letters or messages; and still others have strong artistic talents. The range of experience and developmental stages is broad; yet, in the past, traditional curricula for the different grades have prescribed the same work for all children and have set guidelines regarding the sequence in which skills were to be introduced to the children. Age and/or placement in a given grade have governed the work children were expected to do.

Educators have always been aware of the need to make adjustments in a given curriculum. They have encouraged more mature students to move ahead and have offered extra help to those less experienced or less mature. But they have always felt the pressure of meeting specific deadlines in order to promote children to the next grade. Having children repeat an entire grade when only one or two areas needed extra work has not been entirely satisfactory, nor has it been beneficial to remove children from their own age group. "Social promotions," intended to keep children with their peers, have been one answer to the dilemma. But if the work then proved to be too advanced, late bloomers fell further and further behind. Neither holding children back nor promoting them on social grounds fully served their needs. Placing children in multi-age classes has been one answer.

Now there is a move toward integrating the first four years of school into a multi-age classroom in which children can work at their own pace and in their own sequence of learning. These "family groupings" – based on children of mixed ages and levels of development – foster continuous progress and offer children the opportunity to move ahead in areas of strength while taking extra time with difficult topics.

Eliminating the need for annual promotions within the guidelines of a set curriculum allows for greater flexibility of teaching/learning and removes the stress of deadlines. Both the teacher and the children are free to let learning evolve naturally. As we have emphasized before, this means neither the abandonment of discipline nor the adoption of an attitude "that anything will do." But it does mean that attention will shift from the curriculum to the learners. Though the curriculum will be used as a general guideline and resource for goal-setting, the children, rather than the curriculum, will determine the sequence and pace of learning.

Whether working in a combination grade (K-one, one-two, two-three) or in a four-year nongraded primary system with the kinds of family groupings based on age or level of maturity described later in this chapter, teachers will find that the mix of children working at different levels becomes the stimulus for greater independence of learning, a lot of peer modeling, and good social integration among children of differing ages. In such a setting, the spirit of cooperation that is an important element of teaching the learners' way comes to the fore. In fact, establishing a positive climate for learning is crucial to making family grouping successful, and in this chapter we will offer some specific suggestions for working with children in such mixed-age groupings.

As in the rest of the book, our discussions are based on firsthand experience. We began our joint work when Margaret was teaching a combination of kindergarten and grade one, and her early successes in teaching kindergarten children to read became the impetus for expanding our work to grade one and all areas of teaching. Since then, Margaret has taught for years in multi-age classes, including a kindergarten-grade-one-grade-two grouping. Her experience and that of colleagues working in multi-age classes in the upper levels of primary school form the basis of this chapter.

Both teachers and parents who are unfamiliar with the benefits and joys of family grouping have expressed their worries and fears. The examples shown below are readily answered by reference to the list of strengths.

Worries and fears about multi-age classes

Teachers' concerns
- A curriculum that stretches over several grades is too vast to be handled by one teacher.
- The programs for children of different ages are too diverse.
- There will be too much work preparing and teaching lessons.
- It will be like doing two or three jobs instead of just one.
- Organizing the classroom will be too difficult when you have so many different groups.
- I will have too many reading groups.
- How can I handle promotions when children are working at such diverse levels?
- Discipline will be a problem. The bigger children will bully and override the little ones.
- Distractions will disrupt learning as children of different levels work together in one classroom.
- Children at the mid-level in the class will look ahead at the books and writing of the older children and will then be bored.
- The most advanced group of children will not be sufficiently challenged. Their curriculum will be watered down.

Parents' concerns
- My child will not receive proper instruction in such a mixed group.
- My child should not be grouped together with a bunch of younger/older children.
- How can the teacher keep discipline when s/he has that many different jobs to do?
- There will be too many distractions for serious work when all those little kids are in class along with the older ones.

■ How can you challenge the older children when you have to keep your eyes on the little ones?

Strengths and benefits of multi-age classes

Years of working in multi-age classes that had family groupings and gave teacher and children the opportunity to work together for two years have convinced us of the many benefits and strengths inherent in the nongraded primary.

■ Family grouping helps the teacher keep the focus on the children. S/he teaches children, not a curriculum.

■ All children are ready to use written language to communicate. Because they are, they can participate in most of the interesting activities that capture and hold their interest.

■ The basic school work children do is the same for all ages. The teacher is relieved of teaching several versions of the same lesson because peer modeling becomes a strong part of the learning environment, one that encourages all children to learn to read and write in order to communicate.

■ Integrating the day – weaving reading, writing, and arithmetic into all activities during the day – builds the foundation for full, functional literacy and frees the teacher to work with individuals and small groups who need or want extra attention.

■ Since the children initiate and suggest many of the topics for discussion and study, there is no question of coaxing a class of bored children into completing assignments. Lessons arise out of the children's own interests.

■ The independence of working on projects and group activities inculcates thinking, learning, and problem-solving skills and frees the teacher from the need to plan the children's every move.

■ The children themselves become the keepers of classroom rules. As new groups of children arrive, their more experienced peers introduce them to classroom routines, privileges, responsibilities, and rules.

■ Skills emerge naturally and in the children's time-frame.

■ That kind of natural development makes for smooth progress and easy transitions from job to job and level to level. Children are free to surge ahead or linger based on their needs.

■ If the teacher establishes a climate of cooperation and consideration, older children will not only model learning and social behaviors, but will also become reading buddies,

playground protectors, and research partners. Confidence and self-concept are enhanced as children learn to get along with a wide range of people.

- The excitement of working with interesting, novel ideas and projects keeps the classroom buzzing with language that expands children's vocabulary and thought.

- The freedom to participate in work intended for more advanced children shows younger children where they are headed and what new challenges and excitement lie ahead. Since they are not required to perform at that level, they can enjoy participating at their level without any stress or anxiety.

- The entry/presence of young children adds new spark and enthusiasm to the entire group. The spontaneity and creativity of the young children contribute to the work done by more advanced children.

- Peer teaching stimulates all children and fosters the full development of special intelligences and interests in projects that are flexible in scope and time.

- Because evaluation is based on observing children closely, children will receive more individual attention and teaching that is geared exactly to their needs.

- Social skills and empathy develop in family groupings in which the teacher becomes a model of positive ways of interacting and dealing with interpersonal problems.

- When work is activity-based and closely connected to the children's interests, attention spans are long and concentration is intense. Skills are internalized in ways that move far beyond the ability to give right answers on a worksheet.

- Family grouping exemplifies constructivist ways of learning. As they interact with each other, the teacher, and the learning environment, children generate rules of reading, spelling, grammar, writing, and problem solving. They become active, self-initiating learners who are confident in their ability to take on new and unfamiliar learning tasks. They enjoy learning and they move ahead at their own pace and in their own way.

The transition to teaching in a multi-age classroom involves an attitude change and a new way of looking at learners. If you see the change as a challenge and the children as effective, curious learners, new ideas for teaching them will blossom forth. When the

***How to make
the transition
to teaching
multi-age classes***

usual restrictions of timetables and fixed curricula are removed, your teaching will take on new excitement.

If you adopt the same attitude for your own growth as the one you apply to the children – allowing for gradual development, initial gross performance, and building on strengths – the challenges and risks of your new way of teaching will enhance rather than detract from your joy of teaching.

Adapting the learning climate to the needs of family grouping

Teaching the learners' way fits family grouping

When teaching the learners' way, family grouping is simply a logical extension of the philosophy and practice of fitting teaching to the children's ways of learning. By extending the ages and developmental levels of children in a class, the learning environment comes even closer to approximating the natural learning environment at home where children learn from peers and are constantly surrounded by new challenges that extend their overall knowledge, language, social skills, ability to solve problems and think creatively.

Modeling, practice, and feedback as the main ways of teaching keep the focus on the kind of communication that children of diverse ages respond to readily. Just as at home parents don't talk separately to each of their children, so teachers need not deliver separate lessons to children in their classes. In fact, as we describe later on in this chapter, by modeling reading, writing, thinking (aloud), and problem solving, we simply invite children to participate at their own level much as they participate at their own level in activities at home.

Mixed ability grouping in most of the classroom activities enhances peer modeling and fosters continuous learning at the children's own pace. The spirit of cooperation allows each child to participate in group projects at his/her own ability and level of development. If Stewart is a particularly good artist, then he will contribute illustrations to a writing project that is carried out mostly by more advanced writers. If Sarah is the most knowledgeable speller in a group, she will supply standard spelling for work that needs to be accurate for publishing. This type of sharing of responsibilities and jobs gives all children the sense that they are part of the team and that they are making solid contributions. Their self-confidence is enhanced, and they see themselves as effective learners – a feeling that can be sadly lacking when all children are supposed to advance at the same pace and in the same way.

The ongoing assessment and close observations of children's progress that are integral to teaching the learners' way are ideally suited to working with children of differing ages. The focus on strengths and steps forward satisfy the needs of teachers, parents, and supervisors far better than matching of achievements against fixed standards and time lines. The knowledge that the children's work will demonstrate different "levels of knowing" will reassure the teacher that children are progressing, even though their work seems to show "lapses" from performing well in one setting to a lower level in another. That reassurance, along with the joy and excitement of teaching children who are eager to participate in the interesting daily activities, will help to convince teachers who feel hesitant about taking on integrated classes that family grouping works well for them and the children. Then they are ready to create the positive learning climate that undergirds the learners' way of teaching.

Accepting family grouping as natural and beneficial

Since we have a long tradition of grouping children by age for purposes of schooling, a first step in setting a favorable learning climate is to accept that family grouping is both natural and beneficial. A look at how children learn outside school makes it clear that only in school are they confined to learn in the exclusive company of children of their own age. Everywhere else, siblings, neighbors, friends, parents differ in age. Families certainly have a mix of ages, and this mix allows young children to learn rapidly. They have models of varying ages and levels of development to follow, and their own attempts at doing what "the big guys" do are accepted and encouraged. In that light, moving toward the nongraded primary looks much more natural.

Think of your own learning and try to recall the excitement of learning from a more experienced peer, someone you looked up to but who was not so far above you to take on the aura of a teacher. Perhaps a sport, hobby, or simply playing a game provided the opportunity to watch, then emulate, your hero. Did you find that learning more satisfying than following a structured lesson? Did it have lasting benefits? For young children, being allowed to stay up late like the big kids or go camping for the first time is apt to bring out "grown-up" behavior better than any admonition to stop acting like a baby. Watching a child trailing after a group of older children at play reveals the most amazing concentration, attention span, and persistence at trying something new and difficult.

Inherent in these examples is the knowledge that children learn well in learning communities that offer peer modeling as well as work or play that moves beyond their own experience. Curiosity, interest, the desire to do "what Jim and Bonnie are doing" activate learning and persistence. At the same time, the effort and stress for the "teachers" are minimal. Both teaching and learning function naturally and effectively.

As at home, family grouping in school means that activities are shared by everyone regardless of age. Whether reading, writing, participating in morning meeting, or working on special projects, all children participate – functioning at their own levels. During writing workshop, emergent writers may content themselves with drawing a picture and printing their names, while experienced writers produce coherent paragraphs, stories, or reports. When reading, children pick their own books or join unison reading to the extent that they can. In math activities, less experienced children may simply manipulate the concrete materials provided and make patterns with them while their older classmates move through the entire activity. Remembering how eager children are to emulate their peers, you find that all children derive benefits from the work and are ready to move on to their next level that much sooner because they have observed other children perform well.

Along with academic learning, children derive social benefits from the family grouping. In setting your classroom climate, cooperation and mutual consideration are of prime importance. Modeling courtesy, considerate behavior, and ways of getting along with children of differing ages help to build the children's confidence in school and out. Keeping children together and with the same teacher for two or more years removes the anxieties of deadlines, the fear of failure, or losing friends. The noncompetitive atmosphere leaves late bloomers ample time to catch up to their more mature peers and the focus on strengths and all steps forward keeps learning positive. Children model themselves after their teacher and will often give positive feedback to their classmates: "That looks great!" "I really like..." "That's a beautiful picture."

Children's confidence will also be fostered by the independence of learning that you inculcate when teaching the learners' way. Treating all children as responsible members of their learning community – regardless of age – encourages them to take charge of their own work. Since you are not talking down to any of them but offer the same interesting materials or lessons to all children, they react in kind and show themselves to be independent workers. That independence of learning and the children's willingness to work on their own will free you to work with individuals and small groups to make certain that children at all ability levels receive specific attention and are challenged to move ahead.

Creating the right physical environment

To accommodate children of divergent ages, you will need to rearrange your classroom to make space for physical movement and ease of sharing. Tables set in neat rows take up extra space and inhibit peer interaction. Pushing tables together into sets of four or six will give children the opportunity to work together and will also create space for carpeted areas, centers, and storage of the wide range of books and materials required to satisfy the needs and interests of all your learners. If you are lucky enough to have round or hexagonal tables, they will work even better to bring children together for sharing and cooperative projects.

Flexible seating that may be changed as the need arises enhances peer modeling and teaches children to get along with each other. If they keep their belongings in special baskets or boxes that can be carried easily, the children can move freely from one area to another. To vary the seating arrangement, we put out name tags to show children where they will sit that day or week, and a special table or group of tables becomes the space to call together small groups for small-group teaching. If some of the children decide to work on a special project, they may want to sit around the same table for the duration. But there will be no fixed grouping by age or ability level. Giving the children a choice from time to time adds fun and shows you what friendships are forming and who has found a reading buddy or writing partner.

Along with other centers, you may want to set up a special library corner as a quiet space to give children a chance to read or write quietly without being interrupted. The children themselves can stock the center with books brought from home or the library, and you may want to add items of special interest from time to time. Nonfiction materials, novels, or poetry will attract your independent readers to extend their voluntary reading during choosing time, particularly if there is also an inviting space.

Using teachable moments to create a community of learners

At home, children learn to talk, solve problems, and think through their daily interactions with their parents and siblings. There are no special lessons about taking things apart, thinking about cause and effect when you tip over a glass of water, or figuring out what approaches work when trying to join a group of older children at play. Talking and learning skills evolve in the context of everyday life, and children of all ages not only acquire specific knowledge but, more important, develop highly effective problem-solving and learning strategies.

The activity-centered climate of the nongraded primary class offers the same integrated learning. Along with new information, children continue to evolve their thinking, learning, and problem-solving skills. Showing a film about the Inuit way of life to two primary classes provided a particularly graphic example of the high-level learning children accomplish when they are free to pursue a special interest. The film was intended for upper elementary levels and contained a segment on the construction of igloos. Comments included remarks about the architectural soundness of igloos and the fact that the Inuit had evolved the perfect structure, given the materials they have available. Comments about structural features, angles of placing snow blocks, and the accurate proportions of the various parts caught the children's imagination.

When the two teachers noticed the excitement of the children, they decided on the spot to build on that interest with a follow-up activity and suggested a building project. Giving the children the choice to work singly or in teams, they asked them to build the best igloo they could out of materials available in the two classrooms. Without worrying about differences in age, children formed teams and began to plan and then build igloos using blocks, bricks, Styrofoam cubes, boxes, and Plasticine. The two teachers stood back to give the children full scope in their creative work. Within the teams, discussions about structural work, problems of strength,

Bins and shelves aid movement around the classroom

Baskets that hold the children's belongings can be moved easily.

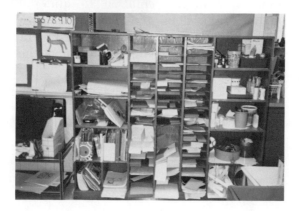

Open shelves keep writing supplies in easy reach.

stability, and durability accompanied the construction work. At the end of the afternoon, everyone participated in evaluating the various structures. Though the film was clearly intended for older, more advanced students, all of the children from two classes encompassing kindergarten to grade two participated and interacted with each other and the building materials.

Respecting the children's ability to take in advanced information, going with their expressed interest, making time for an exciting project, standing back to let the children do the work, all combined to create a learning situation that fostered independence and higher level thinking skills. The physical construction work proceeded on the basis of analysis of the information offered, synthesis of the various aspects to be considered, integration of several factors, and finally evaluation of both the process and finished products. Trial-and-error learning was coupled with critical analysis of what works/does not work and why; problem solving included physical and oral work; cooperation among team members promoted the expression of opinions and discussions about problems and solutions.

Imagination and right-brain thinking added much to the analysis and synthesis of available information. Children did not limit themselves to single solutions but opted for building, drawing, sculpting, and combinations of these to achieve their goals. Attention spans were stretched far beyond that to be expected of 5-year-olds or even 7-year-olds, and the cooperation between two classes added extra interest.

In this instance a film provided the impetus. At other times, books, visits to a museum, or an interesting travel souvenir brought from home will inspire children to undertake research, explore interesting questions or problems, and foster extended reading and writing for a group of children or the entire class. Building on teachable moments, being open to change timetables or lesson plans at a moment's notice, and integrating all learning create the same effective learning community that home has been for toddlers. Problem solving, critical thinking, discussions, and evaluation become natural parts of everyday learning for children of all ages.

Making room for peer modeling enhances the learning climate

When you have a classroom filled with children of roughly the same age, peer modeling is not nearly as extensive as it is in family groupings. Younger members of the group are eager to learn what their older classmates are doing; more mature children band together to form special interest groups to work on projects and learn from each other. But they also become reading buddies, spelling mentors, and art partners for the younger children in the class.

Since projects form such an important part of day-to-day teaching, children who have special intelligences or knowledge about topics like gardening, pet care, a trip to Hawaii, at times become the models or information givers for a group of children or the entire class. And they are not always the older students. In fact, producing books, dioramas, or special presentations often bring children of differing ages together as a team, and the learning within those groups has a wonderful mutuality.

Children understand and value knowledge and standards of performance. They take age into account when working with each other, but they also take critical looks at work that obviously is not up to the usual standard of a fellow student. Margaret observed a group of children gather around Chris whose printing had become quite careless. Taking their lead from Margaret's way of commenting, they informed him that he was able to do much better than that. When Chris objected, Peter pointed out that before moving into grade two Chris had made far neater numerals and that his 4s and 6s did not look nearly as good as before. Chris reluctantly agreed and proceeded to improve his printing. No one had suggested this interaction; nevertheless children chose to comment, and they did so in the same matter-of-fact voice that their teacher uses when discussing work.

Cooperation and sharing are as natural in school family groups as they are at home. The production of books, presentation of plays or reader theater, the creation of new centers, and the stocking of the library corner invite cooperative learning that often brings mature and emergent learners together. Children themselves choose their partners, and they do not confine themselves to children of their own age or level of performance.

Building cooperation among children makes learning safe and productive

Whether grouped by age or in family groupings, children respond best to the teacher's modeling of courtesy, consideration, and cooperation. As you demonstrate attentive listening, genuine caring, and quiet ways of talking, children tend to follow your lead. But the introduction of mixed-age grouping may require some extra effort to make children aware of effective ways of working together. From time to time you will need to remind more advanced readers or spellers to give other children a chance to speak up or to do a job without a chorus of voices in the background. Similarly, you will need to provide opportunities for your independent readers and writers to work on more challenging tasks than those suitable for whole-class participation.

When learning is based on modeling, practice, and feedback, even your youngest learners participate from the outset. They are used to watching others and base their own activities on those observations. As they develop independence of learning and accept responsibility for moving from news time to writing workshop and from there to center time, they will free your time to work with individuals and small groups to meet special needs, teach specific lessons, or extend and challenge the learning of your mature students.

Flexible grouping aids both continuous learning and continuous entry

To make certain that all children receive the personal attention, challenge, or reassurance they need, the nongraded primary will include a number of different groupings. Depending on the size of the school and the number of students at the various levels, there may be both two-year and three-year groupings. Unless classes are quite small in number, extending the integration over the four years from kindergarten to grade three could overtax the teacher's ability to meet the needs of all children. But we have found age groupings that span three years quite workable.

If the student body is large enough to permit the inclusion of two-year groupings, options to move children to the next level that fits their particular needs are that much greater. Children who advance rapidly could move from the first level to a class that would approximate the usual grade-two-three combination and complete the primary years in three years; children who are ready to advance but still need extra support may work best if they are moved to the upper level multi-age class spanning the last three years – the equivalent of grades one, two, and three – in order to continue with some of the lower-level work while being exposed to the full range of the primary curriculum. Late bloomers or more immature children may spend the full three years in their initial class and then move on for one or two years in the upper level group. The combinations can be varied to match the specific needs and intelligences of the children with the special intelligences and strengths of teachers working at the different levels.

In smaller schools there may just be two groupings – early primary and later primary. The former would encompass kindergarten, grades one and two, and the latter grades one, two, and three. Since several teachers will work at each of these levels, there will be the opportunity for team teaching, sharing of special resources, and joint work on special projects as described later on in this chapter. Having several classes working at the same level allows for lateral as well as upward movement of students. Having associate or team teachers certainly opens the door for lots of information sharing and mutual support. The fear of trying out new approaches is reduced when colleagues can consult with each other on what has worked and how to start, and the excitement is enhanced by sharing observations and new insights about children's learning.

If the nongraded primary includes dual entry (bringing in 5-year-olds twice a year) or continuous entry (throughout the year on their fifth birthday), the school year will start with fewer students to make room for the incoming 5-year-olds. In some schools lower primary classes start with as few as ten children in September. Either through continuous intake or the second intake in the new year, the numbers move to the full complement of some twenty-five students. In the meantime, teacher and students have had the opportunity for a lot of individual contact that will enhance learning on all levels and make it both fun and free of stress.

The climate of cooperation that is so important in the classroom makes for smooth entry

There will be a close bond between teacher and students, and before new students arrive, you may find it a good policy to discuss with

the children in your class how they can best welcome the newcomers, make them feel comfortable in school, and help them learn. Suggesting that as experienced learners they have a lot to offer brings out the best in children, and having them participate in genuine discussions about the special needs, hopes, and fears the newcomers will have, establishes a learning community more solidly than simply laying down rules of conduct. In turn, the newcomers may spark new enthusiasm for the learning activities that are fresh and new to them but familiar to the rest of the class.

By sharing the responsibility of welcoming newcomers you reinforce peer teaching and peer modeling. More often than not, the children, rather than the teacher, show inexperienced students where things are, how to do things, how to behave, and what not to do. Encouraging a buddy system whereby two or three children work cooperatively smoothes out the entry process that much more. joining other teachers in special events, group projects or team teaching, enhances academic learning and prepares children to move to the next level to shift to more advanced work and to make room for more incoming 5-year-olds.

Making Easter bunnies can be quite a challenge

Now and then special opportunities come along to reinforce the lesson of cooperation among children of diverse ages. The day before spring break Margaret was asked to teach a grade-three-four class as well as her own. The children, ready for their holiday, were at their most active and excited. Quiet table work or simple story reading did not hold out much hope for captivating more than forty children ranging from kindergarten to grade four. To create a climate of cooperation. Margaret informed the children that she was giving them a challenge. They were to form teams of four to work on a project. Each team had to include one or two of the younger children. They had to be active members of the team and participate fully in the work. The task was to make the largest Easter bunny they could produce using any of the materials available in the two classrooms.

As work got under way with planning, discussing, explaining things to younger team members, looking at books about Easter bunnies, and reading some of the stories to each other, the teams spread out to occupy both classrooms and the connecting hallway. No one had time for recess, though the older boys usually engaged in a game of soccer at that time. Instead, producing their bunny, comparing notes, and sharing equipment and supplies carried the group through the entire morning. The teacher simply walked around among them, commenting here and there on the work of the young artists. Not only did this project keep the younger children fully involved in the work, but toward the end, two teams decided to join forces to create special background effects for their bunnies.

Creativity blossomed as children were left free to develop their own ideas. There was every variety of bunny from Hawaiian bunnies on surfboards to weird rabbits with funky clothes; there were mother bunnies with gorgeous hats, girl bunnies with real woven baskets (based on Mexican weaving), and bunnies with Easter eggs. The concentration, hard work, and effective team participation paid rich dividends in product as well as cooperation.

The Easter parade

Team work, use of all available materials, imagination, and hard work combined to make the Easter bunny project a wonderful success.

At the end of the session, all teams made a presentation telling how their bunny was made, who did what, and how they got their ideas. Some of the older students wrote about their work, and, as a final touch, their teacher brought in measuring sticks asking everyone to take three measures and to compare them with those of other teams. Not only did this work add measurement and math, but it also introduced younger team members to the metric system and its units of measurement.

The bunnies went on display at the school and were solid reminders of a day of hard work, fun, marvelous cooperation, and the productive possibilities inherent in family grouping. Whether spur-of-the-moment or planned in advance, projects of this type demonstrate to teacher and children alike that cooperative, interactive work flourishes when everyone is respected and invited to participate as a full team member.

Adapting activities to fit the varying needs of students

Reading

Story time

Reading aloud to children is an important part of reading instruction at all levels of primary school. In many cases, you will want to call together all the children to listen to a book, story, poem, or magazine article. If the language is rich and varied and the topic absorbing, children of all ages will derive pleasure and learning from these sessions. To make sure that each child feels fully included, give children the opportunity to choose books or stories to be read aloud. Make it a point to give credit to the chooser and remind the children that this is someone's special choice. No matter how often a favorite story is heard, children enjoy the fun of story time. Just as story reading at home makes for feelings of safety, enjoyment, and confidence, so reading aloud in the family grouping at school confers benefits on all listeners.

To extend the reading scope of your more advanced students, include more lengthy works, reading a chapter at a time, picking either the morning/afternoon session when the younger children are not present, or a period during which children have a choice of activity. In the latter case, any child, regardless of age, has the option of listening to the reading.

Another way of adapting oral reading to more advanced work is to encourage children to form their own reading circles to share a favorite book or story. The child selecting the reading material may be the one who is doing the reading, or children in the group may want to take turns. As long as they listen quietly, all children may join the circle, but no one is forced to sit still to the bitter end. When interest has flagged or the reading has proved to be outside of the interest or skill of any of the listeners, they are free to move out of the circle. But as a courtesy to the readers and their listeners, children who do not wish to participate are asked to select a quiet task elsewhere in the classroom.

Visitors to the classroom, parents, reading buddies, student teachers – anyone coming in – can extend the scope of story time by reading aloud to one, two, or more children. Since, within the requirements of completing given tasks, children are free to choose activities, they have the option of joining these oral reading sessions and often do so. If the visitors bring in their own reading materials, interest may widen and extend to new topics or authors.

At the upper levels of primary school, some of your advanced readers may prefer to read their own novels, stories, or nonfiction materials as their way of having story time. If they are not interested in the choice of the day, they may wish to withdraw quietly to sit by themselves or in a small group to do their own silent reading.

Unison reading

Unison reading of big books, experience charts, or multiple-copy books lends itself well to family grouping. As long as children continue to benefit from oral reading practice – before shifting more fully to silent reading – they can come together in small-group or whole-class gatherings to participate in unison reading. Here the principle of "finding their own level" takes full effect. Fluent, experienced readers will read along with the leader; less proficient, more timid, or inexperienced readers will speak up as they can; some may still simply track the print with their eyes as the leader runs a pointer or bookmark along the lines of print. If you are very familiar with the material read and frequently lift your eyes from the print, these sessions become excellent opportunities to note the level of participation of students in your class.

As with story reading, unison reading is not initiated only by the teacher. Peer reading, spontaneous small groups, reader's theatre, reading buddies, or visitors may all spark unison reading in which one or more children participate. The freedom to move around, to form small groups, and to participate at whatever level is right for each child make unison reading possible at many times during the day for children at all levels.

Book time

Book time will have to be flexible when your class includes children ranging in age from five to seven. Here the silent corner in your room will find full use. Children who have advanced to reading silently for extended periods may want to withdraw to their favorite spot to become immersed in their reading, while those who are still emergent readers will need the opportunity to move around, talk quietly, and exchange books or comments with their peers. If your room is well stocked with books and all kinds of language arts materials, book time and center or choosing time can take place simultaneously to give emergent readers the option to shift from looking at books or stories to working with other language arts material.

At the beginning of the year, when book time may be relatively short, the entire class can participate fully in sitting down with books to be looked at or read. As the time devoted to book time expands throughout the year, less advanced readers or children who still find it hard to sit still for extended periods of time will need the option to move about. Children don't have to sit at their tables during book time but are free to curl up on the beanbag, under your desk, on the floor, or even in the coat closet. They may share quietly and prepare reader presentations. Book time is neither silent nor passive as children choose the reading involvement appropriate to their level of development.

Reading groups

Small-group reading is one way to assure that those children who still need encouragement and help with emergent or developing reading receive personal attention. Though not grouping by age or level, you will want to call together children who will benefit from this personal attention. Unison reading, and individual reading at the children's choice at the end of the session, provide the opportunity to reinforce the work done in larger groups. At the outset, emergent readers tend to turn pages without focusing closely on the print. When working with them during reading group you will have the opportunity to help them use their bookmarks so that they begin to track print with their eyes, and their participation gains concentration and focus.

Small-group reading with four or five children will afford many opportunities to make close observations of the reading development of individual children. Experienced readers who have shifted to fluent silent reading may not want or need group reading time. They often prefer to work on their own reading, writing, or special projects. To give you a chance to take a close look at their reading and to make sure that they do not feel neglected or overlooked, you may on occasion invite them to read to you or their peers.

Writing

Morning meeting

During sharing at morning meeting and news time, all children will have the opportunity to participate. At times you may need to ask more mature or more outspoken children to give others a chance. But if you encourage all to speak up and maintain eye contact with each speaker, you will find that children begin to emulate your model and become more attentive listeners. Once again, you will observe that children will find their own level of participation. Inexperienced speakers will simply give you a brief statement, while those more accustomed to expressing themselves will help with spelling, editing, paragraphing, and commenting on peculiarities of spelling or punctuation.

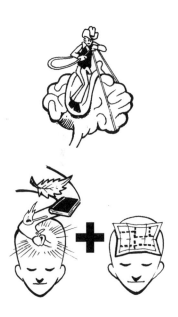

If your class includes children who come only half a day, you may want to have separate news times for them and your more advanced readers and writers.

While older children are busy with writing workshop, children who have just arrived for their half-day class can gather around you for a brief news sharing that gives them ample opportunity to speak up. Once they have shared their news, they will be ready to join the more experienced writers in the writing workshop session. In this way you avoid any difficulties in asking 5-year-olds to sit still for extended periods. But once they have settled into the routine of the classroom, they will derive a lot of benefit from peer modeling if you ask them to join the rest of the children during morning meeting and news time.

Writing workshop

Coupling writing workshop with center or choosing time gives experienced writers ample time to write as much as they wish without making less mature or less experienced children linger over their writing for too long. It becomes important to set flexible guidelines for the amount of work individual children are expected to produce before being allowed to move to centers of their choice. Since writing time becomes a favorite for many children, we rarely hear objections from children when we request differing amounts of work or when we update those amounts as children mature. They quite readily accept that some children are not yet able to write much, print on lines, or produce paragraphs or stories. Though they enjoy modeling their writing after each other, they maintain a great deal of individuality and do not compare their work in a competitive way. But they do like to advance and will tell you or demonstrate to you that they are ready to move ahead to more or more complex work. Being flexible about assigned work does not mean that children will do the least possible. More often it means that they upgrade and increase their writing beyond your expectations.

If there are occasional lapses in this rule of thumb, you can explain your guidelines for required work to the children. When Tyler decided that he would take the lead from Nicky, put down *TOK TOK TO*, and hand that in as his writing work for the day, Margaret reminded him that since he was well able to write complete sentences, that kind of work was not good enough. As Tyler had heard Margaret praise Nicky for his work, she explained that Nicky had just taken an important step – shifting from pretend writing to using letters – that deserved to be acknowledged. Tyler agreed and proceeded to do his own work at his own level.

Though you may want to start separate groups of children on their writing workshop at different times, having them come together as a large group to plan either their individual writing or special group projects can be very productive. Brainstorming ideas, expanding them, suggesting special words, doing idea webbing to aid composition can readily be done by the whole class. Though not all children are ready to use all the ideas or aids in their writing, most will eagerly put forth ideas or suggestions. They enjoy and benefit from the feeling of doing the same work as the older children. Their drawings may reflect what has been discussed, and they may team up with more experienced writers to collaborate on putting together a special book or project.

The administrative work connected with writing workshop can certainly be handled by all children. Shortly after they enter school 5-year-olds will recognize their names in print and will therefore be able to file and date-stamp their own drawings or written work. Getting their own paper, putting out pencils and crayons, and cleaning up afterwards are integral parts of the writing work, and all children will be able to do their share.

Incidental writing

Whether they are still pretend writing, babbling in print, or have progressed to invented spelling and fluent writing, all children will readily engage in the incidental writing that fills the day. Writing letters, making greeting cards, putting up notices or warning signs, making lists, or recording observations of science projects are natural parts of the learning day and can be shared by all. Helping peers in ways that follow the example of the teacher will give the inexperienced writers a boost. When Emily turned to Wendy for help with spelling, Wendy considered Emily's level of writing development and asked, "Do you want that in standard spelling or invented spelling?"

Since writing is as natural a part of in-class communication as reading or talking, emergent writers will be eager to develop their writing skills. The pervasive use of writing to communicate provides the necessary practice to advance writing skills more solidly than the careful presentation of structured lessons about spelling or use of particles of speech. The learning community of the classroom will enhance written communication as effectively as the learning community in the home enhances oral communication and social learning.

Mathematics

Using manipulative work to make math concepts concrete

Throughout the primary grades, children need concrete demonstrations of the math concepts they learn. The progression from concrete learning to more abstract work is as solid a part of the

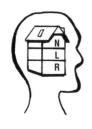

learners' way as the move from gross approximations to finer discrimination of detail. In fact, we have found that the need for manipulative ways of learning is not limited to young children. When working with adult students who have had difficulty with times tables or fractions, we have seen that discovery aha! breakthrough when laying out paper clips as counters – two-four-six-eight – and using coins to look at quarters, three-quarters, seven-tenths, or nine-one-hundredths.

As in reading and writing, all children are able to watch your modeling and listen to your explanations. They will then proceed to work at their own level with the materials you have provided using bricks, blocks, or unifix cubes to count, add, subtract, and develop times tables. While more mature students will follow your lesson with good accuracy, arranging materials in tens, representing large numbers with rows of unifix cubes, and transferring their findings to paper-and-pencil work, less mature children may simply put together rough approximations of what their older peers are doing, create their own versions of the work modeled, or add their unifix cubes to an emerging group project. Their attention spans will be shorter, and they are likely to shift into play, using the materials to make patterns or build structures.

If you stand back and observe how different children work, you will note distinct developmental stages and moves forward as children shift from being unable to count accurately, to connecting numbers and concrete materials, to adding, counting by twos or tens, and from there to more abstract concepts of adding units and tens to represent large numbers. In math, as in reading and spelling, giving the children room to generate their own rules through discovery learning will build a solid foundation for more advanced work. Encouraging them to work their own way, to experiment and "mess about" as Bruner (1957) puts it, makes learning safe, productive, and creative. Work within family groupings sparks cooperative projects and demonstrates to everyone that math, like reading and writing, is an interesting part of everyday living.

Making room for practice

To solidify learning, math needs practice time just as reading and writing do. Once you have demonstrated the lesson of the day – whether to a small group or the whole class – allow ample time for the children to work with both the concrete materials and the paper-

and-pencil task. Do not insist that the work must be done exactly as you showed it, but trust the children to come to the right solutions in their way and in their time. Working together, talking about approaches to problems, comparing notes on solutions are wonderful ways of internalizing thinking skills and problem-solving strategies.

Family grouping is no obstacle to weaving math into everyday discussions and activities. If you include calendar work, counting days, looking at the numbers on the calendar, and making notes of the number of holidays or Sundays in the month, everyone can share. Birthdays offer the opportunity to compare ages, add them all up, make patterns with the numbers, and compare them to each other and that of the teacher or other adults. Cooking, making things, planning money for special events, and counting the number of children absent and present further expand the use of numbers and math. The "corner store" with play money or real coins offers the challenge of making change.

The math center with games, counting materials, scales, and perhaps an old adding machine invites children to apply their growing knowledge. If you have a computer available, math programs with visual effects are sure to generate lots of voluntary practice. To give everyone a chance to use such popular games, children may need to draw names to see whose turn it is on a given day.

Social studies

If the thought of multi-age classes conjures up visions of teaching several separate lessons each time the curriculum lists a social studies topic, think once again of the learning community at home. All of the children are included in the daily activities, and they draw whatever they are ready for from the interactions with others. If the family is visiting a shopping center, Mom and Dad are likely to focus on the stores and items connected with their shopping list, older children may be interested in clothes, books, or sports equipment, and the youngest member of the family is likely to be looking for toys and the ice cream treat that often concludes such a visit. Though the children focus attention on their own interests, they are at the same time learning about not getting too far away from the rest of the family, needing money to pay for goods and services, having to be careful not to run into people who are

*Integrating the
teaching of
specific subjects*

crowding the mall, and a host of other lessons connected with shopping and moving in crowded places. While they are still toddlers riding in shopping carts at the supermarket, children learn about the interesting places where buns, candies, toys, or comic books are to be found. They find out what they can touch and what is out of bounds, and by the time they can walk around on their own, they know a great deal about supermarkets without having had specific lessons or scaled-down versions of the upper level social-studies unit.

In all our years of working with multi-age classes, we have rarely found it necessary to teach separate lessons to make allowances for children's differences in age or experience. Just as we keep in mind what skills will need to be developed in reading, writing, and arithmetic, so we keep our eye on the required topics of the social studies curricula for the groups of children in our class. And just as we foster the development of specific skills and concepts within the context of meaningful reading and writing, so we offer the social studies units in meaningful, integrated ways. More often than not, the children themselves make a suggestion for work that incorporates the lessons they need to learn.

Information on family life, other cultures and their ways, nutrition, and textiles are among the lessons learned by the entire class when we get ready for our annual Mexican Fiesta. As the children prepare for the big day, they read and write about the country, discuss differences and similarities between its customs and ours, prepare some of the special foods from written recipes, and learn a bit about the agriculture or special products of the country in the process. While making costumes, they learn about textiles, weaving, and embroidery. The production of *piñatas* expands into sculpture and ethnic art, and the dances foster the development of rhythm and coordination.

So many lessons, so many levels of performance, and all are pursued eagerly in the spirit of enquiry and the fun of doing interesting work that ultimately leads to a very special day. Neither age nor level of proficiency presents barriers to participation. As they make their *rebozos* and *serapes*, the more mature children will do elaborate decorative work while their less advanced classmates content themselves with producing a fringe at the edge and letting it go at that. The rest of the work shows similar adjustments depending on age, skill, and interest. But all children participate and learn eagerly. If you or the children in your class have resources or interests that include other ethnic groups, you can have special events each year. Inviting parents and other classes to participate is half the fun and adds to the learning.

The same integration of lessons can be achieved with other social studies units as well. If the curriculum calls for a look at specific industries such as logging, fishing, or mining, you can include discussions of weather and the seasons, or anything else that younger children are expected to learn. By broadening your approach to the units to be offered, the learning becomes more interesting for you and the children alike. Resources such as films, books, and special information pamphlets are rarely geared to a narrow focus. With the flexible approach of the learners' way you will encourage the learners of all ages to participate in their way without pressure or anxiety. The fun, excitement, and interest generated by this open approach will spark a lot of reading, writing, and arithmetic work, and you will find that you can check off the various social studies units on your list, confident that children are building their learning skills in meaningful and productive ways.

For even though specific social studies units may be required, the focus of today's curriculum is on developing learning skills rather than on simply gathering facts. Children are expected to learn how to collect information, record data, make hypotheses, draw inferences and conclusions, and to evaluate what has emerged from their work. The safety of being encouraged to work at their own level and the open-ended nature of projects invite all children to work to their capacity without setting limits or curbing creativity.

Science

For science, too, the emphasis is not so much on conveying information as it is on becoming familiar and comfortable with scientific enquiry. Information gathering, learning from observations and experiments, keeping track of observations, measuring and recording data, becoming familiar with scientific terminology, developing enquiry methods, hypothesis testing, and preparing reports are taking precedence over memorizing formulas or the parts of insects or flowers. Acquiring specific information has become the by-product of the constructivist process that characterizes activity-centered learning.

La Cucaracha

1

La cucaracha, la cucaracha,
Ya no quiere caminar,
Porque no tiene,
Porque le falta,
La patita principal.

2

La cucaracha, la cucaracha,
Doesn't venture out at night
Because she hasn't,
Oh, no, she hasn't,
A little candle to light.

3

La cucaracha, la cucaracha,
Has to let her head go bare,
Because she hasn't,
Oh, no, she hasn't,
A little hat she can wear.

4

La cucaracha, la cucaracha,
Often bumps into a tree,
Because she hasn't,
Oh, no, she hasn't,
Glasses to help her to see.

5

La cucaracha, la cucaracha,
Likes it here at South Park School
Because she thinks that,
Oh, yes, she knows that,
Mexican lunches are cool!

Andrew L.

Mexican Fiesta

MENU

Mexican rice: green, red, and spiced
Enchiladas
Tortillas : chopped lettuce, cheese, and onions

Mexican mash
Refried beans
Vegetable tray
Corn bread
Salsa, guacamole, nachos
Cinnamon tea
Ponche de pina
Tropical fruit on skewers
Mexican wedding cookies (made by the children)

PROGRAMME

Welcome
Luncheon
Entertainment
    Game - Señor Lobo
    Songs - Tingalayo
            La Cucaracha, South Park version
    Dance - La Razpa
Piñatas for the children
Thank you

Artwork forms an important part of projects

Andrew's artwork is strong and expressive as a beautiful cover for the Mexican Fiesta program. Though other children of Andrew's age are more advanced in their reading and writing, his work received top honor. This type of acknowledgment of his special intelligence builds the confidence that enhanced Andrew's reading practice.

Showing a video turns into the production of a research report

Far from overloading you with teaching separate science lessons to the various age groups in your class, the nongraded primary will help you experience new excitement and ease of introducing all the children to work that extends well beyond the carefully circumscribed lessons of the past. Margaret's team teacher, Linda Picciotto, showed her kindergarten-grade-one class a video about the sea life near their home. Though the commentary was intended for adults, the children enjoyed the beautiful photography, and their teacher rephrased or discussed the more difficult segments. Everyone agreed that the section on the octopus was most enjoyable, and the teacher's suggestion that it might be interesting to write a "true book" about the octopus was accepted with enthusiasm.

Research activities included reference to the video, reading books obtained from the school library, and a visit to the local Undersea Garden to take a look at live octopuses. The entire class participated in recording the information on large charts. Notes were organized on the basis of categories suggested by the children with some prompting from the teacher. The notes became a synthesis of all the information gathered, including another stop-start run of the video to make time for writing down specifics. In this case the teacher did the recording, and the children ran and then stopped the video.

To demonstrate the nature of rough drafts and brief research notes, the teacher used incomplete sentences, crossed out words, made inserts using a caret to mark the place, and moved items from one category to another as needed. The discussions about where information would fit in best revealed the need for another catch-all category: Interesting Things About Octopuses.

The project extended over several days, and the class produced no more than two or three chapters in one sitting. Editing and proofreading generated spirited discussions and excellent suggestions as evidenced in the example of editing the research note, "push water through their siphons to move."

EMILY: *How about, "They push water through their siphons to move?"*

EVAN: Move *is too boring.* "They use their siphons when they want to move fast."

TEACHER: *Can someone suggest a word we might use instead of* move?

JESSE: Crawl

MARY LOU: Swim

ROBERT: *They are like cannon balls. "They shoot through the water."*

EMILY: *How about, "They push water through their siphons to shoot themselves through the water"?*

ALL: *That's good!*

ALEX: *I think we should say, "They squirt water through their siphons."*

Push won by a narrow margin in a vote taken to decide between *squirt* and *push*.

During discussions of the text, the teacher pointed out the need for a title page, table of contents, and bibliography, and the children agreed that their book should have all the proper pages that regular books have. In this instance the teacher did the final printing using the word processor, but independent writers in a multi-age class could well take on that job, taking turns at typing, proofreading, and editing.

To illustrate both the big-book version and the individual copies, children made two illustrations, one large, one small, to fit the two books. They selected the page they wished to illustrate and signed their drawings, which were then pasted above the text using rubber cement. Small books were bound with a tag-board cover, and the large book was laminated to preserve it for long-term use and enjoyment.

Though the books themselves were produced by the grade-one students, kindergarten children were involved in much of the work and they responded enthusiastically to their teacher's suggestion that they think of writing a joke book about octopuses called *The Untrue Book About Octopuses*. In the meantime the first-graders learned and modeled the entire process of putting together a science report. All children found out about the gradual evolution of an entire book full of scientific facts.

Activity-based teaching develops learning and thinking skills

Whether your science projects consist of growing plants, hatching chicks, observing animals, or doing experiments in chemistry, all children will take interest in the physical work. They can measure growth, chart changes, discuss new developments, hear or read about the development of the embryo in the eggshell, and draw pictures to illustrate their findings. Encouraging full enquiry and interesting fact-finding forays will produce extra excitement and long attention spans. If you allow the children full scope to suggest, discuss, and research topics of interest to them, you will learn along with them and will have ample opportunity to model learning and enquiry behaviors. It has been our experience that some children who are late bloomers in the areas of reading and writing nevertheless have special intelligences in other areas – nature, interpersonal, or artistic – and are quite ready to share their expertise with the entire class.

W hen teaching children whose ages and ability levels range over two, three, or even four years, a focus on specific skills becomes overwhelming and unmanageable. If you keep the learning objectives of one year's work in mind, you can make adjustments to observe how different children progress toward fulfilling those objectives; but when you try to fit your teaching to accommodate two, three, or four separate curricula, your focus will need to shift to the broader goals of literacy, numeracy, thinking and learning skills. Descriptive notes rather than marks on worksheets will form the basis for recording and reporting how children's learning evolves. Continuous progress requires continuous evaluation. Keep records throughout the year that include notes on problem solving, discussions, artwork, social behavior, and willingness to participate in or try new work.

To assess progress draw upon the observational and informal methods of recording steps forward and use your observations as guides to your teaching. As you record how individual children progress along the literacy continuum, you will become aware of areas that need special attention or reinforcement. If your independent readers and writers are shifting to chapter reading and lengthy written work, you may need to work with them on

**Evaluating
progress**

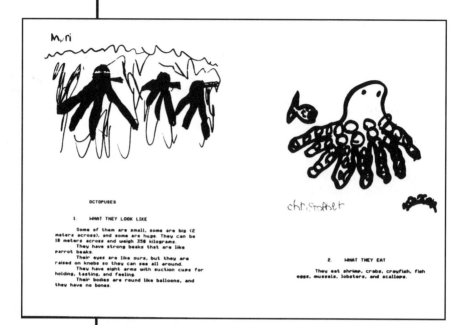

Myri

OCTOPUSES

1.   WHAT THEY LOOK LIKE

Some of them are small, some are big (2
meters across), and some are huge. They can be
18 meters across and weigh 350 kilograms.
They have strong beaks that are like
parrot beaks.
Their eyes are like ours, but they are
raised on knobs so they can see all around.
They have eight arms with suction cups for
holding, tasting, and feeling.
Their bodies are round like balloons, and
they have no bones.

christopher

2.   WHAT THEY EAT

They eat shrimp, crabs, crayfish, fish
eggs, mussels, lobsters, and scallops.

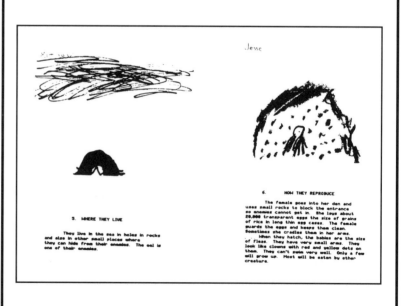

Jesse

5.   WHERE THEY LIVE

They live in the sea in holes in rocks
and also in other small places where
they can hide from their enemies. The eal is
one of their enemies.

6.   HOW THEY REPRODUCE

The female goes into her den and
uses small rocks to block the entrance
so enemies cannot get in. She lays about
20,000 transparent eggs the size of grains
of rice in long thin egg cases. The female
guards the eggs and keeps them clean.
When they hatch, the babies are the size
of fleas. They have very small arms. They
look like clowns with red and yellow dots on
them. They can't swim very well. Only a few
will grow up. Most will be eaten by other
creature.

*Junior scientists do a fine
research job*

*Team work in research,
reporting, editing, and
illustrating produced* The
True Book of Octopuses.
*Children took a keen interest
in seeing that their book was
accurate and the spelling
standard. Writing done on the
side reflects that interest but
shows the children's
own spelling.*

Octopuseis | Octopuseis Can Saey iek. They can Suay oat of tie plasis. They can lay 20,000 eeg.

Octopuses can spray ink. They can squeeze out of tight places. They can lay 20,000 eggs.

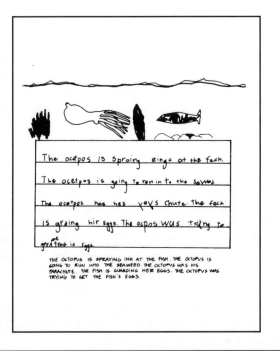

The ocetpos is spraing einge at the fech. The ocetpos is going to ron in te the sewed. The ocetpos has hes yoys chute. The fech is graing hir Eggs. The ocpos was triyng te get the fech is Eggs.

THE OCTOPUS IS SPRAYING INK AT THE FISH. THE OCTOPUS IS GOING TO RUN INTO THE SEAWEED. THE OCTOPUS HAS HIS PARACHUTE. THE FISH IS GUARDING HER EGGS. THE OCTOPUS WAS TRYING TO GET THE FISH'S EGGS.

paragraphing, critical reading, or advanced spelling work. If emergent readers continue to draw heavily on pictures to "read," you may want to have them work with some of the highly predictive, repetitive texts to encourage greater focus on print. If the writing activities of several children focus on dinosaurs, suggesting a research project on the topic may generate new steps forward.

Seeing assessment as a way of keeping track of new strengths and helping children build on emerging skills eliminates the anxiety and worry often connected with assessment. Of course you will want to refer to the curriculum guides and use them as checklists on which you cross off everything that has been taken care of and note what opportunities of learning you need to create to meet additional items. Such reference work will reassure you, your supervisors, and the children's parents that the students are moving forward toward becoming proficient learners and toward entering the next level of elementary school.

Continuous assessment and continuous intake go hand in hand with continuous promotion. The classroom teacher, more than standardized tests, will determine at what point children are ready to move to a higher level – both in classroom work and in promotion to the next level within the school. If children demonstrate during mid-year that they are ready for more advanced work, they can advance to a new class. The cooperation between different classes and teachers throughout the year will have prepared children for working in a number of classroom settings and with different groups of children and teachers. Similarly, teachers are likely to know newcomers to their class from joint class projects so that the transition will be smooth and easy for everyone concerned.

Keeping parents informed

If the nongraded primary is a new development in your area, it will be important to keep parents informed of the new ways of teaching/learning. They may want to be reassured that continuous progress does not mean the abandonment of standards or less learning for their children. Beginning the year with a parent information session – perhaps a tea at which the children serve their parents – then following it up with regular newsletters about new developments, projects the children are working on, and strides forward they are making, will demonstrate that the nongraded primary is fostering learning in a positive way.

Just as you build on strengths when you work with the children in your class, so it will help to take a very positive stand in communicating with parents. No doubt they will have questions and worries, but if you can point to all the solid benefits their children derive from the nongraded primary, parents are likely to become your strong allies, supporters, and helpers. If you remind parents of their own ways of learning and the ways their children learn at home they will see that continuous progress will help rather than hinder their child's learning.

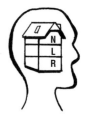

Drawing the parallel between learning within the family and in family groupings at school will draw attention to the benefits of peer modeling. Parents will see the advantage of having children participate in interesting, meaningful work and of working with peers who are more experienced. Once their children are launched into the program, they will note the independence and responsibility engendered by the integrated ways of learning. The absence of anxiety and stress will certainly have the parents' approval. They know their children will learn with greater ease if they are not worrying about what lies ahead – meeting deadlines, getting a poor report card, facing a new teacher, more and difficult work, losing their friends, and/or having to cope with a lot of strangers.

The fact that children are free to move ahead in areas in which they work well without having to wait for other children to catch up will show parents that you are not interested in holding children back. With that, allowing extra time to have children evolve their reading and writing will seem less worrisome. Soon you will be able to point to solid case studies of children who took their time but then moved right along to catch up with their peers.

As soon as they perceive their children's enthusiasm for projects and other learning activities in class, parents will be receptive to your comments about ways of encouraging their children to expand their school learning at home. Seeing their children read, write, and solve problems creatively will make it easier for you to reassure parents that children are indeed learning the basic skills even if they are not taught in the traditional ways. If you discuss the importance of learning and thinking skills, parents are sure to agree with the activity-based work of your integrated classroom.

Your own joy in teaching in an interesting, challenging classroom will be the most telling message to children and parents alike. Because teaching in family groupings makes greater demands on teachers, it is likely that you will receive extra support in the way of reduced numbers of students, extra materials, and the help of aides. If integration is just being introduced in your area, your school district, supervisor, principal, and other teachers will offer you extra training, advice, and reassurance. As a result you will quickly adjust to the needs of children of different ages and levels of ability. Our best advice to you is to trust the children to learn, give them lots of room to develop their own interests and projects, and *hang in there!* Children are wonderfully creative learners as long as you stand back and give them room to learn their way.

Assessing Progress –
Being Accountable

8

New ways of teaching require new ways of measuring progress. When children learn by doing, your assessment needs to shift from evaluating what has been done – the finished product – to what the children are *doing* as they move toward full literacy. Also, since the goals of teaching encompass much more than the acquisition of skills, the range of material that lends itself to giving you clues about the children's progress expands vastly.

Though you will continue to keep your eyes on the skills children acquire, you are relieved of the tedium and stress – for both you and the children – of making constant judgments about right/wrong answers. Instead of wielding a red pen to show what is wrong and looking at stacks of worksheets, you will be looking closely at the learners and how they are moving ahead. The process is much the same as the excitement of watching your own children take their first steps or say their first words. As you watch their learning unfold you do not make judgments about specific skills or right ways of getting started with walking or talking. You simply note what progress baby is making and encourage every small move ahead. That enjoyment in every sign of progress encourages your child to move ahead. A cycle of mutual enhancement – baby trying something new, parent encouraging, baby moving further ahead – helps your child to develop successfully. The same cycle is a vital part of constructivist learning. As you note, enjoy, and acknowledge the children's moves toward literacy, they are encouraged to build on every small success and they feel safe to try new skills and tasks. Assessing progress becomes a positive way of fostering learning.

This chapter describes a number of ways that will help you track the children's progress toward literacy. Since we are urging you to base your assessment of children's progress on observing their ways of interacting with the learning materials, many examples of what children are likely to do at what stage or level of learning are included. Use these descriptions as a kind of yardstick to measure goals or achievements.

What to look for

If building a solid foundation for literacy becomes the principal goal for teaching, then we must take a closer look at what is involved. Some of the sub-goals under that main heading include:

- Reading with fluency and comprehension
- Knowing about the many uses of reading
- Using reading in many different ways
- Learning to write and spell
- Composing and editing their writing
- Being able to discuss and critique text
- Learning from printed text
- Enjoying reading, writing, and research
- Using literacy skills voluntarily

Looking at these broad goals and the fact that children's learning moves from rough approximations to ever greater accuracy makes it clear why assessment is not concerned with right/wrong answers. Just as you don't ask whether a baby is babbling the right way or toddling accurately and according to your expectations, you need not put a value judgment on the ways in which children are using books and print as their skills emerge. Instead of asking, "Is this right?" focus attention on the ways in which children are moving toward fluent reading and writing. As you describe what the children do, you will note each small step forward:

- Geoff is attending to the story during story time.
- Linda begins to mouth some of the words at unison reading.
- Ashley is pretending to read while looking at pictures in a book.
- Bobby says some of the words he hears on the tape.
- All of the children are turning the page and tracking print with their eyes.
- Sarah is memory reading, but points to all the right words.

- Some of the children choose books as part of center time activities.
- During unison reading, most of the children begin to speak up.
- Peter volunteered to read the news on the board today.
- Mandy has shifted to independent reading/to unfamiliar texts.
- Several of the children are practicing the same book again and again.
- Jason shared a page of reading for the first time today!
- All of the children track the lines of print during group reading.
- Most children have picked up good intonation patterns and use punctuation as guides in their reading.
- Children rely on meaning and first consonants more than on pictures.
- Today Marko spoke up to relate reading to his own experience.
- Rosalyn is reading to the other children.

Such descriptions of emergent reading behaviors may be entered in an anecdotal record book to help you keep track of what is going on in your classroom, or may simply be your personal observations throughout the day as you interact with the children. If, along with your broadly based teaching, you are continuing to use fairly structured practice sessions in printing, spelling, or the recognition of sounds, you will make descriptions such as:

- Hua had all the right letters, but some were inverted.
- Danielle is beginning to recognize final consonants.
- Robin is following correct printing procedures more often now.
- Today, Jimmy used many more lowercase letters in his writing.

Thus, describing what the children do as they move toward literacy certainly includes quite accurate detail on specific skills. The crucial difference in evaluating children's progress lies in the fact that you observe the *children's* development rather than the production of *correct answers*. That difference is charted in the comparison of product-oriented and development-oriented assessment (see Table 4). When studying the comparison and the extensive descriptions of children's learning behaviors later in this chapter, keep clearly in mind that in accepting all the rough approximations children produce, you are simply acknowledging every little step forward toward the ultimate goal of fluent, accurate, meaningful reading and writing. You are not abandoning standards.

Our resolve to assess the full range of literacy skills stems from remarks such as, "Your children sure know how to read, but they don't know their long and short vowels." We decided then and there that reading mattered more than the ability to *talk about* long and short vowels. Good readers do not misread *hat* as *hate, rid* as *ride*. They know and use vowel sounds in reading the same way they know and use intonation patterns in talking. They demonstrate that knowledge by *using* reading and writing effectively, not *by talking about* their knowledge.

If you are accustomed to measuring children's performance against set criteria or norms, you may find it difficult at first to describe and accept the small moves forward toward literacy. We spent several years evolving our observation skills and in the process we detected the stages or levels children traverse toward reading, writing, and spelling. To assist you to move toward describing children's behaviors and away from making value judgments, we have included tables that show the gradual evolution of children's literacy behaviors as they move from babbling in print to reading or writing.

If you compare the descriptions with those of children learning to talk, you will note remarkable similarities in all the processes. In each case, the child is playing with sounds, selecting parts to work with, attempting to convey meaning, and moving gradually to the production of accurate units of communication. Being aware of these natural progressions made it easy for us to abandon saying, "No, that is not right," "No, that is not accurate enough," and to shift instead to acknowledging, "You are reading right along with me," "That is a lot of writing you did today, and you made finger spaces too," "If *r* and *m* are all you hear, that's a good way to spell *room* for now." Observing how a child gradually shifted from paying no attention to books, to attending, to memory reading, to recognizing words, and finally to independent reading called for positive comments and encouragement all along the way. Demanding accuracy or being negative about rough approximations was inappropriate and counterproductive. The children were progressing naturally, and they definitely did so with the intent to communicate.

TABLE 4
COMPARISON OF TWO APPROACHES TO ASSESSMENT

Product-oriented	Development-oriented
Assumes that adults must guide the sequence of children's development.	Assumes that children's skills evolve naturally in response to their interactions with their learning environment.
Perceives learning of small finite (right/wrong) steps.	Sees learning as ongoing gradual refinement of skills.
Takes an all-or-nothing stand – mistakes don't count.	Takes an open approach – every small step-up counts.
Evaluates – "is this right/accurate/what I asked for?"	Describes – "the child is working, moving ahead, on task."
Says no to many of the children's responses to tasks.	Says yes to every move toward literacy.
Tends to examine *what* the child has produced/said.	Tends to examine the *how* or *why* of children's work.
Sees errors as red marks.	Sees errors as stepping stones.
Requires word-perfect reading, tends to focus on form.	Accepts same-meaning substitutions, focuses on meaning.
Asks for sounding out, explicit use of phonics in decoding text.	Encourages use of all available cues to meaning – context, pictures, familiar language patterns, and letter sounds.

Levels of knowing

As you observe the children in your class working at reading and writing, you will find they absorb your modeling well. They love to imitate the intonation you use when reading exciting stories or poems, they mimic your hand motions as you demonstrate how to print correctly, and they will happily copy sentences or words that you have printed on the blackboard. But if you look closely you will also notice that the correct answers children give in one setting or the accurate reading of a given book will not be evident when the children are in different settings or when reading unfamiliar books. As we pointed out in chapter 4, there are different *levels of knowing*.

To give you some concrete examples of levels of knowing: we have noted that children who have daily practice in "helping the teacher spell" during news time will readily call out many correct spellings: *today, we, are, ing, ed*. They know those words and endings and are also confident about compound words, silent letters, periods at the end of sentences. Yet when they sit down to do their own creative writing during writing workshop, their invented spelling does not necessarily reflect the knowledge they demonstrated during oral spelling. Children who will call out those endings correctly every time, nevertheless, write *we are goen* or *I laft and laft*. These are children who read fluently and spell many words accurately during oral spelling. Obviously, on one level they know how to spell those words and endings but on another they do not.

You are no doubt familiar with the situation of teaching something that the children seem to understand, when their next move shows you that they really have not yet internalized the lesson. So we are not telling you anything new. But when you base your evaluation of children's progress on close observation of the steps children take in their learning, this knowledge takes on new significance. What the children are showing us in reverting to a lower level of spelling is that they must first progress through *their own* stages in order to evolve their own internal rules. They may have accepted what was demonstrated to them, but their brain needs to do its own programming before that externally acquired knowledge becomes readily accessible in all kinds of situations. Just as a baby needs to move through babbling and playing with sounds before producing intelligible words, so the young speller needs to experiment with sounds to give the brain a chance to move through a series of rough approximations that make sense to it.

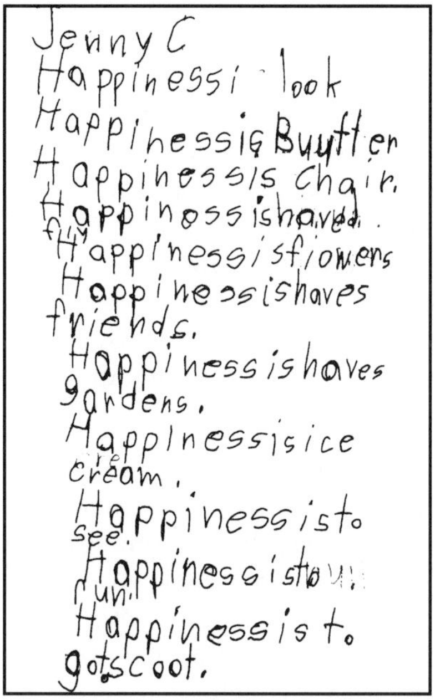

Jenny C
Happiness i look
Happiness is Buutter
Happiness is chair.
Happiness is haved.
Happiness is flowers
Happiness is haves
friends.
Happiness is haves
gardens.
Happiness is ice
cream.
Happiness is to
see.
Happiness is to
run.
Happiness is to.
got scoot.

Lisa Lau
Happiness is having
a birthday party.
Happiness is going
to the circus.
Happiness is playing
at school.
Happiness is having
a cat.
Happiness is having
a beautiful doll.

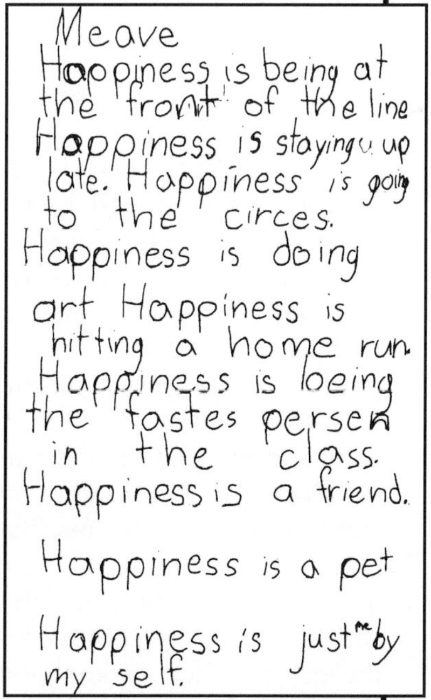

Meave
Happiness is being at
the front of the line
Happiness is staying up
late. Happiness is going
to the circes.
Happiness is doing
art Happiness is
hitting a home run.
Happiness is loeing
the tastes persen
in the class.
Happiness is a friend.

Happiness is a pet

Happiness is just by
my self.

**Each child develops at an
individual pace**

*Personality, level of overall
development, and personal
preferences show clearly when
children choose to do the same
writing assignment.*

*Jenny's writing is still at
the gross performance level on
all fronts. The interesting
aspect of her level of writing
is that she leaves out endings
like ing and small functor
words like a. When she reads
her writing aloud, she fills in
the missing parts. Like a
baby who means to convey a
whole message with two-
word sentences, so early
writing often is showing the
same kind of intent
to convey more with
abbreviated messages.*

*If you recognize such work as
a first step – a "babbling in
print"- you can relax and
trust the young learners to
progress as Maeve and Lisa
have done.*

If you think of baby learning to talk, you realize that there are two skills involved in producing the first words: hearing exactly what has been said and using the speech apparatus to reproduce those sounds accurately. All of us are well aware of the steps baby takes to move from *googoo* to *googy* to *gooky* to *cookie*. Both hearing and saying move through a series of improvements and eventually the child arrives at saying the word the same way adults do. There may have been plenty of models, but the *child* did the internal programming that eventually produced the correct version. Spelling works the same way. You need to know what the word sounds like and have a repertoire of ways to represent those sounds in order to give a written representation of the word.

Based on our observations, inner programming guides spelling (and reading and writing) development only if you give the child both opportunity and encouragement to move through the necessary steps from babbling to phonetic spelling to ever greater accuracy. The modeling of fluent, accurate spelling (and reading and writing) plays a vital role in helping the child move through these stages, just as fluent language in the home acts as the guide to language development. In school, as at home, children must move through those stages if their knowledge is to be usable in all settings, not just in the one in which they first observed it.

Seen in that light, assessing *levels of knowing* becomes highly important and the difference between product-oriented and development-oriented assessment takes on new significance. It clearly is not enough to note that children are giving correct answers on exercise sheets, in oral reading, when copying down words, or spelling words from a list. The question becomes, can they and do they transfer that knowledge readily to new and different situations or do they simply know it at the imitation or product level? Observing the children's small steps forward will tell you far more exactly who has truly internalized what, and where individual children are along that continuum of literacy development. Eventually you will find that the overt knowledge children displayed so readily and joyfully merges with the covert knowledge they built as they labored over invented spelling, their own creative writing, and the move to fluent reading. Though the early show of product-type knowledge is gratifying and exciting, in the long run the only knowledge that is going to lead to full literacy is that which has been programmed internally by the child. That is the type of knowledge you are looking for when observing the development-oriented behavior.

Levels of knowing are part of adult learning as well. Do you have big words in your vocabulary that you understand readily but don't feel comfortable using in your talking or writing? Do you understand what a coach is telling you or demonstrating but find yourself unable to move in exactly the right way? Are you an accurate speller when you write but hesitate when you are asked to spell a difficult word orally? In all of these cases you know or understand at one level but cannot immediately transfer that knowledge to other ways and settings.

At a simpler level you may be aware that you don't recognize people in unfamiliar settings. People you met at the office may not look familiar when you see them on a beach. Piaget speaks of "conservation" and has demonstrated in his experiments that, at a given level of overall development, children who "learn" that the weight of a piece of clay remains the same no matter what shape it has, do not transfer that knowledge to new situations. He called this lack of transfer *lack of conservation*. Most of us studied those experiments but we did not necessarily see the principle in action while watching children in class. The lack of transfer of reading, writing, or spelling skills from one setting to another is a good example of lack of conservation. What a child "knows" in one setting is not yet sufficiently assimilated to be used in another setting. The overall developmental level asserts itself and, like Piaget, we find that children need to take their time to move to the next level.

Just as the ability to use oral language represents a continuum, so the ability to use written language evolves gradually along a continuum that tends toward ever greater accuracy and variety of use. But the process is not simply a linear move upward. Along the way, children induce and then refine rules that help them apply their new learning to new situations. As new material is assimilated, there will be regressions and plateaus in learning. Some children will move so quickly that they appear to skip a level altogether, others will linger so long at one point that they appear to be stuck. But eventually, all children will progress along the continuum *if they are allowed the freedom to proceed their way and at their pace.*

The literacy continuum

In over twenty years of closely observing children in class, we have abstracted the stages children traverse as they move toward literacy. Comparing these levels with those that linguists have described in connection with oral language learning, we have been conscious of the similarities. The descriptions we are offering below are not theories but the record of the children's ways of moving toward literacy.

Stages of oral language development

1. Gurgling, squealing, crying, conveying feelings with sounds
2. Babbling, using recognizable language sounds – playing with sounds
3. Adopting the intonation pattern of language spoken in the home; babbling speech-like sounds though not yet using words
4. Expressing meaning through intonation without using actual words: questions, requests, demands, protests
5. Using one-word statements and rudimentary diction to convey messages
6. Changing to two- and three-word sentences – primarily using nouns and verbs
7. Saying longer sentences using functor words and more accurate diction
8. Overgeneralizing patterns – "I bringed..."
9. Evidencing the internalization of rules: word order, sorting out pronoun references, accurate use of tenses
10. Moving toward greater accuracy of diction, language, and fluency

Stages of writing/composing

1. Drawing pictures to convey meaning
2. Combining letters and numbers randomly on page
3. Placing strings of letters left to right, top to bottom on page
4. Segmenting letters into word-like units
5. Writing one-word sentences: *FLURS* – Read: "I planted the flowers."

6. Moving to two- and three-word sentences: *ALLISS BTHDAY* – Read: "It is Allissa's birthday today," or *CAT DOG* – Read: "I have a cat and a dog."

7. Composing longer sentences, some compound: "I love cats Som KIDS in my class have TheaM anD I'm Gld to Be at School."

8. Generalizing patterns of familiar models: stories, poems, nursery rhymes

9. Evidencing the internalization of rules: placing periods at end of sentences; shifting writing style to fit topic; varying sentences

10. Writing fluently and coherently – continuing to evolve

Note: Items 1 through 4 are "babbling in print." Children say message "while writing" or "read" it when finished. They intend to convey meaning.

Stages of spelling/printing

1. Pretend spelling, using letter-like forms and scribbles

2. Babbling in print, producing strings of letters including some numbers

3. Grouping letters into word-like units, making word patterns

4. Using one-letter spelling: *U R* – Read: "You are"

5. Using two- and three-letter spelling: *W WNT HM* – Read: "We went home."

6. Using phonetic spelling based largely on consonants. *MM = Mom*

7. Expanding phonetic spelling to include some vowels: "We want to the Cirks."

8. Overgeneralizing known patterns: *BRITE, NOO = bright, new*

9. Evidencing internalization of rules: Vowels are part of each word; double consonants change vowel sound; silent *e* affects sound

10. Moving toward greater accuracy and larger repertoire of spelling patterns

Stages of reading

1. Listening to stories
2. Picture reading, describing pictures
3. Going through motions of reading: turning pages, tracking print with hands, rehearsing silently
4. Pretend reading: becoming aware of need to scrutinize print, making up story, or drawing on memory
5. Using memory reading, sometimes tracking print with hands but not eyes
6. Scanning for meaning and saying individual words (mostly nouns and verbs) during unison reading or while reading alone
7. Listening for repetitive parts of story and chiming in for a few words – usually nouns and verbs – while scanning text with eyes
8. Generalizing knowledge gleaned from practicing with familiar texts to unfamiliar ones: words, phrasing, style
9. Evidencing internalization of patterns of written language and rules of phonics. Using context, syntactic patterns, knowledge of subject matter, and sounds of letters and words to derive meaning from print
10. Reading with fluency and expression (intonation indicates comprehension)

By observing children closely at the beginning of the school year, you will soon discover where they are on the literacy continuum. You can then build upon the knowledge and experience each child brings.

The importance of seeing each child unfold

At times, educators unfamiliar with fitting teaching to the learners' way voice the opinion that such a system of instruction may be fine for children who have a good background in literacy learning but is not suitable for children whose home learning did not include literacy skills. If that type of instruction meant no more than reading stories and allowing invented spelling, such opinions might be correct. In fact, it encourages children to build upon their own, natural learning strategies, and development-oriented assessment becomes the crucial element in seeing that all children receive the help, encouragement, time, and materials they need to move to full literacy.

Since development-oriented assessment does not limit itself to examining what children do in one setting but moves on to examine what they do in all kinds of settings, you quickly become aware where each child is functioning on the literacy continuum. You do not make assumptions about children's knowledge and you do not confuse product knowledge – right answers on worksheets – with the deeper knowing that flows from inner programming. Knowing that each child needs to move through all, or certainly most, levels if they are to fully internalize what they learn, you make all kinds of extra learning opportunities available to children who come to school unfamiliar with books and print. (The beauty of development-oriented assessment is that you note and acknowledge even the smallest steps forward as the child progresses along the literacy continuum.) Both you and the child take pleasure and pride in undertaking a journey that other children completed at home. For them, reading the first word or beginning to spell will be the culmination of a great deal of home learning; for the uninitiated, there will be many steps before they read the first word or print the first letter.

Far from being too difficult or not suitable for children who are unprepared for beginning reading, constructivist teaching opens the door fully and makes progress toward full literacy as natural an evolution as progress toward talking was at home. But for development-oriented assessment to become functional, you may need to sharpen your skills of observation.

How to see what you are looking at and hear what you are listening to

When we first began our research we found that looking isn't necessarily seeing and listening isn't necessarily hearing. If that sounds strange, think of watching different kinds of sports. If you know the game well, you see far more than the novice who does not appreciate the fine points of the players' moves. In addition, you recognize the reasons behind certain plays, appreciate the skill involved in a particular play, and anticipate what is likely to happen next. Though both of you are observing the very same actions, you see and hear far more of what goes on in the game than the novice. As a result, the action on the field is much more likely to hold your

Writing bursts out of the "pupa stage"

Kelly V.

September:

Kelly begins with drawing. Though she can print her name, she is still babbling in print. Her letters are well formed, progress from left to right, and are in a fairly straight line. Her message, dictated to the teacher, fits the picture.

November – The breakthrough!

Kelly continued to draw and print along the same lines from the first day of school until November. On the 26th she burst out of the pupa stage and all of the knowledge she had accumulated over the months showed itself at the same time: beginning consonants, finger spaces, names, even complete words and some vowels.

Writing flows without the need for a picture. Kelly uses wide lines and for the first time makes clearly defined spaces between words. Beginning consonants are in place for to, my, pay, TV, saw. Vowels are correct in today, dad, I, Alissa, and Raffi. The words Dad, Alissa, Raffi are complete. Capitals and lowercase are intermixed but used correctly in TV, I, Alissa, Raffi. There is even the beginning of editing in the repetition of PTV.

Kelly v. eTTsW N soa

I see a rainbow.

Ke llyv.
to b MT DaD iASP I
P T To PTV.
I SyV Allss ASyy Ra ffi
WeAS b

Today my Dad gets his Pay T.V.
I saw Alissa at the Raffi Concert

Assessing Progress –
Being Accountable

Kelly v

Me   and Carla and D a D and J. .oon
wht   SKe.   LiSa is SK. MY
MoM wnt to wSLrv .

Kelly v

M y To th   is   iot
MoM. Our   you going
to . Pit   -it inDr
your   Pilo.

My DaD wnt to
My Gran DaDs to
Pic him iP to
Tac him to Fa g is
Bit l

Writing continues to evolve

Kelly V.

January:

Kelly has moved to quite sophisticated composing. She knows about words, sentences, and paragraphs. All of the words are clearly separated by spaces; each sentence ends with a period, and the topic of skiing begins and ends the writing. Whistler – wslre – is a ski resort.

Eleven of the seventeen words are completely correct and the remainder are easily recognized. Only four words have missing vowels, and capitals are used with greater accuracy than before. Kelly self-corrected the reversed J in Joan and did some erasing to make her work neater.

March:

Kelly has graduated to dialogue and definite paragraphing to separate different parts of her composition. She ran out of time, ending her page "but I" yet still produced thirty-two words of which nineteen are spelled correctly.

All of the beginning consonants are correct; most of the ending and median consonants are correct; pic and tac are good approximations; vowels are becoming good approximations. The substitution of our for are is a common one among children and is based on the difficulty of hearing the distinction between the two words. Kelly has shifted to regulation lines and is leaving spaces between her lines to make her printing more legible.

full attention and stir your feelings. You are involved in seeing and hearing; the novice may be simply looking and listening. Since observing the young learners in our classes has moved away from simply spotting right/wrong answers, we have become far more skilled at seeing and hearing what the children are actually doing in response to learning materials or activities.

In terms of classroom management, seeing and hearing have become our principal ways of timing our interactions with the children. Body language, facial expressions, pauses, enthusiasm, hesitance, or eagerness to try signal when to urge children to go ahead, leave them to continue by themselves, offer help, give an on-the-spot mini-lesson, or abandon all else to plunge wholeheartedly into an activity for the rest of the session. Close observation and timing of our intervention – or lack of it – give children the freedom to set their own pace of learning and us the opportunity to note and record progress being made. The children's moves forward may not be on our lesson plans or schedules for the day, but the subtle shifts in behavior that signal a child's need to sit quietly to digest new knowledge or puzzle over a project can help you support his/her pace of learning.

So much of truly vital learning is internal to the child. By seeing and hearing with openness and care we assume responsibility for noting and recording progress. In traditional assessment we frequently put the onus on the children. To prove that they have learned to read or write, we often require them to *talk about it* or to *deal with it piecemeal*. Both are far more abstract and advanced than simply reading and writing. No doubt many of the so-called failures or poor performances are simply the failure of tests to assess what it is the children do. Careful observation – seeing and hearing – allow us to note the many subtle moves ahead that each child is making but that are missed in testing that equates reading and writing with sub-skills and the ability to classify them. We are calling the small steps forward children make "step-ups" to indicate that they represent moves ahead however small.

Blocks to seeing and hearing

When we started to fit our teaching to the children's ways of learning, we saw ourselves as good listeners and observers but soon found that we had – and still have – much to learn. Blocks to clear perception abound. Here are some of them:

- The sheer **pressure of numbers** can make it hard to focus on individual children. Giving individual attention to so many children is no mean feat. But if they have adopted independent ways of learning, your task will be easier.

- **Thinking about lesson plans** and what to do next may get in the way of seeing and hearing learning behaviors. Like the children, the teacher focuses best on one thing at a time. Being too concerned with the lesson of the day may make it difficult to capitalize on a child's excitement about a personal experience or a new step forward.

- **Looking for specific answers** may block an appreciation of valid responses. Children have a keen sense of hearing and translate what they hear into spelling. They may suggest *wiell* as the spelling of *while* or produce contractions like *sprised* and *fraid*.

  L seems to be hard to hear as a median consonant, and *100 mios a nour* is a good representation of the actual sounds the child hears when saying "A hundred miles an hour."

- **The demand to use specific methods** or tests to measure progress can obscure a wealth of information supplied by children. Working with letters or sounds in isolation reveals little about children's ability to use them effectively in context or about their newly developed desire to use written language to communicate.

- **Preconceived ideas about what children should be able to do** at specific points may cloud perception of their small step-ups. Assessing a child's progress on the basis of his/her age, what his/her siblings or peers did or do, may keep you from seeing the areas in which the child is progressing.

- A conviction that **one particular route to a goal** is the best one may blind you to other ways. If word-perfect reading seems paramount to you, the children's use of their own language patterns or personal experience to help them understand their reading may go by unnoticed.

- **Doubts about a child's ability** to perform a given task may obscure step-ups in learning. If Kelly imitates other children's responses or copies their written work, that may be a big step forward from not participating at all or guessing randomly.

Blocks to seeing and hearing can be both internal and external. Both can be detoured or cut down to size.

How to improve seeing and hearing

Becoming aware of the difference between looking and seeing, listening and hearing, will take you a giant step in the right direction. It will foster the *intent* to see and hear and will encourage you to describe what you are observing. We find that focusing on the children's strengths and step-ups more than on areas of weakness greatly enhances our perceptive powers. Without ignoring areas that need work, the focus on strengths helps to encourage further progress. If Ken is good in sports, that intelligence can become the focal point for artwork, reading, writing, or special projects – *at his choice*. If Jill is a meticulous printer but needs more practice with spelling, encouraging her to use her printing skills in many ways will provide practice in spelling. Noting what words have been left out during reading and writing will give you interesting insights into children's effective ways of paying closer attention to nouns, verbs, and adjectives than to words that carry less meaning.

By watching for the meaning of children's messages more than for their form, you will discover – as we did – that, at all levels, children strive to communicate. To take the whole context into account when trying to understand or decipher a child's message, look at the children's pictures, try to recall information about their home, the trip they just took, or the special events they talked about. Children assume that you know what they are talking about and often leave out parts they deem nonessential. At home, a parent uses the total setting to understand and respond to the baby's early one-word sentences. You can do the same in class.

Taking time out to observe other teachers and their interactions with children can also be highly productive. Here, too, the key is to be nonjudgmental. Your aim is greater awareness and sensitivity, not finding imperfections or faults. So whether you are listening to tape recordings of your work with children or watching other teachers, notice and describe activities and strengths more than shortcomings.

The benefits of sharpening your observation skills will soon multiply. As you become more aware of the ways in which children learn, you see and hear still more clearly, and you will find it easy to note every step-up. As in watching your favorite sport, your observations will become ever more knowledgeable and exciting because you bring clarity of vision and strong background knowledge to your work. To speed you on your way, we are sharing examples of some of our classroom observations. You will soon be adding examples of your own.

Clues to look for in children's behavior

Early stages – emergent reading and writing

Since you are well aware of such standard indicators of progress as knowledge of letters, sounds, or the ability to print, we are listing the more global indicators of the children's moves toward literacy. Traditionally, many of these have not been included in the assessment of progress, yet they are the soil from which the more detailed knowledge will spring. Without that nourishing foundation the detailed skills may not take root but may remain at the surface and not evolve and flourish. Recognizing and acknowledging these step-ups is particularly important with children who have little or no background in literacy and its skills when they come to school. They need to move through more levels along the literacy continuum than their more experienced peers and you will want to recognize, praise, and rejoice in even the smallest move forward. Both you and the children will thrive in a climate that acknowledges success at every turn. In such a positive environment all children will strive to move toward full literacy. As they observe your modeling and the many examples of fluent reading and writing around the classroom, their step-ups will move them ever closer to accurate, fluent reading and writing.

Step-ups toward literacy

Indicators that the child is looking for meaning
- Making up a story while looking at pictures
- Retelling a story read earlier
- Expecting you to read a piece of pretend writing
- Talking while scribbling to indicate "I am writing a message"
- Asking questions about stories, events, or characters
- Reacting appropriately to labels or directions
- Imitating intonation patterns of other readers
- Pretending to read a book or story

Becoming familiar with written/book language

- Repeating interesting words from books or stories
- Singing refrains heard in books
- Putting word cards together to copy nursery rhymes or other text
- Copying or tracing print
- Using letter or word cards in pretend writing
- Playing with ABC building blocks to make sequences
- Writing or scribbling on blackboard

Demonstrating interest in books/print

- Browsing through books
- Going to the library to look at books
- Asking questions about books or stories
- Wanting to know more about a topic
- Wanting to find more books in a particular series
- Asking the teacher to find a story about a given topic/character

Taking risks in learning

- Beginning to write though unsure of composition and spelling
- Using invented spelling
- Volunteering news items
- "Helping the teacher" spell
- Trying to draw unfamiliar items
- Asking for help
- Volunteering to read orally (with or without help)

Pretend use of written language – babbling in print

- Memory reading
- Scribbling
- Pretend teaching using teacher's intonation and words
- Sending letters or cards in scribbles
- Pretend reading – babbling with varying intonation while "reading"
- Pretend writing – babbling in print (producing strings of letters)
- Picture reading – making up stories based on pictures

Showing a desire to use written language

- Playing with books
- Poring over books whether able to read a story or not
- Asking for specific stories
- Asking to have favorite books read again and again
- Wanting to have things labeled
- Moving from using toys to word games and books
- Playing with letter or word games
- Asking to be taught (for example, a kindergarten child following you around with a book saying, "Teach me to read like the grade ones")

Achieving ends with printed messages

- Wanting to send/take messages home
- Asking for labels or warning signs such as *don't touch this*
- Wanting captions for pictures
- Wanting to make greeting cards

Understanding book language

- Using book language when pretend reading
- Asking relevant questions when listening to stories
- Using book language – "once upon a time" – when story telling
- Anticipating phrases or refrains
- Inferring endings or sequences of events

Developing sense of sequence

- Putting blocks, cards, or pictures into sequences
- Using flannel board to show a progression of events
- Moving through books in right sequence
- Drawing a set of pictures to illustrate a story
- Retelling stories or events in proper sequence
- Role-playing in sequence – getting up, getting breakfast, and so on

Deriving/expressing feelings from/with print

- Displaying eagerness, anticipation, laughter, tears, and other emotions at story time
- Talking about being happy, scared, excited, or sad because of a story
- Trying to show expressions on faces when drawing

Noting and replicating intonation patterns

- Mimicking teacher or other reader when chiming in
- Emulating fluency and modulation of voice when pretend reading
- Picking up accents of fluent readers
- Taking on tone, speed, and rhythm of teacher's voice when pretend teaching
- Changing voice to represent different speakers

Choosing to practice voluntarily

- Using books during free time
- Taking/bringing books (from) home
- Asking to be allowed to continue an activity
- Preferring word/letter games over other toys
- Choosing to write or draw

Hypothesis testing

- Trying out the fit of puzzle pieces
- Engaging in trial-and-error learning with games
- Putting together letters to see if sequence makes a word or name
- Asking for confirmation, "Is that ...?" "Does that say...?"
- Trying different approaches in problem solving
- Using initial consonants to guess words or names
- Asking for confirmation of spelling guesses, "Does *dad* start with a *d*?"

Imitating literacy behaviors

- Imitating teacher's reading or writing
- Pretending to follow written directions
- Pretend reading to dolls or pets
- Pretend making/following a shopping list

Role-playing

- Playing storekeeper or customer
- Becoming the teacher
- Taking on roles of characters in stories
- Taking turns being *guesser* or *tester* in letter games

Using the environment to aid learning

- Looking at pictures or other special aids around the classroom to arrive at the meaning of words or signs
- Using knowledge of products to guess label meanings
- Referring to familiar stories to find words or letters
- Using the environment to get ideas for artwork or games
- Watching others to check own performance

Participating actively

- Joining games, projects, story time voluntarily
- Chiming in during unison reading
- Giving information to group members when working together
- Volunteering to talk during sharing time
- Sharing after book time

Listening attentively

- Making eye contact when listening
- Demonstrating by actions that a message was received
- Sitting still during story time
- Following directions accurately

Demonstrating enjoyment of reading-type activities

- Showing animation and enthusiasm when interacting with printed materials
- Playing inventive games matching words and letters
- Having favorite books and stories
- Wanting teacher to come to look at work, patterns, artwork, and so on
- Wanting to read to others – "Can I read this part to you?"
- Learning and/or reciting poems and nursery rhymes

Using all senses to learn

- Writing in sand table
- Jumping on ABC jumping mats (paper or plastic hopscotch grids made by teacher)
- Acting out stories
- Becoming big, small, thin to be like characters in stories
- Interacting fully with the environment of the classroom
- Making puppets to fit a story
- Following a recipe during cooking time

Showing a sense of rhythm

- Bouncing, clapping, foot-tapping to music
- Using intonation patterns in a rhythmic way
- Reciting or singing with a definite rhythm
- Jumping, hopping, or skipping effectively
- Moving appropriately when rhythms change

Demonstrating pattern perception

- Noting likenesses and differences in letters, words, pictures, stories, books, and so on
- Classifying objects into groups
- Arranging items in specific order (blocks, toys, colors, and so on)
- Creating patterns with blocks or letters
- Using familiar language patterns to anticipate what comes next

Developing manual dexterity – fine motor skills

- Improving skills to draw, cut, color, trace, or put together
- Showing greater dexterity in handling fine equipment
- Beginning to print letters
- Demonstrating greater precision in overall movements
- Putting together puzzles with ease

Using music and dance

- Joining in movement games
- Singing along
- Joining circle games
- Learning words of new songs
- Using a singsong voice to recite

Integrating art and writing

- Asking to have captions for pictures
- Drawing illustrations for stories
- Fitting stories to pictures
- Dramatizing stories in plays and puppet shows
- Making murals of story characters
- Representing stories in dioramas

Developing memory store of written language

- Memorizing poems or nursery rhymes
- Quoting standard beginnings and endings
- Anticipating phrases and idioms
- Recognizing rhymes

Recognizing uses of print in daily events

- Being familiar with such things as invitations, grocery lists, labels, phone numbers, letters, newspapers, books, notes to and from home, directions for making things, and so on

Using fantasy and imagination

- Entering into games of make-believe
- Building villages and towns with blocks and toys
- Using blocks or other objects to represent cars, houses, people
- Creating stories or landscapes with blocks and toys
- Using materials in imaginative ways

Recognizing similarities and differences

- Comparing sizes, shapes, colors of objects
- Spotting words or letters that look alike – "There are three *m*s in that."
- Noting different ways letters are arranged

Classifying

- Talking about the fit of an item in a group
- Arranging items into categories and sub-categories
- Grouping items together in different ways
- Arranging and rearranging groups of items

Step-ups toward the more detailed skills of early reading and writing

Once children begin to read and write, some of the clues to look for become more conventional. But here, too, it is important to note the global behaviors that give evidence of the move toward full literacy. (Many of the behaviors listed above under emergent reading will continue to be clues as well.)

Recognizing words

- Spotting the same word in several places in a message
- Distinguishing words from numbers and distinguishing words from drawings
- Recognizing familiar words in unfamiliar contexts

Integrating print with artwork

- Illustrating written work
- Using print in decorative ways
- Creating greeting cards
- Choosing books because of beauty of illustrations and language
- Creating plays including script, costumes, and props

Learning from print – using it to gain information

- Reading about hobbies, sports, animals, and so on
- Doing research
- Following directions or recipes
- Checking rules for games
- Seeing an interesting picture and wanting to read its caption
- Using the dictionary and encyclopedia to look things up

Initiating projects

- Wanting to make books – copying and/or writing them
- Starting special projects – research, producing plays, designing games
- Asking to be allowed to do work that differs from rest of class
- Volunteering to read and write

Doing research

- Looking words up in a dictionary
- Reading several books on the same topic
- Growing bean plants, then measuring and recording growth each day
- Observing the behavior of animals
- Charting the progress of chicks hatching
- Checking in the library for information on a specific topic
- Putting together a report on a topic
- Questioning a resource person

Practicing voluntarily

- Wanting to reread the same story many times
- Taking books out to recess
- Reading/writing during choosing time
- Taking books home

Persisting at tasks

- Trying more than one approach in problem solving
- Wanting to work on projects for hours – even weeks – at a stretch
- Wanting to continue a task the following day

Evolving spelling patterns

- Spelling words like *the, day, we* rapidly during oral spelling
- Giving endings – *ing, ed* – as one unit
- Transferring known spelling patterns to new words – *their, kind*
- Using phonetic spelling – *fyu = few, u = you*

Demonstrating awareness of conventions of print

- Writing from left to right
- Using punctuation marks and capitalization
- Centering headings
- Using upper- and lowercase letters
- Keeping letters the same size when printing

Using print for practical purposes

- Writing diaries (often carried on over the weekend as well)
- Writing letters/sending messages
- Developing scripts for plays
- Describing science projects
- Describing inventions on Invention Day
- Keeping a record of activities or special events
- Using books to find out about topics of interest
- Following recipes or directions for making things

Using print to record/preserve messages

- Helping to create experience charts
- Keeping a journal
- Writing reminders

Evolving a writing style
- Copying style used by other children
- Copying style of reference books or stories
- Converting earlier copied work into own words
- Varying writing style to fit the task – stories differ from reports

Devising new ways to say/do things
- Making up new endings for stories
- Using someone else's ideas and building on them
- Using toys in unusual ways
- Inventing new rules for playing games

Increasing syntactic complexity
- Lengthening sentences when dictating or writing
- Joining two sentences together with conjunctions
- Developing variety in sentences
- Using different opening phrases for sentences
- Editing written work to make it sound better
- Noting that all sentences start with the same word, then changing some

Showing an eagerness to advance
- Demonstrating curiosity and inquisitiveness about books and print
- Seeing other children at a new stage and wanting to get there too
- Wanting to ask questions, make things work
- Being willing to tackle unfamiliar reading and writing
- Choosing "difficult" books as reading or reference material
- Expressing confidence in ability to handle a new job
- Becoming independent in progressing to new tasks

Being helpful and cooperative
- Helping peers with spelling, reading, or reference work
- Being careful not to step on other children's work
- Offering to help, clean up, stay after school
- Settling disputes without teacher's help
- Considering other people's needs and feelings
- Sharing favorite jobs to give others a turn
- Taking turns in talking and sharing news

Sharing interests
- Working cooperatively on projects
- Discussing books and written work with peers, teacher, or visitor
- Alerting others to material of interest, "Tina would like this..."

Seeing themselves as readers/writers
- Joining freely in reading and writing activities
- Wanting to create own writing and stories
- Talking about their own reading and writing
- Using reading and writing to communicate with others

The above descriptions of children's reading and writing behaviors are just samples of the observations you will make in your own class as you assess progress. They are step-ups that focus on development more than on finished products. As children become more proficient in reading, writing, and spelling, you will be watching for more familiar and conventional indicators of growth, such as paragraphing and greater sophistication in diction and style of writing. But in the spirit of development-oriented assessment, you will continue to focus your attention on step-ups rather than on errors or deficiencies. In grades two and three children will respond to positive feedback with the same enthusiasm and productivity as they did in kindergarten and grade one.

Since process-oriented teaching is based on close observation of children's work, you may actually be more ready than product-oriented teachers to account for progress. But no matter how clearly you see each step-up along the way to literacy, there will be the need to offer more traditional evidence that children are acquiring – or are at least moving toward – mastery of specific skills. To fulfill that need we are suggesting a variety of ways of being accountable.

Being accountable to others

Standardized tests

Do you remember the agony of being put on the spot to give the answer the teacher had in mind? Can you recall feeling after a test that you didn't really show what you knew but instead exposed areas of uncertainty? Have you had students who are competent but fail to display that competence in their test results? If your answer is yes to any or all of these questions you know that tests have their limitations. But formal tests, given at intervals, have a valid place in accountability for student learning. Ongoing daily assessment of children's work may eliminate much of the anxiety and negativity often associated with tests, but to validate the effectiveness of your new way of teaching, it becomes important to use standardized tests that make it possible to compare the performance of your students with that of students in more product-oriented classes.

Just as it is poor practice to go against the grain of effective functioning with the children's learning, so it is poor practice to go against the grain of established or required ways of showing accountability. Our own practice and our strong advice to teachers is to accept and administer any and all tests your district or school require, whether standardized tests, mastery tests, or special norm-referenced tests. Since children in our classrooms are used to being helpful and cooperative in their day-to-day work, we find it necessary to tell them that these tests are designed to show what they can do all by themselves, thus they must not consult each other or give help. If procedures used in the test are unfamiliar to the children because they have not had experience filling in worksheets or exercise forms, we give them some practice before the test to familiarize them with the format and/or instructions they will encounter. Over the years we have found that even though our focus has been on overall literacy development, children in our classes have performed satisfactorily – often exceptionally well – on skill tests examining word attack skills. Scores on comprehension and vocabulary tests are usually well above average. In short, use of the standard tests not only fulfills your local requirements but reassures everyone, including you, that all is well with children who rely on their own effective ways of learning.

Recording progress with observation instruments

Once launched on fostering literacy through constructivist approaches we wanted to monitor closely how children were progressing. The eagerness to participate and the successes achieved by children left little doubt about the effectiveness of the new approach; yet there was not enough quantitative information to reassure us, supervisors, and parents that concrete learning was taking place. Nor did we have a clear enough view of the sequence of individual children's development to allow us to see if definite stages could be discerned.

To keep a written record of children's progress, we developed two observation instruments: the **Individual Profile of Emergent Reading** for emergent readers, and the **Individual Profile of Early Reading Development** for beginning readers. Both feature observable behaviors of children interacting with learning materials and both use simple check marks, minus signs, or blanks to indicate a child's ability/inability to perform or the lack of opportunity to observe.

Use of these observation instruments sharpened our listening and observation skills and augmented our confidence when discussing children's progress with parents and supervisors. Over a period of time these written records revealed both the children's individual style of learning – whether auditory, visual, or a combination – and some overall patterns. For example, once the **Profile of Emergent Reading** showed about 30 percent check marks (regardless of how distributed over the various categories) the child was on the verge of reading.

Refer to pages 316 and 318 for copies of the two observation instruments for individual children. You may wish to develop your own checklists, but whether you use ours or your own, you will find that the specific items help you to keep your attention on what children in your class actually do rather than on your lesson plans. No doubt you will have your surprises, chuckles, and occasional delightful insights into the ways children think and develop. If individual profiles for thirty or more children prove to be too time-consuming, single out a few children for specific close observation – those whose work is either particularly advanced or slow to emerge will need extra attention. You may also want to fill out observation records for children whose parents are insistent about being well informed.

An example of a whole-class version of one checklist is also illustrated on page 320. Whole-class checklists contain the same categories and descriptions but provide room for checking all the children in your class. Each checklist contains just four behaviors to be observed. They are repeated three times to give you the opportunity to observe all children or to make successive observations over several days to note progress. After a given activity we are generally able to fill in the charts for the entire class in a matter of a few minutes.

When using whole-class profiles begin by filling in the children's names at the top of the page. (If you plan to use these whole-class profiles regularly, make multiple copies of the names and simply paste them in place instead of writing them out each time.) On the day you want to record your observations, fill in the date and record your observations using the marks shown. If you do not have a chance to observe all children, make the same observation again on the next day. You will find that it takes only a few minutes to complete the profile and that its use sharpens your awareness of children's reading/writing behaviors. Once you know the children in your class well, you may want to reduce the list of children to be observed to the few whose progress you want to monitor closely in order to give extra support.

Once you have become accustomed to carefully noting children's learning behaviors, you will probably find that you no longer need to keep such detailed records and may want to abandon the use of observation lists altogether. We use them now and again for children who need extra attention, mostly to demonstrate to parents that June/Jim is making progress even though slowly. Student teachers coming into your classroom may find the observation instruments helpful, and the children at times take a keen interest in their own records. One of the attractions of these checklists is the fact that records can be kept unobtrusively, without worrying the children or interfering with their classroom work.

Informal measures of progress

"Time on task" is acknowledged to produce progress. A record of the amount of reading children do will tell a lot about their progress toward literacy. With the help of aides, parent helpers, visitors to the classroom, student teachers, or the children themselves, you can keep a simple chart of children's reading activities. Parents can augment this record by reports of the reading children do at home. Trust will stand you in good stead here. Both parents and children are generally quite eager to report accurately, but if you make the records a matter of competition and gold stars, children may get the impression that this is a contest rather than a record-keeping activity and accuracy may go by the board. If you include both the number of books or stories and the titles, your records become indicators of growing sophistication in reading as well as increasing amounts of practice. The same book or story entered repeatedly reveals the extra practice children need to internalize the patterns they will use for more varied and independent reading later on, but can also become a signal to you that a child may need some extra encouragement to move ahead. Hence even a simple chart may become a diagnostic tool that helps you use the children's work as a guide to further teaching.

Filling in anecdotal records as shown here will take less time than scoring and keeping track of worksheets. Making entries either daily or two or three times a week as needed offers greater flexibility to note such landmarks as "Billy volunteered to read for the first time today" or "Krista is beginning to write in her diary." As with the observation checklists, we find that a few minutes here and there are all we need to chart progress or note puzzling or interesting behaviors. The anecdotal record is a fine place to record the oral- and listening-skill building of children that is so important in overall literacy development but often receives little attention in school records. Willingness to speak up in a group, to participate in a play, or to go to the library to ask for a reference book may all be significant milestones in a child's development and are definitely worthy of note.

Writing becomes its own record

As the children begin to print and compose, their writing and special projects become means of measuring progress. The development of motor skills, printing, spelling, artwork, composition, independence of thought, or the evolution of writing styles readily emerge from the written pages and become evidence of steps toward greater proficiency. Sending written work home can be a fine way to reassure parents that school work is not all fun and games but is producing notable steps forward. If the early writing you send home shows the children's invented spelling, stamp the copy DRAFT to let parents know that this is not the finished product but merely one step along the way. Examples of written work done over a period of time will be an even better means of demonstrating the many step-ups toward accurate spelling and composing. Keeping a folder of written work produced by a child over a period of time becomes solid evidence of progress throughout the year. We make it a practice to collect the children's writing month by month and to have those folders available for conferences with parents, supervisors, or the children themselves. If you would prefer to send

Tara	Feb 8 - Chicken soup - good reading needed very little help	Feb 10 - The Three Bears - looked at pictures - good substitutions
Jenny P.	Feb 8 - Henny Penny - very good reading - retold story	Feb. 10 - Story By Noodles - needed some help
Jenny C.	Feb 8 Oh My! - good reading enjoyed this	Feb 10 - The Carrot Seed - good try - uses pictures
Meave	Feb. 8 - very fluent reading of Henny Penny - talked about story	Feb. 10 - Billy Goats - very nice - retold story
Ann	Feb. 8 - Splosh - on her own, no help needed - related to her story	Feb 10 - Mixed up Signs - fluent, good comprehension - asked questions
Luvena	Feb 8 The Digger Wasps - improved - asked questions about wasps	Feb. 10 - Chicken Soup - read with obvious enjoyment - good rythma
Melody	Feb. 8 - absent	Feb 10 - Brown Bear - wants to read it to K's.
Cristina	Feb 8 - Gingerbread Boy - Great! - going to follow up with picture	Feb. 10 - Fire Fire - with enjoyment - figured out rhyming words
Laura	Feb 8 - What is Big? - good try guessed at new words	Feb. 10 - One Potato - had fun - needed some help
Jennyn	Feb. 8 - What is Pink? - good, trying hard	Feb. 10 - Mr. Pine's Sign - Good reading obviously enjoyed this
Samantha	Feb 8 - What is Big? - knew story guessed at it.	Feb. 10 - Three Bears - getting words - needed help

Teacher's anecdotal record of individual children's work

To keep track of individual children's progress, the teacher maintains a record of the books children are reading at specific dates. Anything else that is noteworthy is included in this record. To make recording easy, the pages of the notebook are trimmed back so that the children's names can be seen in the margin. This ongoing record offers the opportunity to chart each child's progress and to note how s/he is progressing compared to other children or to the progress made by children in previous years.

Tara	May 18 Funny Old May - excellent reading	May 24	The Turnip - nice reading today!
JennyP	May 18 Mouse's Song - very nice reading	May 24	Read to Me - enjoyed reading this - corrected (self)
JennyC	May 18 - Wanted to be read to today	May 24	Home for a Bunny - with help - strong desire to read
Meave	May 18 - Mouse's Song - excellent reading	May 24	Funny Old Man - good comprehension - new all words
Ann	May 18 - Chocolate Cake - good corrected own error	May 24	Animal Babies - read with obvious enjoyment
Luvena	May 18 - One, Two, Three - read beautifully with rythmn	May 24	Kittens & Bears — asked questions - wants to put on play
Lisa	May 18 - Old Woman ~ Pig - good reading - asked questions about words	May 24	Noisy Nora - good reading
Melody	May 18 - Park in Spring - good reading	May 24	Brown Bear — often reads old favorites
Cristina	May 18 - read Bozo again - enthusiastic about reading story	May 24	To New York - asked questions - read story twice
Laura	May 18 - Three Little Bugs - nice & smooth	May 24	Old Friends - read with enthusiasm
JennyM	May 18 - rather haltingly today - read in unison	May 24	Fun! Fun! Fun! - enjoyed this - needed some help
Samantha	May 18 - read with her delightful English accent - wants to read to other kids	May 24	read chapt. from Spraggles - very fluent

Sept. 23
- some K- children are giving me beginning consonants, ending consonants, capital letters + periods at the ends of sentences
- children are zeroing in more on words and sentences + some are just responding to the meaning words + sentences when read to them.
- attention span is lengthening
- children are not so restless when sitting for news time
- some are becoming more aware of waiting for turn before talking
- beginning to be more cooperative + aware of other children's rights
- more aware of give and take
- I feel the whole class shifting to one of cooperation and sharing
- some children only want to play with toys, others are interested in skill games - eg lotto, Memory, What's Missing, Sequence

- children who are alert + aware eg. when name is called look up quickly - seem to be more aware of the reading process.
- my one fluent reader really captures the attention of the rest of the class when he is reading news from the blackboard

Oct.13 — Two children reading well + putting their own sentences on the blackboard. One child that was taught to blend words in pre-school (eg nut, but etc) + could do it successfully then will not attempt to read this year.
- the flow or integration of the classroom hasn't really happened yet although I feel it is beginning I can physically feel the shift as children become more independent + trustful. Children who did not relate as a group before are

beginning to get a classroom feeling. U.S.S.R. is going well - children settling down to look at books very well.
Children are asking for old favorites (stories) over and over again, rather than reading a new story. I'm reading stories over and over again (at their request) I leave words out more + more + let them anticipate + fill them in.
Oct 17
A father brought in a big wasp's nest still attached to a piece of tree limb with leaves. We started looking at it + decided we didn't know enough about bee's nests so we went to the library + got all the bee books we could find. As we were looking at the books and studying the nest a very big, sleepy looking bee climbed out. What excitement! The children were

a little worried. The wasp was, huge wobbly and scary. We were able to capture the wasp in a jar and study it close up. I noticed that children were looking at books + comparing the pictures etc. to the real thing – a lot of close observation, a lot oof book checking went on. the news on the blackboard was "Stephanie brought a bees nest to school. We are learning about bees nests."

– later " A queen bee crawled out of the nest. She was wobbly. We captured her and put her in a jar to study.

–beginning consonants really well-established in a lot of children, also 'ch + th' for som beginning to recognize final consonants. Also patterns like

–noise level beginning to diminish as children find right level of voice for classroom
–children according to parents can't wait to get to school, but when asked what was their favorite part of the day a few kids said "Playing outside at gym time."

Oct. 30 Some K- children zeroing in on words. Chad is reading fluently. Joanne when asked to draw a picture + dictate a sentence chose to copy down the whole chart story done earlier in the day (6 sentences) Several children copied down the title- 'A Trip to the Apple Orchard'.

–children are playing well together "give and take" happening
–children getting very independent
– taking on a lot of responsibility.

ing. Also capitals and periods - All children recognize first names (on cards) Not all can print their own names yet. - Nicky, Matthew.

My Jason is really beginning to talk now. -can say a few words - He spends an hour a week with E.S.L. Teacher

Wed – Plans changed quickly this morning – a lovely big dog called Casey followed his Mistress Stephenie to school today. I tried to make him go home but he wouldn't. Then I phoned S' dad. He came + got dog + we settled down to school. I read several stories about pets that came to school. News on b.b. - was Stephanie's dog came to school today. He followed Stephanie. Her dad

Teacher's anecdotal record

Sample pages show teacher's notes on highlights of a few days in class.

more written work home, it would be a good idea to retain at least one sample per week for each child as your ongoing record of writing development. The writing notebook with its weekly entries is a convenient way to assemble work. You may also want to take the time to make lists of the children's steps forward and staple these lists to the individual writing folders.

Oral reading may be assessed by "miscue analysis"

A modified version of *miscue analysis* (see page 321) can aid your assessment of oral reading. (See sample modified from Goodman and Burke 1970.) The full version is too time-consuming to be used for all children, but an abbreviated version will enhance your understanding and appreciation of children's thought processes. With its theoretical stance that errors are not haphazard but the result of careful thought, miscue analysis looks for strengths and shores up a teacher's ability to reassure parents who want Jason or Kelly to be letter-perfect from the start. Miscue analysis will lend further weight to your more general in-class observations. Use it if you are in doubt about a child's reading development. Marking the book or a photocopy to note which words the child omitted, inserted, substituted, or had supplied by you allows you to count how many words s/he read accurately and to analyze whether the "miscues" preserved the overall meaning and fit the structure of the sentence. Analyzing the reading of your most advanced and fluent readers may help you to accept that letter- or word-perfect reading is not necessarily the hallmark of good reading. The extraction of meaning is. If you observe your own oral reading, you will note that you, too, misread or omit certain words and that you, like the children, will make the necessary adjustment in the syntax of the remainder of the sentence to preserve the meaning or go back to self-correct and make a new start. Miscue analysis teaches you that, far from being signs of weakness, the minor adjustments readers make in their oral reading are actually signs of reading for meaning.

Hang in there!

When assessing progress in a constructivist classroom you have to keep clearly in mind that the specific skills you used to look for as *first steps* become *end products* of a long process of gradual development. Since you are building on the children's natural ways of moving from whole to parts and gross to fine performance, a great deal of learning takes place *before* detailed skills emerge. Those skills may be first steps in the decoding phase of literacy, but if that decoding phase – the accurate use of letters and sounds – is springing from self-programming the children have done while using reading and writing to communicate, then the decoding and spelling skills are *end products* of a lot of solid literacy learning. *So hang in there and trust!* In the long run the children in your class, like the children in a product-oriented class, will learn all about phonology, spelling, and sounding out, but in the meantime they will have learned so much more about being readers, writers, and users of print.

You will find it easier to hang in there and trust if you compare the children's progress to the charts that show the literacy continuum than if you compare their performance to that of children working in a product-oriented classroom. You should glory in the eagerness, joy, and productivity children show in the many step-ups they make toward full literacy. Since you start them with whole language work and are moving toward skill development, it stands to reason that that is how their skills will show up – whole language first, detailed skills later. Of one thing you *can* be certain, all children are becoming readers and writers so their skills are bound to emerge.

INDIVIDUAL PROFILE OF EMERGENT READING

NAME OF CHILD

TEACHER

PERIOD OF OBSERVATION: from   to

TOTAL OBSERVATIONS:

MARKING:
CHECK MARK – CHILD PERFORMS
MINUS – CHILD DOES NOT PERFORM
BLANK – NO OPPORTUNITY TO OBSERVE

DATES //////////////

Use of models

Watches others to learn about reading behaviors
Copies actions/responses of teacher or children
Rehearses silently to approximate reading behavior of teacher or peers
Begins to say some words when listening to others read
Joins in to "read" a refrain or familiar passage

Imitates sequencing
Leafs through book from front to back
Tracks oral reading from left to right
Tracks print with hands or eyes while others read
Prints from left to right

Differentiating parts – language development

Develops oral fluency
Communicates freely with teachers and peers
Describes pictures or events accurately
Dictates news items, picture captions, or personal messages
Uses words learned from reading or classroom activities – expands vocabulary

Demonstrates knowledge of words
Gives only one word when asked to say or read a word
Recognizes some words on sight
Leaves spaces between words when printing
Gives one word at a time when dictating a sentence

Acquires knowledge of letters
Begins to print letters instead of using wavy lines
Names letters accurately when seeing or printing them
Recognizes sounds of initial consonants
Tries to produce/feel the sound of letters when writing

DATES

Integration

Uses the context or setting to aid reading
Uses illustrations as aids in recognizing printed messages
Uses familiar language patterns as aids to reading
Substitutes words that fit the syntax and meaning when reading
Refers to familiar patterns or story lines to anticipate what comes next

Keeps the focus on meaning
Looks for meaning when relating to books and print
Recognizes that print conveys the meaning in books and stories
Relates stories to own experience
Provides appropriate captions or labels for pictures

Shows expanding cognitive development
Remembers stories or sequence of events
Anticipates or infers words from story line
Asks questions about stories or other printed materials
Attends when listening to stories, shows increased attention span

Active involvement and social development

Demonstrates motivation and interest
Handles books, looks at pictures, or plays with books
Takes (brings) books (from) home
Enjoys and uses reading activities
Plays with word/letter games and puzzles

Develops independence
Does not cling to teacher for support or answers
Proceeds to next step in a task without help
Selects new activity when finished with a task
Chooses books or stories to be read

Shows growth in personal development
Relates well with teacher and peers
Uses learning materials appropriately
Accepts responsibility – for own belongings, cleaning up, social interactions
Acts appropriately during book time

Listens attentively
Follows directions accurately
Hears necessary cues, screens out distractions
Discriminates sounds accurately
Demonstrates a sense of rhythm

INDIVIDUAL PROFILE OF EARLY READING DEVELOPMENT

NAME OF CHILD

TEACHER

PERIOD OF OBSERVATION: from   to

TOTAL OBSERVATIONS:

MARKING:
CHECK MARK – CHILD PERFORMS
MINUS – CHILD DOES NOT PERFORM
BLANK – NO OPPORTUNITY TO OBSERVE

DATES

Initial reading – gross performance
Attends to reading
"Reads" from memory
Recognizes some words on sight
Uses familiar phrases as guide to reading

Use of models
Observes teachers and peers in learning situations
Imitates reading/writing behaviors of teacher and peers
Produces the same intonation patterns as fluent readers
Plays teacher, using the teacher's actions and words

Use of feedback
Listens attentively during reading/writing conferences
Asks for comments or questions during authors' circle
Asks questions about words, spellings, or story content
Speaks up to give positive/constructive feedback to peers

Practice
Reads/writes during center or choosing time
Pays attention to books during book time
Participates in plays or other presentations
Helps with producing sentences during news time

The move from whole to parts
Surveys stories before reading them
Scans lines of print for meaningful units to aid fluent reading
Thinks of message first, before worrying about words and spelling
Uses familiar story lines as guides to story reading and anticipating words

DATES

Spelling – differentiating parts
Recognizes/provides initial/median/final consonants when writing or spelling
Converts spoken language to written symbols phonetically
Invents own spelling patterns
Begins to recognize vowel sounds

Use of letter-sound correspondence
Comments on sound-alike words during news time or writing workshop
Relies on beginning consonants to sound out unfamiliar words
Notes similarities between words and their sounds
Generalizes known spelling patterns to new words

Use of language patterns in reading and writing
Reads in phrases instead of word-for-word
Converts text to own language patterns
Self-corrects misreadings to fit syntax and meaning
Develops distinct writing styles to suit the different purposes of writing

Reading for meaning and enjoyment
Relates books and stories to own experience
Uses books to gain knowledge
Reads aloud to other children or adults
Demonstrates comprehension by retelling parts of stories

Independence
Moves from completed task to new one without help
Self-corrects reading as necessary to preserve meaning
Generates ideas and initiates own projects
Selects books and activities independently during center or choosing time

Motivation and interest
Takes (brings) books (from) home
Has favorite authors or reading topics
Prefers reading/writing to playing when given a choice
Talks about books and stories with others

Writing
Writes to add meaning to drawings
Composes complete sentences and messages during writing workshop
Writes spontaneously three or more sentences
Uses writing purposefully during or outside of writing workshop

WHOLE-CLASS PROFILE OF EMERGENT READING

TEACHER

MARKING:
CHECK MARK – CHILD PERFORMS
MINUS – CHILD DOES NOT PERFORM
BLANK - NO OPPORTUNITY TO OBSERVE

STUDENT'S NAMES

Date

Copies actions/responses of teacher or other children
Rehearses silently to approximate reading behavior of teacher or peers
Begins to say some words when listening to others read
Joins in to "read" a refrain or familiar passage

Date

Copies actions/responses of teacher or other children
Rehearses silently to approximate reading behavior of teacher or peers
Begins to say some words when listening to others read
Joins in to "read" a refrain or familiar passage

Date

Copies actions/responses of teacher or other children
Rehearses silently to approximate reading behavior of teacher or peers
Begins to say some words when listening to others read
Joins in to "read" a refrain or familiar passage

Totals:

MODIFIED "MISCUE ANALYSIS" *
MARKINGS TO RECORD CHILDREN'S READING BEHAVIORS

To use these markings when children are reading to you, make some photo-
copies of the pages the children will read and either mark the pages as you go,
or tape record the children's reading, then mark the pages afterwards. As you
focus closely on the reading behaviors of individual children, you will find
that the children's self-corrections, words they ask for, or changes they make
tell you a lot about their overall reading and progress. The important point to
keep in mind is that you are not trying to find errors but are describing carefully what it is a child does when reading.

Child's behavior	*Text and your notation*	*Comment*
Substitution	**mom** He called his mother. above the line.	Write the word.
Omission	We (always) went swimming.	Circle the omitted word.
Insertion	at He hit the ball. ∧	Show location and word inserted.
Reversal	'Come here,' mother said.	Draw curved line around words.
Long pause	She came in/the door.	Insert a slash to show pause.
Word supplied to child	They wanted to go camping. ∿∿∿	Draw a wavy line under words you supplied to the child.
Repetitions		Draw a line from right to left to the point at which the reader began to repeat; then mark the reason for the repetition.
Correction	Ⓒ We played ball in the park. ∧	(Child read sentence as though it ended after ball.)
	Ⓒ Here (it) is.	(Child omitted *it*.)
Anticipating difficulty	Ⓐ Now this is/ridiculous.	(Child paused then started again.)

*Modified from Goodman and Burke 1970

Positive Teacher-Child Interactions Generate Energy

9

Though we began with "the basics"– teaching reading, writing, and spelling – years of observing children blossom forth clearly revealed that we did not stay there. Once we reached our goal to develop a way of teaching that would build on the children's own way of learning, we realized we had reaped much more than we had dreamed, but it took us a while to recognize the full import of the change. Adapting teaching to the children's way of learning has generated a new and positive energy in our classrooms that translates into joyful, productive learning for everyone.

Children who come to school eager to learn to read and write, maintain that excitement and curiosity. Those who are less interested, fearful, apathetic, or hostile recapture their natural curiosity and desire to learn. The climate of delight and co-creative teaching spark a joy and eagerness that simply did not exist in our classrooms before. Now reading, writing, discussions, thinking, and planning are natural parts of the children's day, and they take that active involvement in learning home with them.

Children move toward full literacy with ease and joy when their learning is based on communicating with others, on solving problems, and on facing new and interesting challenges. They pursue reading for the joy of it. Stories, reference material, their own writing are familiar and highly useful sources of learning and entertainment. Writing is pursued avidly and imaginatively. Even in grade one, children evolve research skills and understand that to find information they have a wide range of sources available both in and outside the classroom.

Gone are stress, fear, anxiety, boredom, and frustration. Books and materials used by children and teacher alike have moved far beyond the limited range of basal readers with their stilted language and limited vocabulary. Children are free to build on their individual intelligences and interests and, not surprisingly, surge ahead in the acquisition of all language skills.

When we started our joint work, our underlying goal was to teach in a way that would inculcate a love of reading. We wanted to see children acquire the ability to read a wide range of materials and to use that ability actively and voluntarily to learn, explore, solve problems, and simply enjoy. We reached our goal, and then we discovered unexpected bonuses. Writing flourishes, and spelling evolves to a level children rarely achieved in our previous grade one classes. Artwork is strong and expressive. The children's imagination, spontaneity, and creativity expand rapidly. Self-confidence and a willingness to face challenges of learning abound. Children are resourceful, cooperative, helpful, and sociable. Clearly, learning to read by reading and write by writing had an influence on overall development.

Twenty years of practice and class upon class of children have confirmed our initial research hypothesis that, given the opportunity, children will learn as effectively in class as they do when first learning to speak at home. By shifting our teaching approach to modeling, practice, and feedback and creating a classroom environment that is safe for learning and exudes trust in their ability to learn, we free the children's capacity to learn. With that freedom children take charge of their own learning, much as they did at home and with the same pervasive results.

Building on the learners' ways works in other teaching areas as well

A look at other systems of teaching that build on the same principles of learning has shored up our confidence. Our experience is not isolated and our hopes not simply empty dreams. Suzuki calls his method of teaching the violin the "mother tongue" approach and has amply demonstrated that all children have the capacity to learn to play and play well. Zoltan Kodaly (originator of the Kodaly method of teaching singing and reading music) went still further. His aim was to give back to the people of Hungary their joy and appreciation for music. Thirty years of work has seen his hope realized. In that case, too, effective learning in one field – singing – enhanced overall learning but particularly learning in mathematics. The parallels between the Kodaly method of teaching music and the learners' way of teaching of reading and writing are striking. (See Table 5.) Both methods foster effective, joyful learning; both have pervasive benefits for teachers and students alike.

But we would like to sound the same warning Kodaly instructors have given. Fostering learning the natural way is not a matter of techniques or "quicky" gimmicks. To be successful requires a shift in outlook and philosophy. Patience, careful preparation on the part of the teacher, and a lot of planning behind the scenes create the open atmosphere that gives children the opportunity to learn freely. Understanding the ways in which children learn and the willingness to look and listen carefully are crucial. Giving children the chance to initiate much of their own learning takes courage and perseverance. But the rewards are well worth it – the excitement and interest generated in the climate of co-creative teaching will never let you go back to the old ways of rigid lesson plans and guided reading.

When analyzing just what has changed in our classrooms as a result of adapting teaching to the learners' way, we concluded that the most profound change rests in the transformation of energy. Visitors are always struck by the atmosphere of productivity and purposeful activity that pervades classrooms in which children are free to learn their way. On closer examination we find that this transformation of energy functions at all levels.

Productivity, success, and the excitement of discovery keep teacher and children energized and always ready to explore new learning. You will understand this phenomenon if you have had the experience of being bone tired, reading a book, or watching a TV show and suddenly coming alive, full of energy and attention, because you found an idea or scene totally absorbing and stimulating. When you are involved in your favorite activity your energy becomes almost inexhaustible – in fact, you *can* dance all night. We experience this type of positive energy each day we work with children.

*New learning –
new energy*

TABLE 5 • COMPARING THE KODALY METHOD OF TEACHING MUSIC WITH THE LEARNERS' WAY OF TEACHING READING

*Learning to sing**	*Learning to read*
Instruction begins with familiar songs. The teacher models singing and invites the children to sing along.	Instruction begins with familiar stories or nursery rhymes. The teacher models reading and invites the children to read along.
Enjoyment and appreciation are key goals of teaching.	Enjoyment and interest are key goals of teaching.
Components – rhythm, sounds – are taught in the context of knowing the songs.	Components – letters, sounds, words – are taught in the context of knowing the reading material.
Physical involvement – clapping, hand signals, moving to music – are part of learning to sing.	Physical involvement – singing, talking, moving, writing, drawing – are part of learning to read.
Songs that are part of the children's heritage – not material created for pedagogical purposes – are deemed essential to teach children to appreciate and enjoy music.	Classic children's literature, enjoyable stories, rich in language and meaning – not basal readers – lay the foundation for a love of reading.
All children are trusted to sing in tune. By grade two none sing out of tune.	All children are trusted to learn to read. Some may be slow, but they all learn.
At each stage, learning moves from the whole to the parts. More complex songs are learned and enjoyed *before* the intricacies of musical notations are introduced.	At each stage, learning moves from the whole to parts. Children learn about stories, sentences, words *before* they learn to spell and sound out.
Close observations of how children learn to sing have shaped the curriculum. Child development – not subject logic – guides teaching.	Close observations of how children learn to read have shaped the curriculum. Child development – not subject logic – guides instruction.
Teacher and learners cooperate in learning variations.	Teachers and learners cooperate in initiating new learning.
Individual work aids children to develop their skills.	Individualization of instruction helps children evolve.
The teacher works behind the scene to plan instruction.	The teacher works behind the scene to create a rich environment.
Success with singing enhances other learning as well.	Success with reading enhances overall learning and development.
The ultimate aim is to lead children toward love and knowledge of music from the earliest school years to adulthood.	The ultimate aim is to lead children to lifelong literacy and love of reading.

* (Choksy, 1974)

Teacher energy is recharged daily

Though putting more energy into teaching than ever before, we find the work less tiring. That seeming paradox finds its explanation in the transformation of the energy we use in teaching. Instead of being drained, it is recharged and stimulates our interest and enthusiasm. The energy we used to expend on trying to keep the children in their seats or working on teacher-assigned jobs they often disliked is now freed up to interact with the children in meaningful, productive ways. Children who are free to move about and work on jobs of interest to them don't need to be "kept under control" – they are too busy to create havoc. The strain of imposing our will or rule on active, curious children has been replaced by the excitement of sharing learning experiences, being helpful, and observing the progress children make. Each day is new and different. Instead of being fraught with anxiety about accurate performance, for teacher and children alike each reading session produces a surge of excitement at new steps forward, at re-experiencing familiar pleasures, and sharing enjoyment or interests; each writing session releases new creative energy and the sharing of ideas.

Shifting the teacher's role from expert and boss to co-learner and facilitator frees up energy normally used in trying to be – or appear to be – knowledgeable about and on top of every situation. Just think of the ease of feeling free to say, "I don't know much about .... Why don't we try to see what we can find out about that." Or "Why don't you ask your dad [brother, friend] if he would come in and tell us about that [show pictures/demonstrate how to do that]?" That approach frees us to become genuine learners and opens the classroom to any number of co-teachers – peers, visitors, parents – who can provide new and exciting input. It lets us work with individual children on projects that hold excitement and novelty for us as well as the children. Our own joy in learning and discovery is picked up by the children just as readily as our frustrations and anxieties used to be. Needless to say, the effects of positive modeling are far more pleasing to all concerned.

The willingness to shift at a moment's notice from the lesson plan of the day sparks excitement. If a chick suddenly makes the first hole in its shell, or if a child bubbles over with excitement about a camping trip or the tractors that are digging a huge hole next door to his house, the entire class may surge ahead in discussing, drawing, writing about that memorable event. Lack of attention span, interest, or motivation among children ceases to be an energy drain.

There is an important psychological by-product to this responsive way of interacting with the children. Since the teacher responds to feelings of excitement, curiosity, eagerness, sadness – whatever – the children's need to draw attention to themselves by acting out or whining fades away early in the school year.

Being flexible and taking cues from the children about their special interests and needs generates creativity, spontaneity, and revitalized interest in drawing up lesson plans. Though a lot of time and energy is spent on planning learning materials and centers throughout the year, then changing them as interests or the season suggest, the work involved both challenges and satisfies the teacher's creativity, ingenuity, and resourcefulness. Enthusiastic children are marvelous teachers and appreciative participants.

Interactions generate positive energy

Creativity has become the serendipitous by-product of our shift to teaching the learners' way. As the children evolve their reading and writing skills through interacting freely with the teacher, each other, and the learning materials, they begin to evidence greater spontaneity, creativity, and productivity in their work. Sparked by their enthusiasm and wide range of questions and interests, we find our own imagination, spontaneity, and innovative techniques growing apace.

The relaxed, open interactions have turned a tug-of-war of wills into mutual cooperation that gives greater scope for self-expression to children and teacher alike. Children's moment-to-moment interests and needs become the cues for shifts in lesson plans. The dull routine of a set sequence of skill-drills is replaced by joint explorations and ever-changing topics. Though as teachers we keep our scope and sequence in mind to make sure children learn such required subjects as contractions and past-tense endings, the flow of conversation, projects the children undertake, and the daily news sharing become vehicles for practice.

Teaching takes on a conversational tone as the interactions between teacher and children move away from the lecturer-student roles. The tension of having to talk about and apply rules of spelling or grammar dissolves when the teacher simply mentions them each time an apostrophe, capital letter, silent *e* or the like occur. Soon children recognize these parts of writing and display their knowledge gleefully as they make a game of spotting them or stating the rule at news time. In writing conferences they discuss standard spelling and conventions of composition without worry about "making mistakes."

As the teacher relinquishes control over the children's every move, so the children release the teacher. Since the interactions in class suggest to the children that they are responsible, purposeful workers, they take on those qualities, freeing the teacher to move around the classroom to interact with individuals or small groups. Work goes on among the rest of the children whether the teacher keeps an eye on them or not. In fact, observers have expressed amazement at the fact that the teacher can stand and talk with them, work intensively with one or two children at a time, or even leave the room altogether without any noticeable effect on the overall activity in the classroom. The independence and mutual cooperation of children does not draw on the teacher's energy but flows from the children's interactions with the overall learning environment.

The abundance of books, games, and all sorts of learning materials around the classroom is readily available to all children, and their physical need to move around, manipulate things, and examine their environment is met as fully as possible within the bounds of school rules and the requirement to keep down the noise level. Satisfying the needs of curiosity, kinesthetic sense, comfort, self-expression, freedom to choose and to share generate that impulse to learn, so essential to learners who will continue to meet an ever changing world with expanding demands on their flexibility. Remarks like, "We can't do that," "We haven't learned that," or "That's too hard" are rare. Children are always willing to try and exude confidence in their ability to tackle jobs.

They exhibit the same confidence in their interactions with visitors to the classroom. The principal, parent helpers, student teachers, custodian, visiting teachers, local firefighter, police officer, or nurse, reading buddies from higher grades, university professors – anyone coming into the classroom – is readily consulted or drawn into activities. The young readers and authors are generally delighted to share or demonstrate their talents, and since none are *required* to do so, the fears or tensions of having to perform are absent. Instead, a sense of ease and cooperative learning prevails.

Extending the classroom through frequent field trips certainly serves to augment the interactive energy. The opportunity to move outside, to touch, smell, explore, and talk about new or familiar places and experiences gives rise to research projects, library research, and lively discussions. Trips to a local store, farm, museum, beach, or park, or a visit to someone's garden or special workshop can often be arranged without the need for transportation. Parent helpers or teaching aides join the fun.

Whether on field trips, in class, or during interviews, interactions with parents, too, are filled with positive energy. Whether English-speaking or not, highly educated or little concerned with academic matters, parents feel welcome in the classroom and enjoy their children's progress. Here again interaction augments the positive energy. As the teacher and children share the excitement of learning with parents, so parents keep the teacher posted on reading, writing, and artwork that the children do at home. Younger brothers and sisters become eager visitors to school and we get reports of children trying to convince parents they should be allowed to go to school even though sick.

Teacher qualities that generate positive energy

Patience and the willingness to hang in there when little or no learning seems visible are prime requisites for maintaining positive energy. Time and time again we receive confirmation that by trusting a child to learn, a sudden surge forward will occur after a long interval of quiet internal work. The willingness to let children set their own learning pace pays big dividends in solid learning, but it takes a lot of self-discipline to stand back to give the child time and space to do it alone. Standing back and watching for the right moment to make a suggestion, give encouragement, or let the child continue comes only with time and practice. Timing becomes a matter of awareness of each child's personality, learning style, and of the overall continuum of learning to read and write.

Standing back to give the children room to learn does not mean that the teacher has relinquished responsibility for the classroom. From the first day of school, s/he sets the rules of conduct both by example and by spoken rules. If the enthusiasm and excitement carry children into too noisy or otherwise disruptive behaviors, the teacher reestablishes order by reminding the children that they are disturbing others. Part of the "safety" of the classroom is based on the clear understanding that the teacher is in charge and will keep activities on an even keel. Children need and want clear guidelines and react well to sound reasoning behind rules of conduct. Being firm without being punitive or negative adds that air of stability to an otherwise noisy classroom. In school, as at home, natural learning does *not* mean lack of discipline.

Similarly, openness and warmth do not mean overwhelming children or rushing in too close when a child wants to stand back. In personal interactions, as in learning situations, the positive energy is generated by a clear message and demonstration on the part of the teacher that s/he is there for the children but will neither hover over them nor gush affection when a child shows no inclination to be fussed over.

A sense of humor and willingness to relax and enter into the fun of playing when the occasion presents itself certainly add to the positive climate. Willingness to make mistakes and be corrected makes trial-and-error learning a two-way street and sparks learning for everyone.

Willingness to ask for help falls into the same category. Parents and visitors to the classroom become generous helpers and contributors when approached the right way. The principal, supervisor, and other resource people in school and the larger community are often happy to give time or materials to the children. These helpers, like the children, respond well to the one overriding quality in the natural learning environment, that of building on strengths.

Success invigorates children and teacher alike

That positive feeling of looking for and rejoicing in every little step-up – every success – pervades the classroom and infuses teacher and students alike with boundless energy. The certainty that all children are making progress assures that their learning blossoms. Neither teacher nor students know apathy or boredom as they learn together. Instead, the excitement of new discoveries sweeps everyone along to the next level of learning – and then the next. As the children acquire literacy and thinking skills, the teacher gains deeper insight into their ways of learning, and there arises a feeling of awe at the marvelous capacity each and every child brings to learning. The climate of delight is invigorating indeed!

Bibliography

Armstrong, Thomas. 1994. *Multiple Intelligences in the Classroom.* Alexandria, Va.: A.S.C.D.

Baratta-Lorton, Mary. 1976. *Mathematics Their Way.* Reading, Mass.: Addison-Wesley.

Brewster, Chris, and Don G. Campbell. 1991. *Rhythms of Learning: Creative Tools for Developing Lifelong Skills.* Tucson, Ariz.: Zephyr Press.

Brooks, Jacqueline Grennon, and Martin G. Brooks. 1999. *In Search of Understanding: The Case for Constructivist Classrooms.* Alexandria, Va.: A.S.C.D.

Brown, Roger, and Ursula Bellugi. 1964. "Three Processes in the Child's Acquisition of Syntax." *Harvard Educational Review* 34:133-151.

Bruner, Jerome S. 1957. *On Knowing: Essays for the Left Hand.* New York: Basic Books.

Caine, Geoffrey, Renate Nummela Caine, and Sam Crowell. 1994. *MindShifts: A Brain-Based Process for Restructuring Schools and Renewing Education.* Tucson, Ariz.: Zephyr Press.

Caine, Renate Nummela, and Geoffrey Caine. 1991. *Making Connections: Teaching and the Human Brain.* Alexandria, Va.: A.S.C.D.

_____. 1997. *Unleashing the Power of Perceptual Change: The Potential of Brain-Based Teaching.* Alexandria, Va.: A.S.C.D.

Calkins, Lucy M. 1983. *Lessons from a Child: On the Teaching and Learning of Writing.* Exeter, N.H.: Heinemann.

_____. 1994. *The Art of Teaching Writing.* Portsmouth, N.H.: Heinemann.

Campbell, Don G. 1988. *Introduction to the Musical Brain.* St. Louis, Mo.: MMB Music Inc.

_____. 1997. *The Mozart Effect: Tapping the Power of Music to Heal the Body, Strengthen the Mind and Unlock the Creative Spirit.* New York: Avon Books.

Choksy, Lois. 1974. *The Kodaly Method.* Englewood Cliffs, N.J.: Prentice Hall.

Clay, Marie M. 1979. *Reading: The Patterning of Complex Behaviour.* Auckland, New Zealand: Heinemann.

Damasio, Antonio R. 1994. *Descartes' Error: Emotion, Reason, and the Human Brain.* New York: Grosset/Putnam.

De Beauport, Elaine. 1996. *The Three Faces of Mind: Developing Your Mental, Emotional, and Behavioral Intelligences.* Wheaton, Ill.: Quest Books.

Diamond, Marian Cleeves. 1988. *Enriching Heredity: The Impact of the Environment on the Anatomy of the Brain.* New York: Free Press.

Diamond, Marian Cleeves, and Janet Hopson. 1998. *Magic Trees of the Mind: How to Nurture Your Child's Intelligence, Creativity, and Healthy Emotions from Birth Through Adolescence.* New York: Dutton.

Donaldson, Margaret. 1978. *Children's Minds.* New York: Norton.

Duckworth, Eleanor. 1987. *"The Having of Wonderful Ideas" and other Essays on Teaching and Learning.* New York: Teachers College Press.

Edelman, Gerald M. 1992. *Bright Air, Brilliant Fire: On the Matter of the Mind.* New York: Basic Books.

Ferguson, Charles A., and Dan I. Slobin, eds. 1973. *Studies of Child Language Development.* New York: Holt, Rinehart and Winston.

Forester, Anne D. 1975. "The Acquisition of Reading." Unpublished Master's Thesis, University of Victoria, Victoria, B.C.

_____. 1975. "Learning the Language of Reading – An Exploratory Study." *Alberta Journal of Educational Research* 21:56-61.

_____. 1977. "What Teachers Can Learn from Natural Readers." *The Reading Teacher* 31:2.

_____. 1980. "Learning to Spell by Spelling." *Theory into Practice* 19:3.

Forester, Anne D., and Norma I. Mickelson. 1979. "Language Acquisition and Learning to Read." In *Applied Linguistics and Reading,* ed. R. Shafer. Newark, Del.: International Reading Association.

Gardner, Howard. 1985. *Frames of Mind: The Theory of Multiple Intelligences.* New York: Basic Books.

_____. 1991. *The Unschooled Mind: How Children Think and How Schools Should Teach.* New York: Basic Books.

_____. 1999. *The Disciplined Mind: What All Students Should Understand.* New York: Simon and Schuster.

Gentry, J. Richard. 1987. *SPEL is a four-letter word.* Richmond Hill, Ont.: Scholastic.

Gilmor, Timothy M., Paul Madaule, and Billie Thompson, eds. 1989. *About the Tomatis Method.* Toronto: Listening Centre Press.

Goleman, Daniel. 1995. *Emotional Intelligence: Why It Can Matter More Than IQ.* New York: Bantam Books.

Goodman, Kenneth S. 1986. *What's Whole in Whole Language?* Richmond Hill, Ont.: Scholastic.

Goodman, Yetta M., and Carolyn L. Burke. 1970. *Reading Miscue Inventory.* Newark, Del.: International Reading Association.

Graves, Donald H. 1983. *Writing: Teachers and Children at Work.* Exeter, N.H.: Heinemann.

_____. 1994. *A Fresh Look at Writing.* Portsmouth, N.H.: Heinemann.

Harste, Jerome C., V. A. Woodward, and Carolyn L. Burke. 1984. *Language Stories and Literacy Lessons.* Portsmouth, N.H.: Heinemann.

Hart, Leslie A. 1975. *How the Brain Works: A New Understanding of Human Learning, Emotion, and Thinking.* New York: Basic Books.

_____. 1983. *Human Brain and Human Learning.* New York: Longman.

Healy, Jane M. 1990. *Endangered Minds: Why Our Children Don't Think.* New York: Simon and Schuster.

Holdaway, Don. 1979. *The Foundation of Literacy.* Toronto: Ashton Scholastic.

_____. 1980. *Independence in Reading.* Toronto: Ashton Scholastic.

Jensen, Eric. 1996. *Brain-Based Learning & Teaching.* Del Mar, Calif.: Turning Point Publishing.

_____. 1998. *Teaching with the Brain in Mind.* Alexandria, Va.: A.S.C.D.

Jourdain, Robert. 1997. *Music, The Brain, and Ecstasy: How Music Captures Our Imagination.* New York: William Morrow.

Luria, Aleksandr R. 1976. *The Working Brain.* New York: Penguin Books.

McKeown, Margaret G., and Isabel L. Beck. 1999. "Getting the Discussion Started." *Educational Leadership* 57(3): 25–28.

Moerk, E. L. 1977. *Pragmatic and Semantic Aspects of Early Language Development.* Baltimore: University Park Press.

Newman, Judith. 1987. *Looking at Children's Writing.* New York: Scholastic.

Perkins, David. 1999. "The Many Faces of Constructivism." *Educational Leadership* 57(3): 6–11.

Piaget, Jean. 1955. *The Language and Thought of the Child.* Cleveland, Ohio: World.

Restak, Richard M. 1979. *The Brain: The Last Frontier.* New York: Doubleday.

_____. 1984. *The Brain.* New York: Bantam Books.

_____. 1988. *The Mind.* New York: Bantam Books.

_____. 1991. *The Brain Has a Mind of Its Own: Insights from a Practicing Neurologist.* New York: Crown Publishers.

_____. 1995. *Brainscapes: An Introduction to What Neuroscience Has Learned about the Structure, Function, and Abilities of the Brain.* New York: Hyperion.

Schachter, Daniel L. 1996. *Searching for Memory: The Brain, The Mind, and The Past.* New York: Basic Books.

Scherer, Marge. 1999. "Perspectives: The C. Word." *Educational Leadership* 57(3):5.

Smith, Frank. 1971. *Understanding Reading.* New York: Holt, Rinehart and Winston.

_____. 1986. *Insult to Intelligence.* New York: Arbor House.

Sprenger, Marilee. 1999. *Learning & Memory: The Brain in Action.* Alexandria, Va.: A.S.C.D.

Springer, Sally P., and Georg Deutsch. 1981. *Left Brain, Right Brain.* San Francisco: Freeman Co.

Sylwester, Robert. 1995. *A Celebration of Neurons: An Educator's Guide to the Human Brain.* Alexandria, Va.: A.S.C.D.

Tough, Joan. 1976. *Focus on Meaning.* London: Allen and Unwin.

Vygotsky, Lev S. 1962. *Thought and Language.* Cambridge, Mass.: MIT Press.

Wells, C. Gordon. 1981. *Learning Through Interaction: The Study of Language Development.* Cambridge, U.K.: Cambridge University Press.

Wheatley, Margaret J. 1992. *Leadership and the New Science: Learning about Organization from an Orderly Universe.* San Francisco: Berrett-Koehler.

Children's Books

Alderson, Sue Ann. 1991. *bonnie mcsmithers you're driving me dithers.* Toronto: Annick Press.

Allard, Harry. 1974. *The Stupids Step Out.* Boston: Houghton Mifflin.

Barchas, Sarah. 1975. *I Was Walking Down the Road.* Richmond Hill, Ont.: Scholastic.

Gilman, Phoebe. 1997. *The Balloon Tree.* Toronto: Firefly Books.

Herriot, James. 1993. *The Christmas Day Kitten.* New York: St. Martin's Press.

Karlin, Nurit. 1985. *The Tooth Witch.* New York: Lippincott.

Martin, Bill. 1996. *Brown Bear, Brown Bear, What Do You See?* New York: Henry Holt & Co.

Peet, Bill. 1974. *Huge Harold.* Boston: Houghton Mifflin.

_____. 1983. *How Droofus the Dragon Lost His Head.* Boston: Houghton Mifflin.

_____. 1979. *Hubert's Hair-Raising Adventure.* Boston: Houghton Mifflin.

_____. 1984. *Pamela Camel.* Boston: Houghton Mifflin.

Westcott, Nadine B. 1980. *I Know an Old Lady.* Toronto: Little Brown.

Other great books by Anne Forester and Margaret Reinhard!

On the Move
Teaching the Learners' Way in Grades 4-7

"This is a beautifully inspiring book for teachers and parents..."
– Consortium for Whole Brain Learning.

For intermediate teachers who want to use the literature-based approaches that have proven so successful in the primary grades, *On the Move* describes a typical classroom day, and provides practical suggestions for creating a climate of active and meaningful learning, integrating reading and writing into social studies, science, and other content area subjects. How to assess progress and maintain discipline while encouraging choice and flexibility are also addressed.

360 pages, illustrated • $19 • 1-920541-96-8

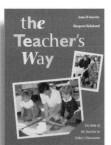

The Teacher's Way
The Role of the Teacher in Today's Classroom

For teachers of grades K-4

"Celebrating successes, encouraging student growth, increasing student interest, decreasing discipline problems, and fostering friendly parent relations are the road signs along The Teacher's Way." - Educational Leadership

The Teacher's Way is an accessible, comprehensive source book that redefines the role of the teacher of the future. Practical classroom ideas are presented alongside theories on which they are based. Using real teaching experiences, the authors acknowledge and celebrate both the multi-age nature of every classroom and the unique personal background each child brings to learning.

352 pages, illustrated • $20 • 1-895411-67-X